Law and the Professional Educator

Book I: Fundamentals of Education Law

THIRD EDITION

Isaac Ersoff

Eastern Oregon University

NUTHACH PRESS

Published by NUTHATCH PRESS
Sisters, Oregon 97759

ISBN: 0-9724843-0-2

To Resa
and
Our Families

About the Author

Isaac Ersoff was born in Miami, Florida. His professional career began in 1976 and has encompassed four areas: music, teaching, law, and higher education. While his activities in these areas have overlapped, for the sake of clarity each is discussed separately below.

Music

In 1976, Isaac became the principal tuba player with the Miami Beach Symphony. He attended the University of Miami School of Music and the Eastman School of Music. He engaged in freelance work in New York, Florida, Missouri, and Oregon, and held positions with the Miami Brass Quintet, the Florida Pops Orchestra, and the Southwest Missouri State University Faculty Brass Quintet.

While attending Eastman, he met the lovely and talented violist Resa Ryan, and the two were married in 1979. Finding that life as professional classical musicians was not to their liking, the couple decided to become professional educators.

Nevertheless, Isaac's musical career continued, with his focus shifting to composition and experimental music. He and his brother developed a music production and publishing company and by 1990 Isaac had become a member of the board of directors of Miami's Expo-Mental Festival (which sponsors an annual series of experimental music performances).

Isaac's musical endeavors reached their zenith (or perhaps their nadir) when he joined two other local producers to form the trio "Scraping Teeth." In 1993, SPIN Magazine named them "The Worst Band in America." After the ensuing "15 minutes of fame," Isaac finally turned away from music and devoted his efforts to more sound pursuits.

Teaching

Isaac began part-time, foreign language teaching in private religious schools in 1976, and began full-time teaching after obtaining his Bachelor of Science in Education from the University of Miami. From 1983 to 1989, he was a regular education teacher. He taught science, math, and music in grades 6-12, and also spent one year teaching a self-contained 5th grade class.

During these years, Isaac concluded that he was not satisfied with his training in two areas of great interest to him: educational psychology and educational methodology. He began intensive study in these areas and, developing a high level of expertise, eventually entered the field of special education and obtained his Master of Science in Special Education from Western Oregon University.

Isaac's first special education position was as a teacher and department head at Merrick Educational Center from 1989 to 1992. Merrick is a state-of-the-art center for special education in the Miami-Dade County Public Schools. The broad scope of the Merrick program required Isaac to teach all regular education subjects from kindergarten through 12th grade, while also serving as a special education teacher at these grade levels. Another unique aspect of the center is the high degree of death and dying - many students have serious injuries or chronic illnesses and the center's student mortality rate often exceeds three students per month.

Upon moving to Oregon in 1992 Isaac took a hiatus from school teaching, but returned to the profession in 1997. He held positions as a special education teacher and as a handicapped learner specialist at all levels - elementary, middle school, and high school. His approach was inclusive, providing as much support as possible to regular education teachers through co-planning, team teaching, modeling, and other collaborative techniques. Isaac's secondary special education program design has been recognized as a model design. Additionally, during the 1999/2000 school year, Isaac returned temporarily to Miami to design and implement an alternative education program for incarcerated adolescents in grades 8-12.

Law

Isaac obtained his Doctor of Jurisprudence from Willamette University College of Law. He is a member of the Oregon State Bar. His practice focuses on education law and special education, but has also included emphasis in the areas of disabilities, negotiation, contract, employment, and collective bargaining. He also practiced in the corporate arena, serving for a time as in-house counsel for the Oregon Brewing Company (d.b.a. Rogue Ales).

In addition to his work in traditional legal areas, Isaac also holds a Certificate in Dispute Resolution from Willamette, and served his internship under the renowned labor arbitrator Carlton J. Snow. Isaac's emphasis in arbitration is on public sector labor disputes, primarily focusing on school district and state college issues. A related emphasis is his focus on collaborative bargaining.

Higher Education

Isaac is an assistant professor of education at Eastern Oregon University. He is also an instructor with the School of Education at Oregon State University. Previously, he was an adjunct professor of law at Willamette University and also served as Willamette's coordinator of disability services for graduate programs. Additionally, Isaac serves as a consultant to individuals and to educational institutions and organizations, and also provides an array of continuing education options to professional educators. Some of the topics in which he specializes include:

- Effective Methodology for Heterogeneous Classrooms;
- Effective Inclusion Practices;
- Special Education Program Organization and Design;
- Social Skills and Positive Behavior Programs: School-Wide and Classroom Success;
- The IDEA and Transition: Best Practices for Self-Awareness and Self-Advocacy Instruction;
- Collaborative Collective Bargaining for Professional Educators; and
- A Model for Continuous, Convenient, and Quality Professional Development for Teachers, School-Level Administrators, and District-Level Administrators through Partnerships between Districts and Institutions of Higher Learning

The author hopes that you enjoy this text. He appreciates your questions, comments, and suggestions. Please feel free to contact him via email at: Isaac@Ersoff.com

Additional List of Cases

Appendix A contains complete or moderately edited cases of import in the law of education. Additionally, the following is a list of cases cited or quoted within the text of the chapters themselves. The list is organized by chapter and topic.

Chapter Two: Mandatory Schooling

Pierce v. Society of Sisters, 268 U.S. 510 (1925).

Chapter Three: Constitutional Basics

Board of Education v. Pico, 457 U.S. 853 (1982)
Carey v. Piphus, 435 U.S. 247 (1978)
Fuentes v. Shevin, 407 U.S. 67 (1972)
Goldberg v. Kelly, 397 U.S. 254, 271 (1970)
Goss v. Lopez, 419 U.S. 565 (1975)
Greene v. McElroy, 360 U.S. 474, 496-97 (1959)
Hazelwood School District v. Kuhlmeir, 484 U.S. 260 (1988)
Mathews v. Eldridge, 424 U.S. 319 (1976)
Milliken v. Bradley, 418 U.S. 717, 744-45 (1974)
Mullane v. Central Hanover Trust Co., 339 U.S. 306, 314 (1950)
San Antonio School District v. Rodriguez, 411 U.S. 1 (1973)
Tinker v. Des Moines School District, 393 U.S. 503 (1969)
West Virginia Board of Education v. Barnette, 319 U.S. 624 (1943)

Chapter Five: Religion

Cooper v. Eugene School District, 301 Or 358 (1986)
County of Allegheny v. ACLU, 492 U.S. 573 (1989)
Everson v. Board of Ed. of the Township of Ewing, 330 US 1 (1947)
Lee v. Weisman, 505 U.S. 577, 580 (1992)
Lemon v. Kurtzman, 403 U.S. 602 (1971)
Lynch v. Donnelly, 465 U.S. 668 (1984)
Newdow v. US Congress, 9th Cir App (2002)
San Antonio School District v. Rodriguez, 411 U.S. 1 (1973)

Chapter Six: Discrimination in General

Brown v. Board of Education, 347 US 483 (1954)
Plessy v. Ferguson, 163 US 537 (1896)

Additional List of Cases, continued

Chapter Eight: Privacy

Board of Education v. Earls, US Supreme Court (2002)
Gonzaga University v. Doe, US Supreme Court (2002)
New Jersey v. T.L.O., 469 U.S. 325 (1985)
Vernonia School District v. Acton, 115 S.Ct. 2386 (1995)
West Virginia Board of Education v. Barnette, 319 U.S. 624 (1943)

Chapter Nine: Torts

Bell v. Board of Education of New York, 687 N.E.2d 1325 (N.Y. 1997)
Dean v. Town of Waterford, 523 A.2d 1059 (Md. App. 1987)
Eisel v. Board of Ed. of Montgomery Co., 597 A.2d 447 (Md. 1991)
Gonzaga University v. Doe, US Supreme Court (2002)
Gonzalez v. Mackler, 241 N.Y.S.2d 254 (App. Div. 1963)
Price v. Young, 580 F. Supp. 1 (E.D. Ark. 1983)
Titus v. Lindberg, 49 N.J. 66, 228 A.2d 65 (1967)

Chapter Ten: Employment Basics

NLRB v. Weingarten, Inc., 420 U.S. 251 (1975)

TABLE OF CONTENTS

About the Author i

Additional Table of Cases . . . iv

Section One - General Introduction to Education Law

Chapter One 1
Why Professional Educators Need to Know About Law

Chapter Two 12
Historical Perspective of Education Law
and General Introduction to Basic Legal Principles
and Laws Affecting Professional Educators

Chapter Three 18
Due Process, Equal Protection,
and Freedom of Expression

Section Two - Protecting Students from Discrimination

Chapter Four 35
Discrimination Defined, Types of Discrimination,
and Protected Categories of People

Chapter Five 41
Religion

Chapter Six 58
Race, Gender, and Other Categories

Chapter Seven 68
Disability and the Individuals
with Disabilities Education Act (IDEA)

TABLE OF CONTENTS, continued

Section Three - An Introduction to Other Fundamentals of Education Law

Chapter Eight 89
Privacy (Including Search and Seizure)

Chapter Nine 105
Negligence and Tort Liability

Chapter Ten 115
Basic Introduction to Employment Issues

Appendices

Appendix A 123
Cases

Appendix B 282
A Note About Child Abuse

Appendix C 284
Laws Affecting Education: Links and Summaries

Appendix D 287
Five Common Forms of Discrimination Found in Schools

Appendix E 289
Quick and Easy Help for Working
with Students with IEPs

Appendix F 297
Internet Links Related to Education and Education Law

Appendix G 299
The Complaint in the Case *Henkle v. Gregory*

References 312

Chapter One

Why Professional Educators Need to Know About the Law

I. Introduction

This is a text for professional educators and students of education, not for lawyers and law students. We train lawyers and law students to "think like lawyers" (to the extent that such a concept is not oxymoronic). We cannot assume that professional educators and students of education have undergone the same training. For the above reasons, this chapter has two goals:

1. To identify the thought process educators should employ in reading this text and in analyzing legal situations which will arise in their professional lives; and

2. To address the basic reasons why professional educators need to know about the law.

II. Thinking Like a Lawyer

In analyzing a given situation, legal reasoning involves four basic steps. Educators should attempt to discipline themselves to fit the situations presented in this text as well as discussion and exam questions into this four-part structure. The ultimate goal is for educators to apply this structure to actual situations that are faced in professional life.

The four basic steps to thinking like a lawyer can be remembered as "IRAC" -- Issue, Rule, Analysis, and Conclusion. First, consider what these terms mean; then we will explore an example.

Issue: When we say "issue," we mean the primary legal issue or issues raised by a given situation. It is important to be able to identify what is at issue and what is not.

Rule: The "rule" is the law governing the issue or issues. Rules are not case specific; they are general rules of law that apply to situations presenting given issues.

Analysis: Once the issue(s) and applicable rule(s) have been identified, the specific facts of the situation at hand must be analyzed in order to determine whether and how the rule(s) should be applied to the facts of the situation. Analysis is the main focus of legal thinking.

Conclusion: Once the facts have been analyzed with regard to the applicable rule(s) of law, we are able to determine how the issue should be resolved. Keep in mind that conclusions are brief, often merely a single sentence.

Consider the following example:

Student is twelve years old. Student's family recently moved from a country in which Spanish is the national language, and speaks Spanish in their home, although Student speaks both English and Spanish. Teacher places Student in the basic reading group. Teacher told Student's parents that all children who speak Spanish at home are placed in this class because they need extra attention and reading help.

Issue: The legal issue is whether the school may place Student in the basic reading group solely on the basis of Student's speaking Spanish at home.

Rule: Title VI of he Civil Rights Act (and therefore the Equal Protection Clause of the 14th Amendment) as well as state laws prohibit student placement based on national origin and require that all students have an equal opportunity to participate in the educational program regardless of their national origin (i.e., placement based on national origin is an illegal form of discrimination).

Analysis: Student's family speaks Spanish at home because they are from a Spanish-speaking country and Spanish is their native language; this is a function of Student's national origin. The school failed to assess Student's reading ability and place Student in a reading group based on ability. Rather, Student's placement is based solely on the fact that Student "speaks Spanish at home". Therefore, Student's placement is based on national origin and deprives Student of the educational opportunity to participate in a reading group on the same basis as other students.

Conclusion: The school is illegally discriminating against Student; it is violating Student's civil rights. It should assess Student's reading ability and place Student in a reading group based upon such assessment.

Note that there are no emotional issues or personal opinions taken into account in proper legal reasoning. The process is a fairly rigid discipline: What is the legal issue? What general rule of law applies? What do the facts of this case require? Public policy, emotion, opinion, and the like are reserved primarily for political discussion and are the proper concerns of legislation, not of legal analysis.

Notwithstanding this basic principle, it is also important to remember that while it may not be appropriate to set public policy within the context of legal analysis and judicial decision-making, it is nevertheless appropriate to interpret the Constitution, laws, and prior court cases in an effort to construe the public policies therein implied. There is often a fine line between identification and interpretation of public policy, on the one hand, and imposition of policy based on personal opinion, on the other hand.

Again, please remember to keep the IRAC process in mind while reading the materials presented in this text.

III. Why Professional Educators Need to Know About the Law

Educators must learn about the law for three basic reasons:

First and foremost is professional responsibility - the ethics of the profession. Public school teachers are public servants. It is their duty to respect and protect the rights of students, staff, and other persons under the Constitution and laws. Additionally, while private school educators may not be public servants, they nevertheless are bound by federal, state, and local laws and have a duty to students and staff to assure fair and proper treatment.

The second reason is liability. There are numerous laws and legal principles involved in the education profession. Educators must avoid behavior that may result in liability on either a personal or district level. Therefore, it is imperative that they have a basic understanding of the law.

The third and final reason is that some states require persons seeking teaching licensure to have specific knowledge of the basic legal principles applicable to the education profession.

IV. Introduction to the Basic Hierarchical Relationships

A. The Respective Roles of the United States Constitution, State Constitutions, Federal Law, and State Law

United States Constitution: The United States Constitution controls legal and governmental issues and practices in the United States. All governmental entities, both federal and state, must follow the rules found in the Constitution. The Constitution sets forth the basic rights of citizens, establishes federal governmental entities and the powers and responsibilities of those entities, and identifies the rights reserved to the states.

State Constitutions: Like the federal government, each state has its own constitution setting forth the rights of state citizens, creating state governmental entities, and identifying the responsibilities and powers of governmental entities. The extent of the powers of the various states continues to be debated. States technically retain all powers of sovereign nations except as limited by the United States Constitution. However, the Constitution gives Congress the broad power to "provide for the . . . general welfare of the United States." As a result, the powers of the states are generally limited not only by the Constitution, but also by federal law.

Statutory Law and Administrative Regulations: Congress enacts federal law and state legislatures enact state law. This legislative power is pursuant to the US Constitution and state constitutions, respectively. Additionally, Congress and state legislatures both have created numerous administrative agencies. These agencies regulate specific statutes by promulgating and enforcing administrative rules and regulations pertaining to those statutes. For example, Congress enacted the amended Individual with Disabilities Education Act (IDEA) in 1997. This law controls special education. The federal administrative regulations, which clarify how the IDEA will be enforced, were published by the US Department of Education in 1999. Likewise, each state department of education has enacted (or will enact) its own administrative regulations specifying how the state and its school districts will implement special education in accord with the IDEA and the federal regulations. For the purposes of this course, administrative regulations should be considered as having the same authority as law.

General Constitutional and Legislative Hierarchy: In education law, a general rule with regard to the hierarchical authority of legal provisions is as follows: The Constitution is the highest authority, followed respectively by federal law and regulations, state constitutions, state law and regulations, and local law. (Generally, the local school board or school district enacts policies and procedures that represent the "local law.") Thus, the Constitution controls in all matters. Next, to the extent that federal law exists concerning an issue, if the federal law is constitutional, it will supersede any state provisions. If there is no federal law governing a given issue, the provisions of the state constitution for the state in question will control (again, so long as the provisions in question do not violate higher law, namely the Constitution and/or federal law). Below the state constitution, one looks to state law for guidance. State law will control so long as there is no violation of higher law. Finally, local law (or local school district policy) will control to the extent it complies with all higher law.

Think of this hierarchy in reverse order, starting at the bottom. Consider a question arising about the actions of a given teacher. Now, proceed up the ladder. First, what is the local district school policy? Second, are the teacher's actions and the local policy in accord with state law and with the state constitution? Third, are the teacher's actions, the local policy, and the state provisions in accord with federal law? Finally, are the teacher's actions, the local policy, the state provisions, and the federal law in accord with the Constitution?

The applicable provisions and issues are often fairly evident from the start. Nevertheless, it is important to remember that this hierarchy exists in order to avoid violating rights under a higher law merely because doing so is in accord with a lower law or policy.

B. The Respective Roles of Citizens and Governmental Entities in General

In a very basic and summary manner, the governmental system created by the Constitution as it applies to education law is as follows:

Citizens of the United States: The citizens in this country are at the very top of the system. Citizens have the power to vote. Using this power, they can select the persons who will act as their representatives in the government. Citizens also have numerous rights, such as the right to life, liberty, free expression, free exercise of religion, equal protection, due process, etc. These rights restrain the government. In other words, government may not infringe on the rights of citizens (except under limited circumstances, which will be presented later in this text).

Congress: The Constitution gives Congress enormous power. Congress has the power to propose amendments to the Constitution, to enact laws, to approve and remove Supreme Court justices, to remove the president, to declare war, to tax, etc. Law enacted by Congress, if constitutional, is binding on every person and governmental entity in the country.

The Supreme Court and the President: The Constitution provides for a Supreme Court and a President. The Supreme Court is the highest authority regarding interpretation of the Constitution. Its interpretation of the Constitution is binding on all citizens and governmental entities. Its interpretation of federal law is likewise binding (except that if Congress disagrees, it can change the law, as has happened on several occasions). The president enforces the law and has numerous other administrative duties and powers. The president can veto bills passed by Congress, but Congress can override a presidential veto and enact law on its own. Additionally, the president can impose orders that have the weight of law (if they are constitutional and if they are not undone by Congressional law-making).

Federal Administrative Agencies: Congress has created numerous federal agencies. These agencies enact and enforce administrative regulations. Administrative agencies are not part of the constitutional framework. Rather, Congress creates agencies through legislation. Thus, the authority of federal agencies is determined by the legislation creating them. Most agencies are part of the executive branch and are administered under the supervision of the president. The agency of primary concern in education law is the US Department of Education.

The States: As explained above, the extent of state powers continues to be an unanswered question. Nevertheless, each state does have a constitution defining the rights, responsibilities, and powers of state citizens and governmental entities. The internal state hierarchies generally mirror that of the federal government: citizens at the top, followed respectively by the legislature, a supreme court and an executive, and various local entities.

State Administrative Agencies: State legislatures have created state counterparts to the federal agencies. State agencies related to education law usually include a state department of education, which regulates education itself, and a state department for teacher certification and licensure.

The Local School District: The various states have delegated local authority regarding education to local school districts. The districts are run by elected school boards. Most local school boards hire an administrator (superintendent) to run the day-to-day school district operations. Local school districts are subject to state control and local policy is subject to state and federal law.

School Personnel: Local school districts operate local schools which are staffed by various school personnel. The various types of school personnel include administrators, teachers, counselors, specialists, maintenance workers, bus drivers, and other people who work in the schools and in the school district offices and departments. The actions of such personnel are subject to the policies of the school district, state law, and federal law.

NOTE

The reader should take note that the above-described hierarchy places professional educators at the bottom of the decision-making process. Most major decisions regarding educational policy are made by politicians and bureaucrats, not by professional educators.

C. The Roles of Courts

There are two court systems of concern in education law: federal courts and state courts. Additionally, administrative agencies have adjudicative authority regarding many education law issues.

Federal Courts: The United States Supreme Court was created by the Constitution. The federal court system, on the other hand, was created by Congress, which has the authority to legislatively control the jurisdiction of federal district courts and federal courts of appeal. The federal court system is divided into districts. For example, the Ninth District includes Oregon, Washington, California, Idaho, Nevada, Alaska, and Hawaii. Within each district there are trial courts, called "district courts," and appellate courts, called "courts of appeal." Cases are brought in district courts and appealed to courts of appeal. From courts of appeal, federal cases are appealed directly to the Supreme Court. (But with few exceptions the Supreme Court is not required to hear most cases; it picks and chooses which cases it will hear. If it does not pick a case, then that case is over; the decision of the court of appeal becomes final.)

State Courts: Most state court systems are set up just like the federal system. Cases are initially brought in a trial court and may be appealed to a court of appeal and then to the state supreme court. Most state supreme courts have some degree of discretion similar to that of the US Supreme Court regarding which cases they will accept.

Administrative Agencies: Much law today is in the form of administrative rules. Such rules often require that parties take disputes to administrative adjudication. Other rules provide parties with a choice to pursue an administrative hearing (rather than imposing such a requirement). In any event, most administrative adjudications may be appealed to the respective court system (state or federal).

The Hierarchy: Within the state and federal court systems, the decisions of higher courts always bind the lower courts. This is the doctrine of *stare decisis*, which is the policy of courts to stand by previous precedent in deciding a particular point. However, *stare decisis* is limited. First, courts will stand by precedent only regarding points a court has actually decided; they will not extend the doctrine to *dicta* or *ober dicta* (see note 3, below). Second, courts are bound only by their own previous decisions (with some exceptions, see note 1, below) and by decisions of higher courts in their own jurisdiction.

In other words, if the Supreme Court says that a tomato is a vegetable (which it did in a case arising in the 1800's), then all federal courts must consider tomatoes vegetables; there is no choice left to the lower federal courts. Likewise, if a state supreme court says that same-sex couples cannot be deprived the legal benefits bestowed on married couples (as the Vermont Supreme Court did in 1999), then all lower courts in Vermont must follow that rule; again, the lower courts have no authority to do otherwise.

A difficulty arises when considering the relationship between state and federal courts and between courts in different federal districts. The situation is easily understood when we separate the inquiry into decisions regarding state law and decision regarding federal law. Also, remember that authority moves from the top down. Trial court decisions are binding on no one other than the parties to the case. Decisions by courts of appeal are binding on trial courts. Decisions by supreme courts are binding on courts of appeal and on trial courts. (Note that in some states, the names are mixed up. New York calls its trial courts "supreme.")

First, consider decisions regarding state law. The rule is simple: decisions by a state supreme court bind all other courts, both state and federal, with regard to the laws of that state. (Note that the US Supreme Court does not decide matters of state law, so it is not involved.) Below the state supreme courts are the state courts of appeal. Absent a state supreme court ruling on a particular issue, the decisions of the state court of appeal are binding on questions of state law. Absent a decision by a state court of appeal or a state supreme court, a decision by a federal court of appeal about a matter of state law will bind federal district courts in the same district. Such a decision will not bind any state courts and will not bind federal courts in other districts.

Second, consider decisions regarding federal law. The Supreme Court hears only cases involving the Constitution and federal law. It does not decide matters of state law. Its decisions regarding federal law and the Constitution are binding on all federal and state courts, period. Below the Supreme Court, consider the federal courts of appeal. Absent a Supreme Court ruling on a particular issue, a decision regarding federal law by a federal court of appeal in a particular federal district is binding on all state courts and federal district courts in the same district. It is not binding on courts in other districts (although, it may be persuasive to courts in other districts).

Third, do not forget about administrative adjudication. Both state and federal courts give a substantial degree of respect to decisions by administrative agency adjudicators. Courts are hesitant to overturn such decisions, but do have the authority to do so. At any rate, decisions by administrative agencies do provide notice of how regulations will be interpreted and enforced by the agencies.

Please also remember three final points regarding courts:

1. Even though decisions are binding, courts can "change their minds." A court may decide that one of its own former decisions was incorrect and proceed to change its interpretation of the law. Also, it is possible that a court which is technically "bound" by a decision of a higher court may distinguish the facts of a new case from those of the prior case. The court thus frees itself to make a decision on its own, free from the need to follow the prior decision of the higher court (although if the case is appealed, the higher court may disagree with

the distinction and hold the lower court to the precedent from prior rulings).

2. It should be clear that it is often the case that similar state laws are interpreted entirely differently from state to state. Likewise, federal laws and the US Constitution are often interpreted differently from state to state and from federal district to federal district. It is therefore crucial to remember which decision is binding in a particular location. For example, suppose you are a resident of Oregon. Only Oregon Supreme Court and Oregon Court of Appeals cases are binding on matters of state law. On federal issues, the only binding authorities are the US Supreme Court and the courts of the Ninth Circuit (although state decisions on federal law will bind Oregon courts in the absence of federal court decisions on a particular topic). Decisions by other state courts and by federal courts in other circuits are not binding in Oregon; they are merely persuasive.

3. Finally, beware of *dicta*. *Dicta,* or *Obiter Dictum,* refers to statements in a court decision which go beyond the facts of the case. *Dicta* can be likened to mere "thinking aloud" about "what if" the facts were something other than what is actually presented to the court. It is mere statement of individual opinion - albeit that such opinions are those of judges. In other words, because *dicta* is not based on the facts presented in a particular case, it is merely the individual view of the judge writing the opinion; it is therefore not law and it is not binding as legal precedent. Put plainly, *stare decisis* does not apply to *ober dicta.*

(There are no case readings or discussion items for Chapter One.)

Chapter Two

Historical Perspective of Education Law
and
General Introduction to Basic Legal Principles and Laws Affecting Professional Educators

I. Historical Perspective of the Law Relating to Public Education

Education does not appear in the Constitution. There is no explicit constitutional right to a free public education. While numerous federal laws and regulations have gradually begun to establish and define a number of rights with regard to public education, until the latter half of the 20th century, most laws concerning public schools were state laws.

In 1852, Massachusetts became the first state to legislatively establish compulsory education. All students between the ages of eight and fourteen were required to attend school. Horace Mann pioneered the establishment of this system. Mann's view of public education consisted of three fundamental principles: (1) Public education must be secular, not subjugated to "any . . . standard of religious faith;" (2) State legislatures have the power to, and should, require that all children receive a basic, secular education; and (3) State legislatures have the power to, and should, tax all citizens, even citizens without children or whose children attend private schools, in order to fund a free public education system.

Horace Mann's three principles not only define public school education in this country, they provide a broad outline of the issues that have arisen in the area of education law. Each of the three principles has been, and continues to be, the subject of legal dispute and attack. Consider:

1. Numerous cases concerning religious issues and the public schools have arisen and continue to arise. Various groups continue to attempt to impose their own religious beliefs on public school activities and curriculum.

2. A basic education is indeed now compulsory in every state. Parents are required to assure that their children attend school (public, private, or home school). Early cases in the history of compulsory attendance legislation helped to define the limits of state authority regarding schooling. Also, the compulsory nature of school attendance has resulted in a close scrutiny of the actions of public school personnel in order to assure the protection of the rights of students. Such scrutiny has helped develop our approaches to equal protection, discrimination, and due process regarding public school students and personnel.

3. Various groups continue to seek tax exemptions for private school tuition and vouchers enabling the appropriation of public school funds by private parties to pay for private school tuition. Cases and issues concerning these and related school finance matters help clarify the roles of public schools and public education.

By 1900, compulsory schooling had become established across the country. Nevertheless, there had been much opposition. In the 1800's the opposition to free, compulsory schooling took three forms: (1) Poor families, needing the money, often preferred their children to work rather than to attend school; (2) Educators and members of higher socio-economic classes asserted that including the lower classes would have a detrimental effect on the quality of education; (3) African American and other non-white students were denied the equal benefit of a public education due to the opposition by white people to the inclusion of non-white races with white students.

Education was compulsory in all states, but families could send children either to public school or to private school. Oregon, however, decided to be different. In 1923, the Ku Klux Klan and the Oregon Scottish Rite Masons backed a referendum campaign in favor of a unique law requiring all students in Oregon to attend public school. The campaign was really an attack on Catholicism. Most of Oregon's private schools were religious and most of the religious schools were Catholic. The Klan ranted that "somehow these mongrel hordes must be Americanized; failing that, deportation is the only remedy."

The law passed and was scheduled to go into effect in 1926. It was challenged in the United States Supreme Court in the case Pierce v. Society of Sisters in 1925. The Court decided that the law was unconstitutional. From Pierce, we obtain one of the guiding principles of education law. The Court held the law was unconstitutional because, while states may indeed make education compulsory, the Oregon law:

> "unreasonably interfere[d] with the liberty of parents and guardians to direct the upbringing and education of children under their control. . . . [R]ights guaranteed by the Constitution may not be abridged by legislation which has no reasonable relation to some purpose within the competency of the State. The fundamental theory of liberty upon which all governments in this Union repose excludes any general power of the State to standardize its children by forcing them to accept instruction from public teachers only. The child is not the mere creature of the state; those who nurture him and direct his destiny have the right, coupled with the high duty, to recognize and prepare him for additional obligations."

II. Identifying the Issues in Education Law

In a sense, Pierce defines the scope of inquiry in education law: What are our "liberties"; what are appropriate governmental interests; and to what extent will such interests justify government action limiting our liberties regarding the education of children?

Consider a few of our liberties. We enjoy freedom of expression, freedom to practice the religion of our choice or to not practice religion at all, freedom from governmental establishment of religion, freedom of privacy, freedom from unlawful search and seizure, freedom from discrimination based on our race, religion, gender, national origin, disability, etc. We have the right to due process and the right to equal protection under the law. We enjoy many rights or "liberties" based on the Constitution, on laws, and on the legal interpretations of the various courts.

Consider a few of the possible interests the government may have. Government may want to prohibit discrimination based on race, gender, or religion. School officials may want to maintain decorum or a safe environment in the public schools. Legislators may desire to assure that all students with disabilities are included in regular education settings, curriculum, and activities.

Based on these liberties and interests, is it reasonable for the government to mandate that all public schools be desegregated, or do citizens have the right to send their students to segregated public schools if that is what the majority chooses? Is it reasonable for school personnel to deny access to students who misbehave, express anti-government sentiments, or wear hats in school, or do such policies infringe on students' due process rights and freedom of expression? Is it reasonable to require inclusion of students with disabilities in the regular education setting, or does such a mandate interfere with the rights and reasonable needs of non-disabled students and with the academic freedom of public educators? Is it reasonable to require that all school finances, including donations, be distributed equally, or does this unreasonably interfere with a right to donate money or materials to the school of one's choice?

These are some of the issues we will explore. Now it is time to learn the basics.

III. Two Important Notes Regarding the Difference Between Public School and Private School

1. **Public School Educators are "State Actors":** Our rights under the Constitution are rights with regard to the "State." For example, when we say we have freedom of religion, we mean that we are free from the "State" telling us what to believe. It is important to understand who the "State" is. In

general, "State" means all government – federal, state, and local. This includes public school personnel, because teachers, administrators, and other public school staff are part of the government. Therefore, what the Constitution prohibits government from doing, it also prevents school personnel from doing. Public school personnel are "state actors."

Please remember this principle throughout this text as well as throughout your career as a professional educator. To be sure, school personnel are citizens and enjoy the rights of citizenship. But you must be clear on two points: (1) Public school personnel are state actors and students are not; and (2) Therefore, to the extent necessary to protect student rights, it is entirely appropriate to restrict the rights of school personnel.

2. **Laws Also Apply to Private School Educators:** The Constitution does not restrict private entities, but laws do apply to such entities. Therefore, while the primary focus of this text is on public education, many of the principles presented are also applicable to professional educators in private schools. It is important to remember that while constitutional freedoms such as expression, speech, or religion may not apply to students in private schools, it is nevertheless the case that with only very limited exceptions, private schools are also prohibited from discrimination based on the same principles and categories that apply to public schools.

IV. Case for Chapter Two

Please read the edited version of the United States Supreme Court case *Pierce v. Society of Sisters*, found in Appendix A.

V. Discussion Item for Chapter Two

Part One: Hypothetical Facts

School District consists of two geographic areas, North Area and South Area. The majority of students attending school in North Area are from wealthy families. Most students attending school in South Area are from poor families. The two areas have similar racial and religious demographics.

School District wants to provide Internet and email access to all of its students, but cannot afford to do so. The parents at North Area take matters into their own hands. The North Area parents donate money and services sufficient to equip and network a full computer network system at the North Area schools so that all North Area students have complete access to the Internet from school. Each class is provided several computers, the libraries are supplied with several computers, and computer labs at each school contain many computers. All the computers are fully state-of-the-art and are networked to each other and to the Internet.

South Area parents are unable to do what the North Area parents have done. South Area students have no Internet access from school. There are five computers in the computer lab at each South Area school; all of them are obsolete and in need of repair.

Part Two: Discussion Question

As you know, it is clear that courts will not permit school districts to provide different services in different schools based on the race, religion, or national origin of student populations. Nevertheless, courts have been reluctant to interpret discrepancies due to socio-economic status as violations of the Constitution. Notwithstanding the "legality" of the hypothetical situation in School District's North and South Areas, discuss this situation with regard to Horace Mann's notion of what public schooling is supposed to look like in this country (as discussed above). Also, discuss the situation in light of your own views regarding public schooling.

Chapter Three

Due Process, Equal Protection, and Freedom of Expression

I. Introduction

The goal of this chapter is to present an overview of three fundamental aspects of constitutional law as they relate to the education profession:

1. Due Process;

2. Equal Protection; and

3. Freedom of Expression (also referred to as Freedom of Speech and Freedom of the Press).

Note that the present discussion deals with these issues as they apply to the rights of students. The applicability of these issues with regard to employment will be presented in a later chapter.

Also note that much of this discussion is of concern to private schools as well as public schools. These issues are primarily constitutional and therefore primarily concern the actions of educators in the public schools. Nevertheless, educators in private schools should remember that Congress has enacted a great deal of legislation that forbids discrimination not only in the public sector, but in the private sector as well. Please refer to Chapters Five through Eight, on Discrimination, for more about such legislation.

II. Balancing the Interests

As elements of constitutional law, Due Process, Equal Protection, and Freedom of Expression issues arise when government infringes upon the rights of citizens. In education, the issues arise when educators in public schools restrict or otherwise infringe upon the rights of students. In analyzing whether a particular action is permissible, courts apply a balancing test. Courts use different standards depending upon the specific right involved, but each of the standards requires striking a balance between:

1. The right infringed upon; and

2. The governmental interest involved.

According to the highest – or most strict – standard, the government must show that the infringement is necessary in order to accomplish a compelling state interest. At a lower standard, government need only show that the state action in question is reasonably related to a legitimate governmental function.

Unfortunately, Supreme Court cases are not sufficiently consistent to provide a reliable guide in predicting the specific standard that will be applied in a particular case. In general, cases involving constitutional rights such as Freedom of Expression and Free Exercise of Religion are analyzed under the highest standard. This is also the case with discrimination based on certain categories, such as race and religion. However, lesser standards are also often applied.

Notwithstanding court application of lesser requirements, in education the recommended "best practice" is for professional educators is to evaluate their own actions according to the highest possible standard. In other words, educators should consider it professionally improper and potentially illegal to infringe upon the rights of students unless it is necessary to do so in order to achieve one of the interests discussed below.

III. Compelling Interests in Education

In the arena of professional education, courts have recognized four general categories of "compelling interests." Again, action by professional educators that infringes on individual rights should be considered professionally improper and potentially illegal unless it is necessary in order to achieve one of the following interests:

1. **Legitimate Educational Purpose.** Educators have a degree of flexibility in making decisions about instruction, curriculum, homework, assessment strategies, etc.

2. **Maintaining an Appropriate Educational Environment.** Educators have a degree of flexibility in preventing serious disruption of an appropriate educational environment.

3. **Health and Safety.** Educators may need to take action or set policy aimed at protecting the health and safety of staff and students.

4. **Property Loss and Damage.** Educators may need to take action or set policy aimed at preventing property loss and damage.

IV. Due Process

The Fourteenth Amendment contains the "due process clause." The clause states, "No State shall . . . deprive any person of life, liberty, or property without due process of law." This means that government may not infringe upon a citizen's rights unless it has a sufficient reason to do so. In education, due process limits the actions of public school educators with regard to the rights of students. There are two types of due process rights, substantive due process and procedural due process. These are discussed separately, below.

A. Substantive Due Process

This first due process right is "substantive due process." Substantive due process protects citizens' actual or substantive rights. In other words, government may not infringe upon the rights of citizens without meeting the balancing standard discussed above.

Example of Substantive Due Process:

Consider a situation in which a school suspends a student for fighting. Substantive due process deals with the student's right to a free public education. Balance the school's interest in maintaining a safe and educationally appropriate environment against the student's right. Most likely, the school's interest will be sufficient to support the infringement to a certain extent – the student can be excluded from school property – but the school will have to make sure that the infringement does not go too far – it will need to make sure the student continues to receive instruction (via a home tutor, work sent home from school, or some other means).

B. Procedural Due Process

The second due process right demands that government follow fair and proper procedures any time it seeks to restrict a person's rights. This right is called "procedural due process" because it assures a fair procedure. The goal is to assure that government action is fair, rather than arbitrary and capricious. As with substantive due process, the particular procedure required in any given situation depends on the nature of the interests involved.

Procedural due process rules address the risk of error inherent in the truth-finding process. They protect persons not from the deprivation, but from the mistaken or unjustified deprivation of life, liberty, or property. The rules minimize unfair or mistaken deprivations by enabling persons to contest the basis upon which government proposes to deprive them of protected interests. See, e.g., *Mathews v. Eldridge,* 424 U.S. 319 (1976); *Carey v. Piphus,* 435 U.S. 247 (1978); *Fuentes v. Shevin,* 407 U.S. 67 (1972).

In *Mathews v. Eldridge,* the Supreme Court explained that identification of the specific dictates of procedural due process generally requires consideration of three distinct factors:

1. The private interest that will be affected by the official action;

2. The risk of erroneous deprivation of such interest through the procedures used, and probable value, if any, of additional or substitute procedural safeguards; and

3. The Government's interest, including the function involved and the fiscal and administrative burdens that the additional or substitute procedural requirements would entail.

Based on these factors, the inquiry in procedural due process situations is two-part:

First: Is there a protected private interest at issue?

Second: If so, what procedure is due?

IMPORTANT NOTE

It is important to understand that the first part of this inquiry should more properly be phrased "Does there exist a substantive due process issue?" Such wording would clarify that substantive due process is about the specific legal right or interest involved and that procedural due process is about the actual process or procedure that is due in order to protect a right. In other words, the real focus of procedural due process is on the second part of the inquiry. However, as there must be a protected interest in question in the first place before any procedure is due, the substantive question is necessarily prerequisite to, or the first part of, a focus on that procedure.

The case *Goss v. Lopez* is a leading case on procedural due process in professional education. It arose when some students in Ohio were suspended from school for ten days without ever being given the opportunity for a hearing to "determine the operative facts of the suspensions." The Court addressed both of the two parts of a procedural due process inquiry, as follows:

First: Is there a protected private interest at issue? The Court found that the students had two protected rights, a property right and a liberty right, as follows:

> "The Fourteenth Amendment forbids the State to deprive any person of life, liberty, or property without due process of law. Protected interests in property are normally 'not created by the Constitution. Rather, they are created and their dimensions are defined' by an independent source such as state statutes or rules entitling the citizen to certain benefits.
>
> [O]n the basis of state law, [the students] plainly had legitimate claims of entitlement to a public education. Ohio [law] . . . direct[s] local authorities to provide a free education to all residents between five and 21 years of age. . . . Having chosen to extend the right to an education . . ., Ohio may not withdraw that right on grounds of misconduct, absent fundamentally fair procedures to determine whether the misconduct has occurred. Although Ohio may not be constitutionally obligated to establish and maintain a public school system, it has nevertheless done so and has required its children to attend. . . . [Therefore, t]he State is constrained to recognize a student's legitimate entitlement to a public education as a property interest which is protected by the Due Process Clause and which may not be taken away for misconduct without adherence to the minimum procedures required by that Clause.
>
> The Due Process Clause also forbids arbitrary deprivations of liberty. Where a person's good name, reputation, honor, or integrity is at stake because of what the government is doing to him, the minimal requirements of the Clause must be satisfied. . . . School authorities here suspended [the students] from school for periods of up to 10 days based on charges of misconduct. If sustained and recorded, those charges could seriously damage the students' standing with

> their fellow pupils and their teachers as well as interfere with later opportunities for higher education and employment. It is apparent that the claimed right of the State to determine unilaterally and without process whether that misconduct has occurred immediately collides with the requirements of the Constitution." (Emphasis added)

Second: Since protected rights exist, what process is due? The Court held that school officials must give students notice of the action being taken, inform students of the facts upon which the charges are based, and give students the opportunity for a hearing to present their own side of the story. Even when suspensions are for less than ten days, school officials must provide these procedural safeguards prior to imposing a suspension (unless the student poses an imminent threat of danger to other students). The Court said:

> "At the very minimum, . . . students facing suspension and the consequent interference with a protected property interest must be given some kind of notice and afforded some kind of hearing. . . . The student's interest is to avoid unfair or mistaken exclusion from the educational process, with all of its unfortunate consequences. . . . The risk of error is not at all trivial, and it should be guarded against if that may be done without prohibitive cost or interference with the educational process.
>
> The difficulty is that our schools are vast and complex. Some modicum of discipline and order is essential if the educational function is to be performed. Events calling for discipline are frequent occurrences and sometimes require immediate, effective action. . . . But it would be a strange disciplinary system in an educational institution if no communication was sought by the disciplinarian with the student in an effort to inform him of his dereliction and to let him tell his side of the story in order to make sure that an injustice is not done. Fairness can rarely be obtained by

secret, onesided determination of facts decisive of rights. Secrecy is not congenial to truth-seeking . . . .

[T]he Due Process Clause . . . requires, in connection with a suspension of 10 days or less, that the student be given oral or written notice of the charges against him and, if he denies them, an explanation of the evidence the authorities have and an opportunity to present his side of the story. The Clause requires at least these rudimentary precautions against unfair or mistaken findings of misconduct and arbitrary exclusion from school.

There need be no delay between the time "notice" is given and the time of the hearing. In the great majority of cases the disciplinarian may informally discuss the alleged misconduct with the student minutes after it has occurred. We hold only that, in being given an opportunity to explain his version of the facts at this discussion, the student first be told what he is accused of doing and what the basis of the accusation is. . . . Since the hearing may occur almost immediately following the misconduct, it follows that as a general rule notice and hearing should precede removal of the student from school. We agree . . ., however, that there are recurring situations in which prior notice and hearing cannot be insisted upon. Students whose presence poses a continuing danger to persons or property or an ongoing threat of disrupting the academic process may be immediately removed from school. In such cases, the necessary notice and rudimentary hearing should follow as soon as practicable."

At this time, please read the case *Goss v. Lopez* (found in Appendix A) and then return to the following discussion.

Of course, many situations arise in which the stakes are much greater than a mere ten day suspension. In many cases, the type of informal notice and hearing outlined in Goss is insufficient; additional safeguards are required. Over the years, the Court has identified seven basic elements of adequate procedural protections:

1. **Notice:** "An elementary and fundamental requirement of due process in any proceeding which is to be accorded finality is notice reasonably calculated, under all the circumstances, to apprise interested parties of the pendency of the action and afford them an opportunity to present their objections." *Mullane v. Central Hanover Trust Co.,* 339 U.S. 306, 314 (1950).

2. **Hearing:** "The constitutional right to be heard is a basic aspect of the duty of government to follow a fair process of decision making when it acts to deprive a person of his possessions. The purpose of this requirement is not only to ensure abstract fair play to the individual. Its purpose, more particularly, is to protect his use and possession of property from arbitrary encroachment. . . ." *Fuentes v. Shevin,* 407 U.S. 67, 80-81 (1972).

3. **Impartial Decision Maker:** It is essential that the hearing be before "an impartial decision maker." *Goldberg v. Kelly,* 397 U.S. 254, 271 (1970).

4. **Confrontation and Cross-Examination:** "[W]here important decisions turn on questions of fact, due process requires an opportunity to confront and cross-examine adverse witnesses." *Greene v. McElroy,* 360 U.S. 474, 496-97 (1959).

5. **Discovery:** "[T]he evidence used to prove the Government's case must be disclosed to the individual so that he has an opportunity to show that it is untrue." *Greene v. McElroy,* 360 U.S. 474, 496 (1959), quoted with approval in *Goldberg v. Kelly,* 397 U.S. 254, 270 (1970).

6. **Decision on the Record:** "[T]he decisionmaker's conclusion . . . must rest solely on the legal rules and evidence adduced at the hearing. . . . To demonstrate compliance with this elementary requirement, the decisionmaker should state the reasons for his determination and indicate the evidence he relied on." *Goldberg v. Kelly,* 397 U.S. 254, 271 (1970). Note that this means it is improper for the decision maker to rely on information that is not presented in the hearing.

7. **Counsel:** Citizens, and students, have the right to be represented by counsel in due process hearings. *Goldberg v. Kelly,* 397 U.S. 254 (1970). However, it is not required that counsel be provided for those who cannot afford to retain their own representation.

V. Equal Protection

The Fourteenth Amendment also contains the "equal protection clause." The clause states, "No State shall . . . deny any person within its jurisdiction the equal protection of the laws." The right to equal protection is a right to be treated the same as everyone else. For example, if white people get to go to school, then so do people of all other races; if male students get to play sports, then so do female students; and so on. Government may not infringe upon a citizen's right to equal protection unless it has a sufficient state interest to justify doing so. Sufficiency of state interest must often meet the highest judicial standard, government having to show that the infringement is necessary in order to accomplish a compelling state interest.

The amendment was enacted in 1868 and was initially aimed at establishing racial equality, namely between white people and African Americans. However, as with other constitutional amendments, the Fourteenth Amendment contains an enactment clause giving Congress the "power to enforce [the Amendment] by appropriate legislation." Congress has used this power over the years to enact laws providing equal protection regardless of race, gender, religion, national origin, disability, color, and marital status. Additionally, court rulings and state laws require equal protection, to degrees varying from state to state, regardless of sexual orientation and socio-economic status. It is crucial for educators to remember that because most specific, legal prohibition of discrimination is in the form of legislation, discrimination on the basis of these categories is prohibited in both the public and private sectors.

At this time, please read the following equal protection cases (found in Appendix A) and then return to the discussion below.

Brown v. Board of Ed.
Romer v. Evans
Lau v. Nichols

VI. Two Notes: Intent and Equal Protection for the Poor

Intent: Note that intent does not necessarily matter in Equal Protection cases; if a government practice has the effect of discriminating on the basis of a protected category, the practice may violate the Equal Protection Clause. This applies, for example, in situations where a significant portion of a school system is segregated, or where certain programs or activities are segregated. However, allegations of discrepancies from one school district to another do not necessarily represent equal protection violations. "Before the boundaries of separate and autonomous school districts may be set aside by consolidating the separate units for remedial purposes by imposing a cross-district remedy, it must first be shown that there has been a constitutional violation within one district that produces a significant segregative effect in another district. Specifically it must be shown that racially discriminatory acts of the state or local school districts, or of a single school district, have been a substantive cause of inter-district segregation." *Milliken v. Bradley,* 418 U.S. 717, 744-45 (1974).

Equal Protection for the Poor: Another issue that professional educators confront frequently is the difference in the quality of education between "wealthy" and "poor" school districts. In *San Antonio School District v. Rodriguez,* 411 U.S. 1 (1973), the Court decided that different educational opportunity on the basis of wealth did not violate the Constitution. (Additionally, educators should remember that the Court reiterated the fact that the Constitution does not mention education. As such, there is no "fundamental right" to education.) (An edited version of the case *San Antonio School Dist. v. Rodriguez* is provided in Appendix A.)

VII. Freedom of Expression

The First Amendment guarantees free expression and free association. The landmark case *Tinker v. Des Moines School District* established that students in public schools are guaranteed these rights. The Court said,

> "First Amendment rights, applied in light of the special characteristics of the school environment, are available to teachers and students. It can hardly be argued that either students or teachers shed their constitutional rights to freedom of speech or expression at the school house gate. . . . In order for . . . school officials to justify prohibition of a particular expression of opinion, [they] must be able to show that the[ir] action was caused by something more than a mere desire to avoid the discomfort and unpleasantness that always accompany an unpopular viewpoint. Certainly where there is no finding and no showing that engaging in the forbidden conduct would 'materially and substantially interfere with the requirements of appropriate discipline in the operation of the school,' the prohibition cannot be sustained."

At this time, please read *Tinker* (found in Appendix A) and then return to the discussion below.

While *Tinker* places strict limits on the general actions of school officials, educators nevertheless have more leeway when it comes to "school-sponsored activities." According to *Hazelwood School District v. Kuhlmeir,* schools may "exercise editorial control over the style and content of student speech in school-sponsored expressive activities, so long as their actions are reasonably related to legitimate pedagogical concerns." This "editorial control" is not limited to publications. "School-sponsored activities" also include "theatrical productions, and other expressive activities that students, parents, and members of the public might reasonably perceive to bear the imprimatur of the school. These activities may fairly be characterized as part of the school curriculum, whether or not they occur in a traditional classroom setting, so long as they are supervised by faculty members and designed to impart particular knowledge or skills to student participants and audiences."

However, this editorial control is not a license to censor particular points of view. If a school permits the school paper to publish an article asserting a particular opinion, it may not censor an article asserting the opposing opinion. Also, remember that school officials do not have editorial authority over publications that are not "school-sponsored" and may not restrict the distribution of such publications, except in accord with the "compelling interests" discussed above. (Nevertheless, school officials may place reasonable limits on the time, place, or manner of distribution.)

Expression can take forms other than oral or written statements. Consider dress codes, for example. Such codes should only go as far as necessary to achieve compelling interests. Also consider compelled expression. For example, students may not be compelled to pledge or salute the flag. In *West Virginia Board of Education v. Barnette,* 319 U.S. 624 (1943), the Court held that students' liberty of conscience could not be infringed upon in the name of "national unity" or "patriotism."

> "[T]he action of the local authorities in compelling the flag salute and pledge transcends constitutional limitations on their power and invades the sphere of intellect and spirit which it is the purpose of the First Amendment to our Constitution to reserve from all official control. . . . Boards of Education [have] important, delicate, and highly discretionary functions,

> but none that they may not perform within the limits of the Bill of Rights. That they are educating the young for citizenship is reason for scrupulous protection of Constitutional freedoms of the individual, if we are not to strangle the free mind at its source and teach youth to discount important principles of our government as mere platitudes."

Finally, consider censorship of library books or Internet access. In the case *Board of Education v. Pico,* 457 U.S. 853 (1982), the Supreme Court prohibited schools from removing library books merely because school officials "dislike the ideas contained in the books." As the Court explained:

> "[T]he First Amendment rights of students may be directly and sharply implicated by the removal of books from the shelves of a school library. Our precedents have focused not only on the role of the First Amendment in fostering individual self-expression but also on its role in affording the public access to discussion, debate, and the dissemination of information and ideas. . . .
>
> [W]e have recognized that the State may not, consistently with the spirit of the First Amendment, contract the spectrum of available knowledge. . . . [T]he Constitution protects the right to receive information and ideas. This right is an inherent corollary of the rights of free speech and press that are explicitly guaranteed by the Constitution, in two senses. First, the right to receive ideas follows ineluctably from the sender's First Amendment right to send them. The right of freedom of speech and press . . . embraces the right to distribute literature, and necessarily protects the right to receive it. The dissemination of ideas can accomplish nothing if otherwise willing addressees are not free to receive and consider them. It would be a barren marketplace of ideas that had only sellers and no buyers.
>
> More importantly, the right to receive ideas is a necessary predicate to the recipient's meaningful

exercise of his own rights of speech, press, and political freedom. Madison admonished us: 'A popular Government, without popular information, or the means of acquiring it, is but a Prologue to a Farce or a Tragedy; or, perhaps both. Knowledge will forever govern ignorance: And a people who mean to be their own Governors, must arm themselves with the power which knowledge gives.' 9 Writings of James Madison 103 (G. Hunt ed. 1910).

As we recognized in Tinker, students too are beneficiaries of this principle: 'In our system, students may not be regarded as closed-circuit recipients of only that which the State chooses to communicate. . . . [S]chool officials cannot suppress expressions of feeling with which they do not wish to contend.'

A school library, no less than any other public library, is a place dedicated to quiet, to knowledge, and to beauty. [S]tudents must always remain free to inquire, to study and to evaluate, to gain new maturity and understanding. The school library is the principal locus of such freedom. . . . [I]n the school library a student can literally explore the unknown, and discover areas of interest and thought not covered by the prescribed curriculum. . . . Th[e] student learns that a library is a place to test or expand upon ideas presented to him, in or out of the classroom. . . .

[L]ocal school boards may not remove books from school library shelves simply because they dislike the ideas contained in those books and seek by their removal to prescribe what shall be orthodox in politics, nationalism, religion, or other matters of opinion. . . . Such purposes stand inescapably condemned by our precedents."

VIII. Cases for Chapter Three

Please read the edited versions of the following Supreme Court cases, which are found in Appendix A.

Fundamental Cases:

Due Process:

Goss v. Lopez

Equal Protection:

Brown v. Board of Education

Romer v. Evans

Lau v. Nichols

Freedom of Expression:

Tinker v. Des Moines School District

Additional Suggested Cases:

Equal Protection (Education & Wealth):

San Antonio School District v. Rodriguez

Freedom of Expression:

Hazelwood School District v. Kuhlmeier

IX. Discussion Item for Chapter Three

Part One: Hypothetical Situation

A colleague asks you the following question:

"Why it is that schools can ban certain articles of clothing, such as hats at school. Wearing hats is in no way harming the health of students, damaging property, or causing a disruption. I am aware of the need for schools to keep gang activities at a simmer during school hours and on school property, but doesn't an all-out ban on hats infringe on First Amendment rights? Isn't this a form of expression?

"I know of a school that banned any student from wearing a hat at school, to stop gang attire. I find this completely ridiculous. Wearing hats is not going to hurt anyone and banning them will certainly not stop gang violence. What rules, laws, or mandates apply to schools regarding such clothing bans?"

Part Two: Question

How far can public schools go in order to stem gang activity? Is an all out ban on hats permissible? What do you think in light of the materials and cases presented in this chapter? Consider the substantive right at issue, what procedure is due, and whether there exists an equal protection issue.

Chapter Four

Discrimination Defined, Types of Discrimination, and Protected Categories of People

I. Introduction

This goal of this chapter is to introduce the subject of discrimination as it relates to education law by presenting:

1. A working definition of discrimination for the purposes of this text;

2. The major classes of people protected from discrimination; and

3. The historical context in which discrimination law has developed.

Chapters Five, Six, and Seven discuss specific protected classes in terms of the legal requirements placed on educators in order to assure that educators afford these classes of people an equal educational opportunity.

II. Defining Discrimination

According to Black's Law Dictionary, discrimination (in the sense of illegal discrimination) is:

> "[T]he effect of a statute or established practice which [results in] . . . a failure to treat all persons equally where no reasonable distinction can be found between those favored and those not favored."

Note that discrimination therefore has two essential components: (1) *treating people differently*; and (2) doing so *without a reasonable basis.* For the purposes of this text, discrimination will refer to actions in professional education settings that illegally or improperly treat people differently based on the group of which they are a part. Such discrimination can occur in three ways:

1. When discriminatory treatment in public education (i.e., by government actors) violates the right to equal protection (i.e., deprives students of an equal educational opportunity or deprives employees of equal treatment in the workplace);

2. When the actions of public or private educators violates specific laws prohibiting specific discriminatory treatment; or

3. When public or private entities fail to take affirmative steps required by law to eliminate the effects of past discrimination or to create a situation in which all persons are indeed treated equally. For example, in order to assure that persons with disabilities (whether students or employees) have equal educational or professional opportunities, the law requires actions regarding such individuals that are different from action taken regarding persons without disabilities.

Remember that discrimination can therefore occur when educators act in a manner that improperly treats people differently, or when educators fail to act in a manner required by law in order to assure that people are indeed given equal opportunities. Also remember that it may sometimes be appropriate to treat people differently when such treatment is reasonable. Courts decide whether or not differential treatment is reasonable by evaluating whether the entity engaging in the discriminatory behavior has a sufficient reason for doing so (most often applying the "strict scrutiny" or "necessary in order to achieve a compelling interest" standard discussed earlier in Chapter Two).

III. Protected Categories and Historical Perspective

Constitutional interpretations and numerous laws now prohibit many forms of discrimination, but progress has been slow and painful. Consider the seven bases upon which discrimination is generally prohibited. In general, no American citizen can be discriminated against based on that citizen's:

1. Race
2. National Origin
3. Religion
4. Sex
5. Age
6. Disability
7. Marital Status

Professional educators are presumably well aware of this country's tragic history with respect to differential treatment of persons based on most of the above-listed criteria. State and federal governments have carried out systematic policies of conquest, enslavement, and genocide based on race. Incarceration because of national origin was government policy as recently as the 1940's and incarceration of people with disabilities has been even more recent. People of different races and national origin, people with disabilities, youth and the elderly, women, and people of various religions, have experienced an overwhelming degree of treatment as second-class citizens throughout this country's history.

Legal protection has gradually come into existence, but improper and illegal discrimination continues today. Reading any newspaper will confirm the continuation of such discrimination in society. Discrimination also continues in education:

- Consider female participation in school athletics. Girls must be allowed to try out for teams "unless the sport is a contact sport." This is an example of legal, but improper, discrimination.
- Consider holiday displays in public schools. Christmas decorations, parties, and programs are omnipresent

during the month of December. This is an example of illegal and improper discrimination.
Consider conversations you may have participated in or overheard in schools or elsewhere. How many educators have you heard complain about having to include students with disabilities in regular education settings? How many times have you heard professional educators comment on how a teacher or an employee would be desirable for a given position because of their particular sex, age, or race? How many times have you heard educators make fun of students, colleagues, or others based on their sexual orientation? How many times have you heard comments on how students from certain "types of families" or from certain ethnic backgrounds do better or worse academically? If you have not heard such statements, you are either lucky or you wisely avoid staff lounges. Unfortunately, however, if this list were presented orally in a lecture, you would see the veteran teachers in the class nodding at each statement; they would most likely have heard each one of these statements within a single day or week. These are examples of improper behavior, violative of the ethics of professional education.

The "seven protected categories" do not include all categories of peoples historically and presently discriminated against and who need enhanced legal protection. Two other bases upon which discrimination is often legally prohibited include sexual orientation and socio-economic status.

IV. Two Points to Remember About Discrimination in Professional Education

When reading and considering the materials in the remainder of this book, please remember two points:

1. **Educators deal with students.** Students are a legally deemed to be a particularly *vulnerable* segment of society. Courts recognize and presume

that students are subject to a great deal of peer pressure and have a strong "need to fit in." Additionally, remember that we compel students to attend school. Thus, courts presume that students are an audience captive to behavior modification specialists (i.e., professional educators). As a result of these legal presumptions (which are indeed sound and realistic presumptions), educators must be vigilant in their respect for and protection of student rights. Likewise, educators must be ever-aware of the need to analyze and criticize their own behavior.

2. **There is no such thing as "special rights."** Many misguided individuals and organizations have tried to portray anti-discrimination policies and principles as bestowing "special rights." Yet every citizen is a member of each of the protected categories (each one of us has a race, national origin, religion, sex, age, level of ability, marital status, sexual orientation, and socio-economic status). It is therefore improper and unlawful to discriminate against *anyone* on the bases discussed above. For example, when we say that individuals cannot be discriminated against based on religion, we must remember that this applies to all religions (as well as to non-religion, or atheism). The individuals and organizations who use the misnomer "special rights" generally do so for one or more of the following three reasons:

   (i) They may be confused about, or in denial of, the fact that certain groups of people have historically been discriminated against (and that these groups are therefore in need of protection). They may not understand that discrimination laws do not give "special rights" to these groups. Rather, such laws protect these groups from improper treatment. They may think that because such laws arose to protect certain victimized groups that the laws somehow apply only to those particular groups. Yet such laws apply to all groups (i.e., all races, all religions, all national origins, etc.).

(ii) They may be motivated by philosophical or religious beliefs that view imposing such beliefs on others as appropriate and acceptable.

(iii) They may be using the political rhetoric of hate and obfuscation for personal gain.

V. Additional Essential Reading for Chapter Four

1. A Note About Child Abuse (Appendix B)
2. Laws Affecting Education (Appendix C)
3. Common Forms of Discrimination Found in Schools (Appendix D)

VI. Discussion Item for Chapter Four

Based only on the material presented in this chapter (and the related appendices), why is it unlawful discrimination when elementary school teachers transport their students from one part of the school to another by having the students walk in two lines: one for boys and one for girls?

Chapter Five

Religion

I. Introduction

The goal of this chapter is to address the legal rights and obligations of professional educators with regard to religion. Discrimination on the basis of religion is in many respects the most difficult type of discrimination with which educators must deal. In a strictly legal sense, we each have some form of religious belief, whether we adhere to a particular faith, whether we have a more individualized sense of spirituality, or whether we eschew all belief in things supernatural. Whatever our individual religious view, our beliefs (but, as we shall see, not our actions) are equally protected by the Constitution.

For reasons not related to legal issues (but which are explainable in terms of psychology) professional educators in public schools frequently engage in actions that are discriminatory on the basis of religion. While it may be easy to avoid inappropriate behavior related to other issues (such as race, disability, gender, etc.) it is often the case that educators view their own inappropriate and discriminatory practices with regard to religion as being appropriate. Educators often have difficulty separating their religious beliefs from their professional practices.

The basic legal rule governing the actions of professional educators in the public schools with regard to religion is as follows:

> Behavior by professional educators and staff in public schools which can be considered the *practice of religion*, or the *expression of personal religious beliefs* is inappropriate from a constitutional standpoint where such behavior occurs in the *presence of students* or when otherwise acting in one's professional capacity. The terms "religion" and "religious beliefs" in the previous sentence refer to all religious activities *including nonbelief.* This rule applies to all school-related

locations and during all school-related functions and activities. (This is only a basic rule: ***for specificity in any given factual situation, apply the constitutional tests discussed below.*****)**

The particulars of this basic rule will become clearer as you read this chapter and the related cases, but this introductory statement brings us to an important consideration. Please read the rule again and then consider the following questions:

1. Do your own religious beliefs permit you to follow the rule? In other words, can you really avoid such things as wearing religious attire, decorating your room for holidays, or answering student questions about your personal beliefs?

2. Can you live with the fact that it is often necessary to infringe on the religious freedoms of educators in order to protect the rights of students and in order to protect students from discrimination?

3. Can you be neutral about your own beliefs? Can you be truly neutral? In other words, can you behave towards your students in a manner which acknowledges the right of every person to decide for him or herself what to believe? Can you avoid conveying to your students the notion that any particular religious belief, or even that religion as opposed to non-religion, is "true" or "correct?"

4. Can you stand up to the pressure exerted by parents who want to put up Christmas, Halloween, or other holiday decorations, who want to have holiday parties in your classroom, who expect holiday programs, who demand to know why kids learn about evolution rather than creationism, or who demand to know why their kids are being taught about Kwanzaa, Chanukah, Christmas, Native American traditions, etc.? Can you keep your own

practices professional, appropriate, and legal in the face of such parental pressure?

This is what it takes to work in the public schools. This is what it takes to avoid discriminating against your students on the basis of religion. This is what it takes to teach in a manner that is appropriate, professional, and legal.

What if you cannot come to terms with this balance between professional behavior and your personal beliefs? Perhaps you should not work in the public sector. Perhaps you should consider the private sector for your career path as a professional educator.

Now that we have considered the difficulty of the topic, let us proceed. This chapter addresses religion and religious discrimination in three parts:

1. The provisions regarding religion found in the First Amendment of the Constitution;

2. Statutory provisions and local school district policies regarding religion; and

3. General concerns and guidelines regarding religion in education.

II. The Constitution - Establishment and Free Exercise

The First Amendment provides that "Congress shall make no law respecting an establishment of religion, or prohibiting the free exercise thereof . . . ." While the provision originally applied to Congress, its application now extends to all governmental entities as a result of the Fourteenth Amendment. Note that the provision contains two clauses:

1. **The "Establishment" Clause:** Government (including public schools and public school personnel) is prohibited from taking action which "establishes" religion; and

2. **The "Free Exercise" Clause:** Government may not infringe upon the freedom of each citizen to practice whatever religion that citizen chooses (or to refrain from the practice of religion).

The Supreme Court and the various federal and state courts have dealt with numerous cases concerning these clauses. No doubt such cases will also continue well into the future. The basic approach developed by the Court is to balance the two clauses as follows:

- Government may take action to protect and accommodate the free exercise of religion, but may not go too far in doing so.
- How far is too far? When government violates the establishment clause it has gone too far. The Supreme Court broadly defined the establishment clause, as follows:

> "The 'establishment of religion' clause of the First Amendment means at least this: Neither a state nor the Federal Government can set up a church. Neither can pass laws which aid one religion, aid all religions, or prefer one religion over another. Neither can force nor influence a person to go to or to remain away from church against his will or force him to profess a belief or disbelief in any religion. No person can be punished for entertaining or professing religious beliefs or disbeliefs, for church attendance or non-attendance. No tax in any amount, large or small, can be levied to support any religious activities or institutions, whatever they may be called, or whatever from they may adopt to teach or practice religion. Neither a state nor the Federal Government can, openly or secretly, participate in the affairs of any religious organizations or groups and vice versa. *In the words of Jefferson, the clause*

> *against establishment of religion by law was intended to erect 'a wall of separation between Church and State.'"* *Everson v. Board of Education of the Township of Ewing,* 330 US 1 (1947) (emphasis added).

In the time since the *Everson* case, the Court has been quite clear that the First Amendment applies "with full force to the States and their school districts." *Lee v. Weisman,* 505 U.S. 577 (1992). The Court has established the specific guidelines applied to determine whether government action violates the religious provisions of the First Amendment. These guidelines take the form of to three interrelated tests that the Court has used to analyze alleged violations of the Establishment Clause in the realm of public education:

- The "Lemon Test;"
- The "Endorsement Test;" and
- The "Coercion Test."

A. The Lemon Test

In the 1971 case *Lemon v. Kurtzman,* 403 U.S. 602 (1971), the Court developed what has subsequently become known as the Lemon Test. It is a three-part test by which courts judge whether a law, policy, or state action violates the Establishment Clause. With only one exception, the Supreme Court applied the Lemon Test to every Establishment case it decided between 1971 and 1984.

The test is as follows (note that government action is unconstitutional if it violates any of the three parts of the Lemon test):

1. **Purpose:** The intent or purpose of a law or state action must have a legitimate secular purpose. The purpose may not be related to religion (except that government can take limited action to protect or accommodate free exercise).

2. **Effect:** The primary effect of a law or state action must neither advance nor inhibit religion.

3. **Excessive Entanglement:** The law or state action must not foster an excessive entanglement with religion (i.e., government may not become too involved in the activities of religion in general or in the activities of a particular religious institution).

B. The Endorsement Test

In the 1984 case, *Lynch v. Donnelly,* 465 U.S. 668 (1984), Justice O'Connor wrote a concurring opinion in which she developed the "Endorsement Test." The test effectively collapsed the first two prongs of the Lemon Test, as follows:

> "The Establishment Clause prohibits government from making adherence to a religion relevant in any way to a person's standing in the political community. Government can run afoul of that prohibition in two principal ways. One is excessive entanglement with religious institutions . . . . The second and more direct infringement is government endorsement or disapproval of religion. Endorsement sends a message to nonadherents that they are outsiders, not full members of the political community, and an accompanying message to adherents that they are insiders, favored members of the political community." Lynch, at 687-88 (O'Connor, J., concurring).

It is important to understand that while a majority of the Court relied on the Endorsement Test in the case County of *Allegheny v. ACLU,* 492 U.S. 573 (1989), the Court has not formally adopted Endorsement Test. Remember that the if a situation violates the Endorsement Test, it follows that such a situation also violates the Lemon Test. Therefore, in relying on the Endorsement Test in the case cited above, it is best not to view the Court as abandoning the Lemon Test. Rather, one should understand that when a violation of the Endorsement

Test is present, such violation will be sufficient for the court to find that conduct violates the Establishment Clause.

C. The Coercion Test

In 1992, the Court was faced with a situation in which the Establishment Clause was so clearly violated that it was not necessary to resort to the Lemon Test. In the case *Lee v. Weisman,* the Court developed the "Coercion Test" (also referred to as the "Lee Test"). In Lee, the Court held unconstitutional the practice of including invocations and benedictions in the form of "nonsectarian" prayers at public school graduation ceremonies.

The reasoning in the *Lee* case was concisely summarized by Judge Goodwin in the case *Newdow v. US Congress,* 9th Cir (2002):

> "[In *Lee*] the Court first examined the degree of school involvement in the prayer, and found that 'the graduation prayers bore the imprint of the State and thus put school-age children who objected in an untenable position.' The next issue the Court considered was 'the position of the students, both those who desired the prayer and she who did not.' Noting that 'there are heightened concerns with protecting freedom of conscience from subtle coercive pressure in the elementary and secondary public schools,' the Court held that the school district's supervision and control of the graduation ceremony put impermissible pressure on students to participate in, or at least show respect during, the prayer. The Court concluded that primary and secondary school children may not be placed in the dilemma of either participating in a religious ceremony or protesting."

Thus, in *Lee* the Court concluded that under the Coercion Test, "government involvement with religious activity . . . [that] is pervasive, to the point of creating a state-sponsored and state-directed religious exercise" unquestionably violates the Establishment Clause. This is because, "at a minimum, the Constitution guarantees that government may not coerce anyone to support or participate in religion or its exercise, or otherwise to act in a way which establishes a state religion or religious faith, or tends to do so."

At this time, please read the case *Lee v. Weisman,* which is found in Appendix A, and then return to the discussion below.

Remember three important points about *Lee v. Weisman*:

1. The Court recognized the reality that students are often captive audiences. The court recognized that while students could technically elect not to attend the graduation ceremony, the reality is that

   > "in our society and in our culture high school graduation is one of life's most significant occasions. . . . A student is not free to absent herself from the graduation exercise in any real sense of the term 'voluntary,' for absence would require forfeiture of those intangible benefits which have motivated the student through youth and all her high school years."

   The compulsory nature of participation in school activities is not limited to graduation ceremonies. Many so-called "voluntary" activities are in reality compulsory in the sense described in Lee v. Weisman; absence or non-participation would require students to forfeit various educational benefits.

2. The Court also blasted the notion that religious activities are "no big deal." People who impose religious activities on others often try to make this assertion in an attempt to justify their actions. However, as the Court correctly reasoned,

   > "the embarrassment and the intrusion of the religious exercise cannot be refuted by arguing that these prayers, and similar ones to be said in the future, are of a de minimis

> character. To do so would be an affront to the Rabbi who offered them and to all those for whom the prayers were an essential and profound recognition of divine authority. And for the same reason, . . . the intrusion is greater than the two minutes or so of time consumed for prayers like these."

3. Finally, remember that actions of public educators can violate the establishment clause in many ways; it is not necessary to exhibit the egregious behavior seen in *Lee v. Weisman*. While the case is an example of a situation that is "especially improper because the State . . . in every practical sense compelled attendance and participation in an explicit religious exercise," be sure to keep in mind that any action which violates the Lemon Test is unconstitutional.

C. Using All Three Tests in One Case

In the summer of 2000, the Supreme Court decided the case its most recent school prayer case, the case of *Santa Fe Independent District v. Doe* (found in Appendix A). The Court applied all three tests – the Lemon Test, the Endorsement Test, and the Coercion Test – to strike down a school district's policy of permitting student-led "invocations" before high school football games. Citing *Lee*, the Court held that "the delivery of a pre-game prayer has the improper effect of coercing those present to participate in an act of religious worship." Under the Lemon Test, the school district's policy was found unconstitutional because it did not have a secular purpose. Finally, using language associated with the Endorsement Test, the Court concluded that the district's "policy was implemented with the purpose of endorsing school prayer" and emphasized that even non-coercive laws and practices are unconstitutional if they "convey[] a message of religious endorsement."

D. How Do Courts Apply the Interrelated Establishment Clause Tests?

Given the history of the Establishment Clause cases, one may be somewhat confused as to how to apply the three interrelated tests to current and future situations. Fortunately, however, Judge Goodwin provides us with succinct guidance:

> "[Courts] are free to apply any or all of the three tests, and to invalidate any measure that fails any one of them. The Supreme Court has not repudiated Lemon; in Santa Fe, it found that the application of each of the three tests provided an independent ground for invalidating the statute at issue in that case; and in Lee, the Court invalidated the policy solely on the basis of the coercion test. Although [courts] ha[ve] typically applied the Lemon test to alleged Establishment Clause violations . . . [they] are not required to apply it if a practice fails one of the other tests. Nevertheless, for purposes of completeness, [courts may desire] to analyze the school district polic[ies] . . . under all three tests." *Newdow v. US Congress*.

III. Statutory Provisions and Local School District Policies

Federal laws, state laws, and local school district policies also impose requirements on professional educators in order to protect students' religious rights. Note in particular that certain actions by school personnel are not only improper, but can be illegal. Some examples include:

- Wearing religious dress or religious symbols while on the job;
- Displaying a Bible or other religious books in the classroom or reading them during classroom hours;
- Discussing religious matters with students while on campus;

- Permitting holiday programs or decorations (especially if they focus on one particular religion);
- Using class time for activities related to religious holidays; and
- Establishing periods for voluntary prayer or silent meditation.

NOTE – Use the Legal Rules:
A Word of Caution About *Dicta*

It is crucial to follow legal rules, not mere statements of individual opinion - even if such statements are made by judges themselves. In other words, beware of *dicta*. As explained above in Chapter One, *dicta,* or *obiter dictum,* refers to statements in a court decision which go beyond the facts of the case. Since it is not based on the facts, *dicta* is merely the individual view of the judge writing the opinion; it is not law and it is not binding as legal precedent.

The Oregon case *Cooper v. Eugene School District,* 301 Or 358 (1986) shows how dicta can be a trap for the unwary. In *Cooper,* the Oregon Supreme Court decided a case in which a school district sought to prohibit a teacher for wearing religious clothing (*Sikh* clothing, including a white turban). In directly addressing the facts, the court sided with the district, stating that:

> "Parents and lawmakers may and do assume that the hours, days, and years spent in school are the time and the place when a young person is most impressionable by the expressed and implicit orthodoxies of the adult community and most sensitive to being perceived as different from the majority of his or her peers; famous constitutional cases have involved this socializing rather than intellectual function of the schools. In excluding teachers whose dress is a constant and inescapable visual reminder of their religious commitment, laws like ORS 342.650 [which is the Oregon law precluding public school teachers from wearing religious dress] respect and contribute to the

> child's right to the free exercise and enjoyment of its religious opinions or heritage, untroubled by being out of step with those of the teacher."

But then the court delved into the realm of *dicta*; Justice Linde went beyond the facts of the case and delivered his own personal views:

> "'[R]eligious dress' must be judged from the perspective both of the wearer and of the observer, that it is dress which is worn by reason of its religious importance to the teacher and also conveys to children of the age, background, and sophistication typical of students in the teacher's class a degree of religious commitment beyond the choice to wear common decorations that a person might draw from a religious heritage, such as a necklace with a small cross or Star of David. A teacher does not violate the statute by wearing a garment or a color that unintentionally happens to imply membership in some religious group, nor, for instance, by dressing in clerical garb to assume a role in a classroom historical exercise or a performance of, say, George Bernard Shaw's Saint Joan."

The important thing for the professional educator to remember is that Justice Linde's *dicta* is not binding law. Since the case did not involve wearing a "necklace with a small cross or Star of David," his opinion that such actions are not violations of student rights is not binding as legal precedent.

So in making your own decision about wearing so-called "common decorations," do not be lulled into relying on *dicta*. Instead, consider whether attire, if challenged, will stand up in light of the established legal rules. Consider whether the wearer would prevail in a court properly applying the Lemon Test, the reasoning in the *Lee* and *Santa Fe* cases, or even the Oregon court's own test (i.e., whether the attire "is a constant and inescapable visual reminder of [the wearer's] religious commitment [or whether it affords the proper] respect . . . to the child's right to the free exercise and enjoyment of [his or her] religious opinions or heritage, untroubled by being out of step with those of the teacher").

IV. General Concerns and Guidelines Regarding Religion in Education

Professional educators should remember several points regarding religion, as follows:

1. Evaluate actions in accord with the Lemon Test. Remember that if *any* of the three parts of the test is violated, the action in question violates the Constitution.

2. *Student rights outweigh the rights of school staff.* While school staff enjoy the same basic rights as students, "the interest of the State in avoiding an Establishment Clause violation may be a compelling one justifying an abridgement of [rights] otherwise protected by the First Amendment. [It is often the case that a] school district's interest in avoiding an Establishment Clause violation trumps [staff]'s right[s]." *Peloza v Capistrano Unified School District,* 37 F3d 517 (9th Cir 1994), cert den, 115 S Ct 2640 (1995).

3. *Students are impressionable and the courts consistently presume as a matter of law the existence of such impressionability, or vulnerability.* Never lose sight of or underestimate the *irrebuttable* nature of the legal presumption regarding the enormous influence school staff and school activities have on students. Consider what the Ninth Circuit Court of Appeals said in the *Peloza* case in justifying limits on a teacher's own constitutional right of freedom of expression.

   > "While at . . . school, whether he is in the classroom or outside of it during contract

> time, [a teacher] is not just any ordinary citizen. He is a teacher. He is one of those especially respected persons chosen to teach in the . . . classroom. He is clothed with the mantle of one who imparts knowledge and wisdom. His expressions of opinion are all the more believable because he is a teacher. The likelihood of . . . students equating his views with those of the school is substantial. To permit him to discuss his religious beliefs with students during school time on school grounds would violate the Establishment Clause of the First Amendment. Such speech would not have a secular purpose, would have the primary effect of advancing religion, and would entangle the school with religion. In sum, it would flunk all three parts of the test articulated in Lemon." *Id.*

Likewise, restrictions are justified with regard to many of the day-to-day activities of teachers.

4. While teachers may not do so, students are permitted to read religious material, engage in group activities of a religious nature, and engage each other in religious conversation during their free time in the public schools. (Students may not, however, disrupt classes, interfere with the educational process, or engage in discriminatory or harassing behavior against other students under the guise of "free exercise.")

5. If a school permits student clubs to use school facilities during non-school hours, it should permit the same access to student religious clubs.

6. Do not penalize students for absence from school to celebrate religious holidays or to attend religious functions. (Some school districts now provide staff

with a list of the dates of the major holidays celebrated by the ten or twelve more common religions. Such lists can assist educators in avoiding conflicts when planning examinations and important lessons.)

7. Do not permit the use of public school funds or materials by religious schools.

NOTE - College Students and Religion

Students of education often ask whether the rules that apply to public school students also apply to college students in public institutions. According to the US Supreme Court in the case *Tilton v. Richardson,* 403 U.S. 672 (1971), which distinguished between school-aged students and college students, "There is no substance to the contention that college students are less impressionable and less susceptible to religious indoctrination."

V. Cases for Chapter Five

Please read the following Supreme Court cases, which are found in Appendix A.

Fundamental Cases:
Lee v. Weisman
Newdow v. US Congress (The Pledge of Allegiance Case - "Under God" Language)

Additional Suggested Case:
Santa Fe Independent School District v. Doe

VI. Discussion Items for Chapter Five

The questions below requires you to analyze one case (*Lee v. Weisman*) using the rule of another case (*Lemon*). Additionally, you are presented with a situation (which happens to be a real life situation) and asked apply the Lemon Test once again. In order to help you get started, remember that for cases involving the Establishment Clause, the Issue and Rule portions of an IRAC analysis are as follows:

ISSUE: Does [the practice, law, policy, etc. in question] violate the establishment clause of the First Amendment?

RULE: The Supreme Court uses the following three-part test, known as the Lemon Test, to determine whether state action violates the establishment clause:

> In order for a state action to comply with the establishment clause, it must:
>
> 1. Have a secular purpose.
>
> 2. Have a primary effect that neither advances nor inhibits religion; and
>
> 3. Create no excessive entanglement with religion.

Questions:

Use the above issue and rule to provide answers to the following in IRAC format:

1. Evaluate the case *Lee v. Weisman* under the Lemon Test.

2. School District receives and investigates complaints that Biology Teacher frequently engages students in conversations about religion; that Biology Teacher attempts to proselytize; and that Biology Teacher repeatedly denigrates evolution in favor of Biblical creationism. School District issues the following directive to Biology Teacher. Discuss whether the infringement on Biology Teacher's rights is legal. (Hint: This comes from an actual case and the case is addressed above in the chapter.)

> "You are hereby directed to refrain from any attempt to convert students to Christianity or initiating conversations about your religious

beliefs during instructional time, which the District believes includes any time students are required to be on campus as well as the time students immediately arrive for the purposes of attending school for instruction, lunch time, and the time immediately prior to students' departure after the instructional day."

3. Every year the 11th grade students at the local high school complete a social studies project called "All About Me". Students do research and put together displays about themselves, their heritage, their interests, etc. All of the projects are exhibited in the school gymnasium for an "All About Me Night" which is open to parents and the community. Hannah is an 11th grade student who is atheist. She is disturbed by what she views as an escalating global problem of religious-based violence. She decides to do her project as an "anti-religion" project. She criticized all religions as nothing more than murderous hypocrites. One quote especially offended the mostly Judeo-Christian community. In large letters, Hannah's display said "Are we really any better?" and quoted St. Bernard's notorious statement that "The Christian who slays the unbeliever in the Holy War is sure of his reward; more sure if he himself is slain. The Christian glories in the death of the pagan, because Christ is thereby glorified."

    a. If the school permits Hannah to display her project, is the school violating the Establishment Clause?

    b. If the school does not permit Hannah to display her project, is the school violating Hannah's Freedom of Expression?

Chapter Six

Race, Gender, and Other Categories

I. Introduction

The goal of this chapter is to present the basic legal issues of concern to professional educators in avoiding discrimination against students on grounds other than religion and disability. Such categories include race, gender, national origin, age, marital status, and sexual orientation. The legal bases and legal analyses involved in dealing with discrimination on these grounds are simple, perhaps deceptively so. The whole concept can be articulated in one sentence:

> *All* students are entitled to an *equal* educational opportunity.

This seems easy enough to understand and there has been much progress for us to be proud of as Americans. Consider, for example, the category of race. We notice that most students, teachers, and people in general tend to react with dumbfounded disbelief upon their initial viewing of documentary film footage of the Civil Rights Era. Those who did not experience the period often sit and wonder in amazement at it all: the crazed looks on the faces of white Arkansans, Alabamans, even Bostonians; a mob poised to keep a mere handful of young African American children from attending the all white high school in Little Rock; mobs poised for violence against school children. We look at the current multicultural composition of students in the public schools and we feel pleased with how far we have come since those times.

Unfortunately, however, as professional educators we must face the fact that discrimination on the bases covered in this chapter is not mere historical tragedy. Indeed, you will read a document that will take you directly into the continuing nightmare of discrimination: the complaint filed in federal district court in Nevada in the case *Henkle v. Gregory*. Before reading the complaint, consider the following:

1. The facts alleged are disturbing and the language is graphic, but the whole situation is all too familiar. Many of the facts described in the complaint can be witnessed in almost any high school in the country.

2. Note that the defendants are teachers and administrators. They are sued not only in their official positions, but also as individuals. In most cases, professional liability insurance policies covering educators do not cover civil rights violations. Therefore, if these educators lose the case, they may end up in financial ruin.

3. Hopefully you will never see a federal complaint naming you as a defendant. Finances are only part of the dilemma; imagine the personal and professional turmoil these educators must be experiencing as a result of the case. (Of course, if the allegations are true, the educators brought it all on themselves, something it is hoped will be avoided by all educators having read this text.)

4. While the complaint has been edited to eliminate much of the purely procedural aspects, the style is legalistic. Do not be surprised if you find it difficult to follow. (Keep in mind that many law students never see a complaint until their second year of law school.)

Now, please read the complaint in the case *Henkle v. Gregory* (found in Appendix H) and then return to the discussion below.

II. Manifestations of Discrimination in Education

As can be seen from the *Henkle* complaint, discrimination continues to rear its ugly head in our schools.

Consider the following manifestations of discrimination commonly seen in educational settings:

Segregation: Students have historically been segregated based on race and gender. Students of different races and of different gender were placed in separate schools and classes and were taught by different teachers using different materials. Even today, most athletic teams remain segregated by gender.

Exclusion: Students of different races, genders, national origin, marital status, and pregnant students were at various times in our history excluded from all or part of the educational process. Efforts to maintain such exclusion continue. Examples include attempts to exclude students whose parents are illegal aliens and attempts to eliminate programs for students whose first language is not English.

Harassment and Intimidation: Schools have been unsuccessful at protecting students from harassment and intimidation due to race, gender, national origin, and sexual orientation.

Opposition to Affirmative Action: Overcoming discrimination includes taking affirmative steps aimed at balancing unfairness created by previous discrimination. Nevertheless, discrimination now often manifests itself in the form of strenuous opposition to such affirmative measures.

Voucher and "Choice" Programs: Supreme Court decisions in the 1950's established the constitutional rights of children not to be discriminated against on the grounds of race or color. (The landmark case *Brown v. Board of Education* is discussed below.) Some districts tried to circumvent these decisions by implementing voucher systems and closing public schools. Students could use the vouchers to attend private schools of their own "choice." The Court refused to permit this system, holding that closing public schools and paying public funds for students to attend racially segregated private schools violated equal protection. Voucher and "choice" programs continue to be an issue of concern in education. To the extent that such programs are intended to serve political, discriminatory, or religious goals, they pose a serious threat to the quality of public schooling in this country.

The legal issues are many, varied, and complex. Until recently voucher systems were held to violate the Establishment

Clause of the first amendment when used to pay for parochial school tuition. However, the situation changed drastically when the Supreme Court decided the case *Zelman v. Simmons-Harris* in the summer of 2002. The *Zelman* case involved an Ohio voucher program that provides financial assistance to families in any Ohio school district that is or has been "under federal court order requiring supervision and operational management of the district by the state superintendent." The program provides tuition aid for students in kindergarten through third grade, expanding each year through eighth grade, to attend a participating public or private school of their parent's choosing. *Parents may choose to pay the tuition vouchers to either secular or religious schools.*

The Court upheld the voucher program, even though it results in support of religion. The Court decided that,

> "[W]here a government aid program is neutral with respect to religion, and provides assistance directly to a broad class of citizens who, in turn, direct government aid to religious schools wholly as a result of their own genuine and independent private choice, the program is not readily subject to challenge under the Establishment Clause. A program that shares these features permits government aid to reach religious institutions only by way of the deliberate choices of numerous individual recipients. The incidental advancement of a religious mission, or the perceived endorsement of a religious message, is reasonably attributable to the individual recipient, not to the government, whose role ends with the disbursement of benefits. As a plurality of this Court recently observed:
>
>> '[I]f numerous private choices, rather than the single choice of a government, determine the distribution of aid, pursuant to neutral eligibility criteria, then a government cannot, or at least cannot easily, grant special favors that might lead to a religious establishment.'

> '[W]hen government aid supports a school's religious mission only because of independent decisions made by numerous individuals to guide their secular aid to that school, 'no reasonable observer is likely to draw from the facts ... an inference that the State itself is endorsing a religious practice or belief'.' . . .

We believe that the program challenged here is a program of true private choice, . . . and thus constitutional. . . . [T]he Ohio program is neutral in all respects toward religion. It is part of a general and multifaceted undertaking by the State of Ohio to provide educational opportunities to the children of a failed school district. It confers educational assistance directly to a broad class of individuals defined without reference to religion, i.e., any parent of a school-age child who resides in the . . . School District. The program permits the participation of all schools within the district, religious or nonreligious. Adjacent public schools also may participate and have a financial incentive to do so. Program benefits are available to participating families on neutral terms, with no reference to religion. The only preference stated anywhere in the program is a preference for low-income families, who receive greater assistance and are given priority for admission at participating schools." (Internal citations omitted).

You can read the full opinion of the *Zelman* case in Appendix A.

III. The Constitutional Basis for Eliminating Discrimination

The constitutional basis for eliminating discrimination on the bases of race, gender, national origin, age, marital status, and sexual orientation is plain and simple: Equal Protection. As the Supreme Court first articulated in *Brown v. Board of Education,* 347 US 483 (1954),

> "education is perhaps the most important function of state and local governments. . . . It is the very foundation of good citizenship. . . . [I]t is doubtful that any child may reasonably be expected to succeed in life if he is denied the opportunity of an education. Such an opportunity, where the state has undertaken to provide it, is a right which must be made available to all on equal terms."

In other words, the Equal Protection Clause means what it says; we are all entitled to the equal protection of the law.

Brown v. Board of Education

Brown is perhaps the single most important case in the history of education law in the United States. Indeed, it is one of the landmark cases of US constitutional law in general. *Brown* was a unanimous Supreme Court decision overturning the "separate but equal" doctrine first established in *Plessy v. Ferguson,* 163 US 537 (1896). In *Plessy v. Ferguson,* the Court upheld a Louisiana law which provided that "all railway companies . . . shall provide equal but separate accommodations for the white, and colored races. . . ." The Court's decision in the infamous Plessy case provided that

> "The object of the [Fourteenth] Amendment was undoubtedly to enforce the absolute equality of the two races before the law, but in the nature of things it could not have been intended to abolish distinctions based upon color, or to enforce social, as distinguished from political equality, or a commingling of the two races upon terms unsatisfactory to either. Laws permitting, and even requiring, their separation in places where they are liable to be brought into contact do not necessarily imply the inferiority of either race to the other, and have generally, if not universally,

recognized as within the competency of the state legislatures in the exercise of their police power. The most common instance of this is connected with the establishment of separate schools for white and colored children, which has been held to be a valid exercise of the legislative power even by courts of States where the political rights of the colored race have been longest and most earnestly enforced."

Justice Harlan dissented from the majority of the Court in the *Plessy* case. In his dissenting opinion he foreshadowed *Brown*. Justice Harlan stated:

"Our Constitution is color-blind, and neither knows nor tolerates classes among citizens. In respect of civil rights, all citizens are equal before the law. . . . The law regards man as man, and takes no account of his surroundings or of his color when his civil rights as guaranteed by the supreme law of the land are involved. It is, therefore, to be regretted that this high tribunal, the final expositor of the fundamental law of the land, has reached the conclusion that it is competent for a state to regulate the enjoyment by citizens of their civil rights solely upon the basis of race."

Not until 1957, in *Brown*, did the Court finally accept Justice Harlan's view as the correct interpretation of Equal Protection and explicitly reject *Plessy*. The court held that separate is inherently unequal. The Court stated that "segregation of children in public schools solely on the basis of race, even though the physical facilities and other "tangible" factors may be equal, deprive[s] the children of the minority group of equal educational opportunities." The court explained that

"Segregation of white and colored children in public schools has a detrimental effect upon the colored children. The impact is greater when it has the sanction of the law; for the policy of separating the

> races is usually interpreted as denoting the inferiority of the Negro group. A sense of inferiority affects the motivation of a child to learn. Segregation with the sanction of law, therefore, has a tendency to retard the educational and mental development of Negro children and to deprive them of some of the benefits they would receive in a racially integrated school system."

Since *Brown*, the courts have extended gradually this basic equal protection doctrine, to varying degrees, to protect the educational rights of students based on gender, national origin, age, marital status, and sexual orientation. As stated above, the basic rule is that all students are entitled to an equal educational opportunity.

An explanation of equal protection is found in Chapter Two. Please review that section at this time and then return to the following discussion.

The bottom line in evaluating practices that treat students differently based on the categories covered in this chapter is to apply the test for equal protection violations:

First, look at the interest of the makers of school policy. Does it fall into one of the four categories of "compelling interests" with regard to education? In other words, is the interest:

1. Related to a legitimate educational purpose;

2. To maintain an appropriate educational environment;

3. To protect health and safety; or

4. To prevent property loss and damage?

Second, if the interest is indeed a "compelling interest," then look at whether the particular action or policy is necessary in order to achieve that interest.

As discussed in Chapter Three, Courts do not always apply this high standard to discrimination cases; they sometimes apply a less strict standard. Under the lower standard, the state interest need only be "legitimate" and the state action need only be "reasonably related" to the interest. Race and national origin cases almost always use the higher standard. Cases involving other categories are not as predictable. Nevertheless, the ethics of the education profession, as well as prudence in avoiding potential legal liability, argue in favor of educators evaluating their own actions with regard to all of these categories according to the highest standard.

IV. Statutory Protections

Appendix C contains a concise summary of statutory provisions affecting the education profession. Note that federal and state statutes provide strong and specific protection against discrimination on several of the bases covered in this chapter and such protection is in addition to basic constitutional equal protection. Also remember that through the state and federal statutes, most discrimination principles apply to private schools as well as public schools.

V. Cases for Chapter Six

Please read the edited versions of the following Supreme Court cases, which are found in Appendix A.

Fundamental Cases:
Brown v. Board of Education
Romer v. Evans

Additional Case:
Zelman v. Simmons-Harris

VI. Discussion Item for Chapter Seven

Based on the Court's rulings in *Brown* and *Romer*, how should the court rule in the *Henkle* case? Be specific and remember that your analysis should clearly indicate how the reasoning in *Brown* and in *Romer* applies to the alleged facts of *Henkle*.

NOTES:

1. For the purposed of this question, assume that the facts are as alleged in the Complaint.

2. Discuss the Equal Protection issues.

3. Discuss the Freedom of Expression issues.

4. Also, deal with the assertion, made by some students in this course, that *Henkle* "flaunted" his sexual orientation. Specifically, the student comments refer to the allegations that *Henkle* wore buttons stating "We Are Everywhere" and "Out" on his backpack, that he expressed his identity and viewpoints on certain occasions, and that he asserts a right to discuss his sexual orientation with or express pro-gay viewpoints to other students.

To help you get started with this question, consider the following quote from *Tinker*:

> "Any departure from absolute regimentation may cause trouble. Any variation from the majority's opinion may inspire fear. Any word spoken, in class, in the lunchroom, or on the campus, that deviates from the views of another person may start an argument or cause a disturbance. But our Constitution says we must take this risk, and our history says that it is this sort of hazardous freedom - this kind of openness - that is the basis of our national strength and of the independence and vigor of Americans who grow up and live in this . . . often disputatious society."

Chapter Seven

Disability and the Individuals with Disabilities Education Act (IDEA)

I. Introduction

The legal duties of professional educators regarding students with disabilities are primarily affirmative responsibilities. In other words, while the discrimination principles discussed in previous chapters also apply to students with disabilities (i.e., no action or policy may infringe upon the right of such students to an equal educational opportunity), certain laws establish specific duties with regard to students with disabilities that go beyond mere avoidance of discrimination. Thus, discrimination against students with disabilities can occur when educators fail to take required affirmative actions. The bottom line incorporates four basic principles:

1. With regard to students with disabilities, professional educators must take whatever affirmative steps are necessary to assure such students benefit from the regular education curriculum. In other words, students with disabilities are entitled to a "free and appropriate public education."

2. In some cases, the affirmative steps required may take the form of "reasonable accommodation" under the Americans with Disabilities Act (ADA) and under Section 504 of the Rehabilitation Act (Section 504).

3. However, in some cases, such steps may also require "special education" under the Individuals with Disabilities Education Act (IDEA).

4. Students with disabilities have the right to be taught in the "least restrictive environment" possible. This means that students are entitled to be included in the regular education environment, including classes, activities, curriculum, etc., to the greatest extent possible.

The goal of this chapter it to provide an overview of these responsibilities. Additionally, the chapter provides a summary of the procedural requirements of the IDEA.

II. Who is a Person with a Disability?

A person is legally considered to have a disability if *any one* of three circumstances exist:

1. The person has a *significant impairment of a "major life activity"* (education and the ability to benefit from regular education curriculum is considered a major life activity);

2. The person has a *documented history* of such an impairment; ***or***

3. The person is *treated* as though he or she has such an impairment.

III. Reasonable Accommodation

Any person who has a disability is entitled to "reasonable accommodation" aimed at negating the effect(s) of the impairment. Accommodation is not specialized instruction; rather, it is a modification of some aspect of the educational environment. This can include using different teaching methods or materials, changing in the physical environment, implementation of assistive methods, etc. Accommodations are designed to permit students with disabilities to benefit from their regular education experience to the same extent as persons without disabilities.

For example, a student with Attention Deficit Disorder (ADD) may need to take medication during the school day in order to function properly in the school setting. A school with such a student would be required to accommodate this need by storing and properly administering medication provided by the parent. Failure to do so would constitute a civil rights violation; the school would be discriminating against the student on the basis of the student's disability. Here are some additional examples:

Modifying the Teaching Mode

1. Assess the prerequisite skills of students with disabilities
2. Repeat directions
3. Restate information in different ways
4. Provide a multi-sensory approach (verbal and visual prompts)
5. Help students organize materials by using folders, notebooks, assignment sheets, etc.
6. Frequently review key concepts
7. Provide study aids such as outlines and study guides
8. Provide extra help during class, before school, or after school as needed and requested
9. Provide immediate feedback (teacher, peer, student corrects own work)
10. Use classroom contracts
11. Reteach
12. Small group, peer, individualized, or cooperative instruction (by teacher, IA, peer tutor, cross-age tutor, volunteer)
13. Encourage students to share ideas and ask questions related to subjects being taught
14. To ensure understanding, ask students to repeat directions and restate what they are going to do

Modifying the Teaching Setting

1. Preferential seating (i.e., carrel, dividers, close to front, near peer model/tutor, quiet area of class)
2. Post class assignments on board or wall
3. Remind students to write assignment on their own personal assignment sheet whenever new assignments are given
4. When assignments are collected, ask students personally for their work

5. Modifying Evaluative Procedures (Grading and Testing)
6. Consider ability and effort when evaluating quality and quantity of a student's work
7. Provide opportunity for extra time on tests and assignments
8. Provide opportunity for students to retake tests to improve scores
9. If a student exhibits particular difficulty with a unit or subject, permit the student to take all or part of a test open book for partial credit

Modifying Instructional Materials

1. Use materials that:
   a. address only essential skills;
   b. simplify vocabulary of presented information;
   c. are programmed (e.g., computer drills);
   d. repeat and reinforce skills; and/or
   e. provide assignments and tests in segments
2. Reduce amount of work
3. Use more varied materials
4. Use aids (calculator, word processor, typewriter, spell checker, tape recorder, books on tape, graphic organizers, etc.)
5. Modify testing mode/testing setting

Modifying Student Behavior

1. Post class rules and frequently remind students of expected behaviors

2. Reteach the expected behaviors
3. Reinforce positive behavior
4. Use MILD, CONSISTENT consequences for infractions
5. Set goals with individual students
6. Use individual contract

Modifying Home/School Relations

1. Daily/weekly reports home
2. Materials shared with home
3. Regularly scheduled conferences

IV. Special Education

While all students with disabilities are entitled to the reasonable accommodations they require, certain students with disabilities are additionally entitled to receive special education pursuant to the IDEA, which defines such students as children:

> "(i) with mental retardation, hearing impairments (including deafness), speech or language impairments, visual impairments (including blindness), serious emotional disturbance (. . . referred to as "emotional disturbance"), orthopedic impairments, autism, traumatic brain injury, other health impairments, or specific learning disabilities; and
>
> (ii) who, by reason thereof, need[] special education and related services.
>
> [and] for . . . child[ren] aged 3 through 9 . . ., at the discretion of the State and the local educational agency, [children]: (i) experiencing developmental delays, as defined by the State and as measured by appropriate diagnostic instruments and procedures, in one or more of the following areas: physical development, cognitive development, communication development, social or emotional development, or

> adaptive development; and (ii) who, by reason thereof, need[] special education and related services."

Note that the key to the IDEA is that qualified students with disabilities must *require special education* as a result of their disabilities. The IDEA defines the term special education as:

> "specially designed instruction, at no cost to parents, to meet the unique needs of a child with a disability, including - (A) instruction conducted in the classroom, in the home, in hospitals and institutions, and in other settings; and (B) instruction in physical education."

Again, note that the IDEA is in *addition* to the ADA and Section 504; *special education does not take the place of reasonable accommodation, it is an additional required service.* Thus, while special educators endeavor to design appropriate specialized instruction for students who require it, least restrictive environment and accommodation requirements assure that regular educators remain an integral part of the education process for students with disabilities.

V. Inclusion - Least Restrictive Environment

Inclusion means just that: including students with disabilities in regular education classrooms and other school activities. The IDEA mandates that students with disabilities must be educated in the "least restrictive environment" possible. Inclusion is required to the "maximum extent appropriate" for each student with a disability. In defining least restrictive environment, the IDEA imposes upon states and local school districts the duty to assure that:

> "*To the maximum extent appropriate,* children with disabilities, including children in public or private institutions or other care facilities, are educated with children who are not disabled, and special classes, separate schooling, or other removal of children with disabilities from the regular educational environment

occurs only when the nature or severity of the disability of a child is such that education in regular classes with the use of supplementary aids and services cannot be achieved satisfactorily."

Note that the inclusion requirement means that regular educators must be prepared to teach and to otherwise work with students with disabilities in regular education settings. As such, it is crucial that regular educators obtain training and skills with regard to working with such students, and also that regular educators acquire a basic understanding of the related legal and procedural requirements.

VI. The IDEA's Procedural Requirements

The following is a summary of the procedural requirements of the IDEA aimed primarily at providing only the basic information needed by regular educators (counselors, teachers, and administrators) in order to assure that such educators do not run afoul of the rights of students with disabilities. Regular education teachers and administrators should remember that special educators undergo intensive and ongoing training in these issues; they are the experts in this area. In all areas regarding students with disabilities, including, but not limited to, instruction, conferences, behavior, discipline, school activities, and counseling, it is suggested that regular educators seek the input and advice of special educators.

IEP's vs. 504 Plans

There are two types of written plans that must be developed and implemented by public schools regarding students with disabilities. First, students with disabilities requiring only reasonable accommodation must have a written plan under Section 504; this is commonly referred to as a 504 plan. Each public school should have a person (usually an assistant principal or a guidance counselor, but not a special educator) who serves as the school's "504 coordinator." This person should coordinate the development, maintenance, and implementation of 504 plans.

504 plans should be developed by a committee consisting of the student with a disability (if appropriate), the student's parent(s)/guardian(s), the student's teacher(s), the student's counselor, and the 504 coordinator. Additionally, special educators often serve as advisors to 504 committees. The committee develops a plan that identifies and documents the student's disability and the corresponding need for reasonable accommodation. Likewise, the plan delineates the specific accommodations that will be implemented by the school. The 504 coordinator should contact all school staff involved in the provision of accommodations to inform them of the existence of the plan and to make the plan available to such staff. The committee should update the plan at least annually.

For students with disabilities who require specialized instruction, the IDEA controls the procedural requirements. The IDEA process is more involved than that required under Section 504. Instruction and accommodation under the IDEA are provided in accord with a plan called an Individualized Education Program, known as an IEP. A student's IEP is a legal document; it sets forth, in part, the duties and responsibilities of the school district and staff regarding that student. It is the responsibility of special educators, regular education teachers, administrators, counselors, and other professional educators to be thoroughly familiar with the provisions of the IEP for *each* of their students with disabilities.

The remainder of this chapter sets forth the general procedural information that regular educators should know about the IEP/IDEA process.

REMEMBER: Be safe. *Seek the advice of special educators.* Whether you are a teacher, an administrator, or a counselor, you will save yourself considerable time and trouble – and you will do a much better job for your students with disabilities – if you utilize these specialists as the valuable resources that they represent to your school.

For your convenience, the IEP/IDEA procedural requirements are summarized in the table on the following page.

Table: IEP/IDEA Procedural Requirements

Step	Action	Brief Description
1	Identification	Educators are under a duty to recognize the possible presence of disabilities.
2	Intervention	Implement and document appropriate intervention strategies aimed at alleviating the identified concerns.
3	Referral to 504 Coordinator	If intervention strategies do not work or if they should be documented in a 504 Plan.
4	Review by 504 Committee	Is there a disability? Is reasonable accommodation required and/or sufficient?
5	Referral to Special Ed.	Formation of the IEP Team
6	Evaluation	Determine what evaluation is necessary to identify disability and needs.
7	Eligibility	Based on evaluation, is student eligible for Special Education?
8	Design IEP	If eligible, IEP Team designs IEP (services, modifications, etc.) and determines Least Restrictive Environment.
9	Implement IEP	Implementation of all IEP instruction, services, modifications, etc.
10	Monitoring	Monitor student progress and provision of services.
11	Review	Annually – New IEP Triennially – New Evaluation

Other Considerations

Discipline – Follow specific IDEA procedures

Transition – Beginning at age 14, gear IEP towards preparation for post- school life (interests, goals, etc.)

Self-Advocacy – Development of these skills is crucial

Step One: Identification

Schools and educators have a legal duty to identify students with disabilities. This can be relatively simple in the case of obvious physical disabilities. However, disabilities are not always obvious. Educators are under a duty to recognize the possible presence of disabilities based on student academic performance as well as student performance in non-academic school activities.

Step Two: Intervention

Once an educator identifies a concern regarding the performance of a particular student, a period of intervention begins. The educator should implement appropriate intervention strategies aimed at alleviating the identified concerns. The educator should document the concerns and subsequent interventions. The key issue is whether the strategies enable the student to benefit from the regular education curriculum.

Step Three: Referral to the 504 Coordinator

The educator must refer the student for further consideration if either of two situations exists:

1. The intervention strategies work, but the educator remains concerned that the student's performance signifies a possible disability and that the interventions represent accommodations for such disability; or

2. The intervention strategies do not work.

In either case, educators should make a written referral to the 504 coordinator (or to the committee established in the school to deal with such referrals).

Note: An initial referral is usually *not* an IDEA matter. Special Educators may advise or assist the 504 committee or coordinator, but a full 504 consideration should take place before referring the matter for special education. Consideration under Section 504 should remain separate and distinct from the realm of special education. This is because it is inappropriate to implement IDEA procedures until it becomes evident that the student has a need that exceeds reasonable accommodation. Thus, until it is clear that reasonable accommodation is not sufficient to enable the student to benefit from regular education curriculum and activities (i.e., thus indicating that specialized instruction may be required), it is not appropriate to bring students under the auspices of special education.

Step Four: Review by the 504 Committee

When a case is referred, the 504 coordinator should call a meeting of the 504 team. The team should review the documentation provided regarding the concerns about the student and the interventions that have been attempted. The team should decide what additional intervention and evaluation is appropriate and should provide support to teachers and other staff to facilitate the provision of the selected intervention(s).

Over a period of several weeks, the team should closely monitor the information it obtains regarding the student's performance and the effectiveness of the methods implemented to assist the student. It is important to remember that student performance is a function of a variety of factors. Sometimes the particular methods employed by the student's teacher are not effective with regard to the particular student. Other times poor student performance can be a result of diet, family issues, abuse, or a number of other factors having nothing to do with school or with disability. It is the responsibility of the 504 committee to address these issues and determine the real nature of the problem.

Finally, after a period of intervention and monitoring (in most cases not less than six weeks and involving no less than three meetings of the full committee to evaluate progress), the 504 committee will determine three things:

1. Whether the student's performance remains problematic and whether such difficulty is the result of a disability;

2. If the problem is a result of a disability, whether reasonable accommodation is sufficient to enable the student to benefit from the regular education curriculum; and

3. Whether the student's needs are a result of a disability and cannot be met by reasonable accommodation alone (if this is the case, the 504 team should refer the matter to the special education department in the school).

Step Five: Referral for Special Education Evaluation and Formation of the IEP Team

As soon as a case is referred to special education, the matter comes under the control of the IDEA. At this time, a special educator becomes the "case manager" and an IEP Team is formed. From this time forward, all decisions regarding the student's educational program are made by the IEP Team; school and district personnel are specifically prohibited from making such decisions without the Team. The IDEA provides that the IEP Team consist of:

1. The student (if appropriate);
2. The parent(s) or guardian(s);
3. The special educator (i.e., the case manager);
4. The regular education teacher or teachers;
5. A "district representative" (this can be a special educator or an administrator so long as it is someone familiar with special education services in the district); and
6. Anyone else whose presence is deemed necessary or appropriate by the student, the parent(s)/guardian(s), or the district.

Note that regular education teachers are legally required to attend meetings of the IEP Team. (However, at the middle school and high school levels - where students have several regular education teachers - it is often the practice to rotate IEP

Team duties among the various teachers. The IDEA requirement is seen as being aimed at assuring that the Team has access to the regular education perspective, not as being aimed at requiring the presence of six or seven regular education teachers at every high school IEP Team meeting.)

Step Six: Evaluation

The case manager gives the IEP Team members notice and the first meeting is held. The first order of business is deciding whether the matter is properly before the Team. If the Team thinks that the matter should go back to the 504 committee, it can send the case back. Otherwise, the Team decides what type of evaluation is necessary in order to determine the existence of a disability under the IDEA (which contains its own specific set of eligibility categories, as described above in Section IV of this chapter) and what, if any, need exists for specialized instruction.

Step Seven: Eligibility

After the evaluation is completed, the Team is reconvened. At this time, the Team reviews the results of the evaluation. The team looks at whether the results meet the state and federal criteria for the existence of a disability under the IDEA and whether the student requires specialized instruction. If so, the student is considered eligible for special education.

Step Eight: Designing the IEP

If the Team decides that the student is eligible, the Team must then design the student's educational program. The Team determines the student's needs regarding specialized instruction, as well as the need for any related services (*e.g.*, transportation,

speech/language therapy, health services, audiology, occupational or physical therapy, adaptive equipment, interpreters, orientation and/or mobility counseling, etc.). Likewise, the Team identifies any necessary accommodations or modifications that are required in order for the student to be able to participate in and benefit from regular education settings, curricula, or activities. The IEP documents these items, as well a statement of the student's current level of educational performance.

Step Nine: Implementation of the IEP

As stated above, the IEP is an important formal legal document. The case manager must inform the professional educators and other service providers who deal with the student of the existence of the IEP and must make it available for review by such individuals. Likewise, it is the professional and legal responsibility of the educators and service providers who work with the student to access and review the IEP. The district must fully and immediately implement the program established by the IEP. The school and the district must assure that regular educators become and remain familiar with the contents of their students' IEPs and that staff implements all required instruction and accommodations/ modifications contained therein. Note that if a regular education teacher fails or refuses to follow a student's IEP, the educator may be held personally liable.

Step Ten: Monitoring

IEP implementation and student progress in accord with the IEP should be monitored continuously throughout the year. Reporting on student progress towards IEP goals and objectives is required to be completed on the same schedule as such reporting for non-disabled students. In other words, if the school issues report cards at certain times during the year, then reports of student progress towards IEP goals and objectives should be provided at the same times.

Step Eleven: Review (Annual IEP Review and Three-Year Re-Evaluation)

The IEP Team must review the IEP annually. The IEP Team must meet prior to the expiration date (which is one year from the IEP's implementation) and develop a new IEP in accord with the student's progress and needs as exhibited over the year. Likewise, the Team must review the formal evaluation process to determine whether the student remains eligible for special education and, if so, to identify the student's educational needs. The Team reviews the evaluation every three years. The IEP Team has the option to forgo a new formal evaluation if the members feel that there has been no change in the student's eligibility. However, a formal meeting is still required.

Final Considerations: Discipline, Transition, and Self-Advocacy

Discipline

The law recognizes that students with disabilities, whether receiving special education or receiving only reasonable accommodation, should not be removed from school for infractions that are manifestations of their disabilities. Consider two examples:

1. Students with learning disabilities in the area of reading, or with disabilities that result in any number of processing difficulties, may not comprehend written guidelines, or may not be sensitive to "implied" behavioral expectations. Therefore, we may not hold such students accountable for violations of expectations that we have not explicitly presented to the student in a manner assuring comprehension. In other words, a student's failure to comply with such provisions would be a "manifestation of his or her disability."

2. Students with autism, emotional disturbance, or mental retardation may behave in ways that do not conform to our usual notions of appropriate educational decorum. Nevertheless, to the extent that such behavior is a manifestation of the student's disability, we may not discipline the student for such behavior.

The IDEA sets forth specific procedural requirements for disciplinary actions involving removal from school. The IEP Team must meet to determine whether the alleged behavior represents a manifestation of the student's disability. Note that this requirement has the potential to create confusion in that the Team may be inclined to make a judgment regarding the facts (i.e., whether the alleged behavior occurred) instead of limiting its judgment to whether the behavior, if it did occur, is a manifestation of the disability. Also note that even if the behavior is not a manifestation of a student's disability (and the student is subsequently suspended or expelled) the school district must continue to provide services to the student. If the student cannot come to school, then the district must provide homebound instruction, or provide services in another setting. As with all other decisions regarding services to students with IEP's, the IEP Team must determine the appropriate alternative educational setting for such students.

Transition

The IDEA requires that beginning at age 14, IEP's must incorporate the various goals and objectives applicable to student needs regarding transition from high school to post-high school life. Regular educators in middle school and high school should therefore be aware that IEP's will contain such goals and that the education of students with IEP's on these grade levels will involve requirements, curricula, and activities which may go beyond or replace the regular education curriculum.

Self- Awareness and Self-Advocacy

Arguably the most important skills for students with disabilities to acquire before exiting high school are those of self-awareness and self-advocacy. The importance of these skills is readily understood when we consider that when students with disabilities exit high school (or reach the age of 22, whichever comes first), the IDEA no longer applies. The only legal protections available to persons with disabilities in post-high school life are those provided by the ADA, by Section 504, and by various state and local laws. Unlike the IDEA, none of these legal provisions impose any affirmative duty on non-disabled persons or institutions. In other words, employers, colleges, and other entities have no obligation to identify persons with disabilities or the reasonable accommodations such persons require. The obligation to identify one's disability, to demonstrate the reasonableness of needed accommodations, and to enforce one's rights shifts to the persons with disabilities themselves. As you can see, unless we provide students with effective instruction and practice in self-awareness and self-advocacy, there exists a great risk that the protectiveness of the IDEA and IEP processes may inadvertently leave students unprepared for a post-high school life that requires knowledge of one's rights and the skills necessary to assure enforcement of those rights.

Regular educators should remain aware that self-advocacy training is an important part of specialized instruction. Remember that students are in the process of learning these skills; they are not masters of these skills. As such, be helpful to students with disabilities; encourage their efforts to enforce the modifications/accommodations to which they are entitled. As students learn to use self-advocacy skills, they may initially use these skills in an unrefined or harsh manner. Try not to be insulted or become defensive when students attempt to enforce their rights as persons with disabilities. Remember that these students must learn to identify and enforce their rights and that they had better learn this by the time they graduate.

VII. Additional Required Reading

Quick and Easy Help for Working with Students with IEPs (found in Appendix E)

VIII. Discussion Items for Chapter Eight

There are three discussion items for Chapter Eight.

Discussion Item Number One - Having to Hear It

Silently read the following story. You should recognize every word. But do you get the meaning? Can you tell what animal plays a primary role?

Next try having someone read it aloud to you. Does it help?

Many people with learning disabilities can recognize the words in written materials. They just cannot grasp the meaning unless materials are read aloud.

Here's the story:

Dare worsted ladle gull hoe lift wetter murder inner ladle cordage honor itch offer lodge, dock florist. Disk ladle gull orphan worry ladle cluck wetter putty ladle rat hut end fur disk raisin pimple colder Ladle Rat Rotten Hut.

Wan moaning, Murder colder inset, "Heresy ladle basking winsome burden barter end shirker cockles. Tick disk ladle basking Tudor cordage offer grain murder how lifts honor udder site offer florist. Shaker lake! Dun stopper laundry wrote! Dun stopper peck floors! Dun daily daily inner florist! And yonder nor sorghum stenches dun stopper torque wet strainers!"

"Hoe cake, Murder," resplendent disk ladle gull, end tickle ladle basking an stuttered oft.

*   *   *   *

Honor wrote Tudor cordage offer grain murder, disk ladle gull mitten anomalous woof.

"Wail, wail, wail," set disk wicket woof, "evanescent Ladle Rat Rotten Hut. Wares or putty gull goring wizard ladle basking?"

"Armor goring tumor grain murder's," reprisal ladle gull. "Grammars seeking bet. Armor ticking arson burden barter end shirker cockles."

"O hoe! Heifer blessing woke," setter wicket woof. Butter taught tomb shelf, "Oil tickle shirt court Tudor cordage offer grain murder. Oil ketchup wetter letter. End den -- oh bore!"

*   *   *   *

Soda wicket woof tucker shirt court end whinny retched a cordage offer grain murder, picket inner winnow an sore debtor pore oil worming worse lion inner bet. Inner flesh disk abdominal woof lipped otter batting adder rope. Zany pool down a grain murder's nut cup end gnat gun, any curdled dope inner bet.

*   *   *   *

Inner ladle wile, Ladle Rat Rotten Hut a raft adder cordage an ranker dough ball.

"Comb ink, sweat hard," setter wicket woof, disgracing is verse.

"Oh, grammar," crater ladle gull. "Wart bag icer gut!"

"Buttered luck chew whiff, doling," whiskered disk ratchet woof wetter wicket small.

"Oh, grammar! Water bag noise! A nervous sore suture anomalous prognosis!"

"Buttered small you whiff," inserter woof, ants mouse worse waddling.

"Oh, grammar! Water bag mousy gut! A nervous sore suture bag mouse!"

Daze worry on forger nut gull's lest worts. Oil offer sodden, throne offer carvers an sprinkling otter bet, disk curl an bloat Thursday woof ceased pore Ladle Rat Rotten Hut end garbled erupt.

*   *   *   *

MURAL: Yonder no sorghum stenches shut ladle gulls stopper torque wet strainers.

Discussion Item Number Two - Reading Aloud

Can you read the sentence in the box below? Try reading it aloud. Do you sound like a good reader?

In order to demonstrate the way many people with learning disabilities see regular type, three things have been done to the sentence:

First, the following lower-case letters are used interchangeably: p, b, q, d.

Second, instead of being written on one line, the letters are spread-out on three lines. (Read it from left to right combining all three lines as though all letters were actually on one line.)

Third, the sentence has no punctuation, capitalization, or spaces between words.

```
p   yq       ed       he     te    ppo
  ill     as        t   qut          dco
        le      ass            re         rn
```

Discussion Item Number Three: When Teachers Don't Get It

Suppose you are presenting a workshop for teachers on how to include students with disabilities in regular education classes. You are explaining why education is moving away from outdated notions of structure such as that still seen from time to time in secondary classrooms. You clarify that you are criticizing the old-style arrangement of desks into rows, the delivery of "lectures" to which students are supposed to listen while sitting quietly and taking notes, and the difficulty many secondary teachers have distinguishing between curriculum (such as "Plate Tectonics") and materials (such as text books, work sheets, etc.).

As an example of why such a structure is not educationally appropriate, you refer to students with Attention Deficit Disorder, especially those with the additional hyperactivity component. While such a student may have an intellectual ability equal to or exceeding other students, when a teacher fails to properly structure the classroom environment and educational delivery, the student may have difficulties that are a direct manifestation of his or her disability. You stress the importance of understanding the ethical as well as the legal duty to accommodate such students.

Just as you are about to explain that proper structure and delivery (using groups, peer teaming, varied materials, etc.) not only accommodates students with disabilities, but also is better for all students, you are interrupted by an outburst from one of the teachers in attendance at your workshop. The teacher says, "I've used what you're referring to as the wrong approach for twenty-five years and it works just fine. If a kid can't learn in that setting, then he shouldn't be in the class. He shouldn't even be in there!"

How would you respond to such a statement?

Chapter Eight

Privacy
(Including Search and Seizure)

I. Introduction

The goal of this chapter is to present an overview of students' right to privacy. The discussion addresses the general considerations related to the issue, namely:

1. Protection from unwanted intrusion (such as searches, drug testing, etc.); and

2. Protection from unauthorized disclosure of student records and other student information.

II. Fourth Amendment Rights: Protection From Unwanted Intrusion

A. Search and Seizure

The Fourth Amendment prohibits "unreasonable searches and seizures" of our "persons, houses, papers, and effects." For searches and seizures to be justified, they must, according to the amendment, be based upon "probable cause." These provisions apply to students in the public schools and protect such students from unwanted intrusion except where such intrusion is legally justified.

The Supreme Court explained the principles that control the actions of public school officials with regard to searches and seizures in the case *New Jersey v. T.L.O.* The Court ruled that public school officials may apply a lesser standard in determining whether a search is justified:

> "The school setting . . . requires some modification of the level of suspicion of illicit activity needed to justify a search. Ordinarily, a search - even one that may

permissibly be carried out without a warrant - must be based upon "probable cause" to believe that a violation of the law has occurred. However, "probable cause" is not an irreducible requirement of a valid search. The fundamental command of the Fourth Amendment is that searches and seizures be reasonable . . . . Where a careful balancing of governmental and private interests suggests that the public interest is best served by a Fourth Amendment standard of reasonableness that stops short of probable cause, we have not hesitated to adopt such a standard.

We [therefore conclude] that the accommodation of the privacy interests of schoolchildren with the substantial need of teachers and administrators for freedom to maintain order in the schools does not require strict adherence to the requirement that searches be based on probable cause to believe that the subject of the search has violated or is violating the law. Rather, the legality of a search of a student should depend simply on the reasonableness, under all the circumstances, of the search. Determining the reasonableness of any search involves a twofold inquiry: first, one must consider "whether the . . . action was justified at its inception." Second, one must determine whether the search as actually conducted "was reasonably related in scope to the circumstances which justified the interference in the first place." Under ordinary circumstances, a search of a student by a teacher or other school official will be "justified at its inception" when there are reasonable grounds for suspecting that the search will turn up evidence that the student has violated or is violating either the law or the rules of the school. Such a search will be permissible in its scope when the measures adopted are reasonably related to the objectives of the search and not excessively intrusive in light of the age and sex of the student and the nature of the infraction. . . .

> By focusing attention on the question of reasonableness, the standard will spare teachers and school administrators the necessity of schooling themselves in the niceties of probable cause and permit them to regulate their conduct according to the dictates of reason and common sense. At the same time, the reasonableness standard should ensure that the interests of students will be invaded no more than is necessary to achieve the legitimate end of preserving order in the schools." (Emphasis added).

The Court's ruling in *T.L.O.* can be criticized for its assertion that neither the warrant requirement, nor the probable cause standard, is an "irreducible requirement of a valid search." Remember that these two components are explicitly required by the Fourth Amendment. Nevertheless, the Court's ruling is the law as it stands today. As such, public school officials may legally search students upon the mere showing that:

1. At the inception of the search, there are "reasonable grounds for suspecting that the search will turn up evidence that the student has violated or is violating either the law or the rules of the school;" and

2. The scope of the search is reasonably related to the circumstances justifying the intrusion and "not excessively intrusive in light of the age and sex of the student and the nature of the infraction."

At this time, please read the case *New Jersey v. T.L.O.* (found in Appendix A) and then return to the discussion below.

B. Drug Testing

In the case *Vernonia School District v. Acton,* the Court upheld drug testing of student athletes. The Court permitted the School District to require student athletes to undergo urinalysis drug testing on a random basis and with absolutely no suspicion that the individual being tested had committed any violation whatsoever. Such testing was deemed permissible on the grounds that schools must take intrusive actions in "deterring drug use by our Nation's schoolchildren."

At this time, please read *Vernonia School District v. Acton* (found in Appendix A) and then return to the discussion below.

The Court extended a school's ability to conduct suspicionless drug searches in the 2002 case *Board of Education v. Earls*. In *Earls*, the Court decided that school districts can require suspicionless drug testing of all students who participate in any form of extracurricular activity. The following is excerpted from the Court's opinion; the full opinion, written by Justice Thomas, may be found in Appendix A.

> "The Student Activities Drug Testing Policy implemented by the Board of Education of . . . Pottawatomie County (School District) requires all students who participate in competitive extracurricular activities to submit to drug testing. [This includes *all* extracurricular activities, such as band, choir, honor society, etc., not just athletics.]
>
> [Lindsay Earls, who was a member of the show choir, the marching band, the Academic Team, and the National Honor Society] . . . argues that drug testing must be based at least on some level of individualized suspicion. . . . It is true that we generally determine the reasonableness of a search by balancing the nature of the intrusion on the individual's privacy against the promotion of legitimate governmental interests. But we have long held that 'the Fourth Amendment imposes no irreducible requirement of [individualized] suspicion.'
>
> Significantly, this Court has previously held that . . . [w]hile schoolchildren do not shed their constitutional rights when they enter the schoolhouse, 'Fourth Amendment rights ... are different in public schools than elsewhere; the 'reasonableness' inquiry cannot disregard the schools' custodial and tutelary responsibility for children.'

We first consider the nature of the privacy interest allegedly compromised by the drug testing. . . . A student's privacy interest is limited in a public school environment where the State is responsible for maintaining discipline, health, and safety. Schoolchildren are routinely required to submit to physical examinations and vaccinations against disease. Securing order in the school environment sometimes requires that students be subjected to greater controls than those appropriate for adults. . . .

[Earls argues] that because children participating in nonathletic extracurricular activities are not subject to regular physicals and communal undress [as was the case with the student athletes in *Vernonia*], they have a stronger expectation of privacy than the athletes tested in *Vernonia*. [We reject [t]his distinction . . . . In any event, students who participate in . . . extracurricular activities voluntarily subject themselves to many of the same intrusions on their privacy as do athletes. Some of these clubs and activities require occasional off-campus travel and communal undress. . . . We therefore conclude that the students affected by this Policy have a limited expectation of privacy.

Next, we consider the character of the intrusion imposed by the Policy. Urination is 'an excretory function traditionally shielded by great privacy.' But the 'degree of intrusion' on one's privacy caused by collecting a urine sample 'depends upon the manner in which production of the urine sample is monitored.' Under the Policy, a faculty monitor waits outside the closed restroom stall for the student to produce a sample and must 'listen for the normal sounds of urination in order to guard against tampered specimens and to insure an accurate chain of custody.' The monitor then pours the sample into two bottles that are sealed and placed into a mailing pouch along with a consent form signed by the student. This procedure is virtually identical to that reviewed in *Vernonia*, except that it additionally protects privacy by allowing male students to produce their samples behind a closed stall. Given that we considered the method of collection in *Vernonia* a 'negligible' intrusion, the method here is even less problematic. . . .

Moreover, . . . the test results here [do not] lead to the imposition of discipline or . . . [to] any academic consequences. Rather, the only consequence of a failed drug test is to limit the student's privilege of participating in extracurricular activities. . . . Given the minimally intrusive nature of the sample collection and the limited uses to which the test results are put, we conclude that the invasion of students' privacy is not significant. . . .

[T]his Court must [next] consider the nature and immediacy of the government's concerns and the efficacy of the Policy in meeting them. . . . The nationwide drug epidemic makes the war against drugs a pressing concern in every school. . . . Given the nationwide epidemic of drug use, and the evidence of increased drug use in Tecumseh schools, it was entirely reasonable for the School District to enact this particular drug testing policy. We reject the Court of Appeals' . . . test that 'any district seeking to impose a random suspicionless drug testing policy as a condition to participation in a school activity must demonstrate that there is some identifiable drug abuse problem among a sufficient number of those subject to the testing, such that testing that group of students will actually redress its drug problem.' Among other problems, it would be difficult to administer such a test. As we cannot articulate a threshold level of drug use that would suffice to justify a drug testing program for schoolchildren, we refuse to fashion what would in effect be a constitutional quantum of drug use necessary to show a 'drug problem.'

Finally, . . . [w]ithin the limits of the Fourth Amendment, local school boards must assess the desirability of drug testing schoolchildren. In upholding the constitutionality of the Policy, we express no opinion as to its wisdom. Rather, we hold only that Tecumseh's Policy is a reasonable means of

> furthering the School District's important interest in preventing and deterring drug use among its schoolchildren." (Internal citations omitted).

The Court concluded that the drug testing policy reasonably serves the school district's important interest in detecting and preventing drug use among its students, and held that it is constitutional.

Concerns About *Vernonia* and *Earls*

While the *Vernonia* and *Earls* cases are indeed the law, professional educators may express surprise and discomfort with the Court's rulings. On the one hand, the Court may be sincere when it stated in *Vernonia* that in its opinion "[t]aking into account all the factors . . . [including] the decreased expectation of privacy, the relative unobtrusiveness of the search, and the severity of the need met by the search . . . [the policy] is reasonable and hence constitutional." The cases may represent a unique set of circumstances. Indeed, in *Vernonia* the Court specifically "caution[ed] against the assumption that suspicionless drug testing will readily pass constitutional muster in other contexts." On the other hand, the *Earls* shows that the Court did not follow its own cautionary advice.

These two cases are considered by some legal scholars to represent somewhat notorious examples of the Court's willingness to convolute its analysis of the requirements of the Constitution when a majority of the Justices happen to agree with actions which under a proper analysis would violate such requirements. Consider, for example, what Justice Ginsberg had to say in her dissent in the *Earls* case:

> "Seven years ago, in *Vernonia,* . . . [this] Court emphasized that . . . *Vernonia*'s athletes were the 'leaders' of an aggressive local 'drug culture' that had reached "epidemic proportions.' Today, the Court relies upon *Vernonia* to permit a school district with a drug problem *its superintendent repeatedly described as 'not ... major,'* to test the urine of [a student] solely by reason of her participation in a nonathletic,

> competitive extracurricular activity – participation associated with neither special dangers from, nor particular predilections for, drug use.
>
> Although 'special needs' inhere in the public school context, those needs are not so expansive or malleable as to render reasonable any program of student drug testing a school district elects to install. *The particular testing program upheld today is not reasonable, it is capricious, even perverse*: Petitioners' policy targets for testing a student population least likely to be at risk from illicit drugs and their damaging effects. I therefore dissent." (Emphasis added).

Consider also the language employed by the the Court in support of its decisions. First, the Court turned the "compelling state interest" requirement on its head. It asserted in *Vernonia* that

> "[i]t is a mistake . . . to think that the phrase 'compelling state interest,' . . . describes a fixed, minimum quantum of governmental concern, so that one can dispose of a case by answering in isolation the question: Is there a compelling state interest here? Rather, the phrase describes an interest which appears important enough to justify the particular search at hand, in light of other factors which show the search to be relatively intrusive upon a *genuine expectation of privacy*." (Emphasis added).

Nevertheless, upon consideration, it becomes clear that that the Court has inserted the "genuine expectation of privacy" as a mere justification for circular reasoning. The Court is thus enabled to ignore the students' "genuine expectation" that their Constitutional rights will be protected in the absence of a compelling state interest for infringing upon them. Instead, the Court focused on whether requiring students to submit to random and suspicionless urinalysis testing is beyond the bounds of the typical *expectations of privacy*. Is there an adjective pungent enough to describe the Court's conclusion that such a requirement is permissible because there is "an element of 'communal undress'" inherent in participation in athletic and other extracurricular activities?"

Consider next the Court's further undermining of the "compelling interest" analysis. It reduces the "compelling interest" standard to a standard of mere "reasonableness" by cautioning that with regard to suspicionless drug testing, "[t]he most significant . . . question is whether th[e] intrusion upon privacy is one that . . . *a reasonable guardian and tutor might undertake*." (Emphasis added).

Finally, consider that the Court "noted that the primary guardians of *Vernonia*'s schoolchildren appear to agree [with the drug testing policy]. *The record shows no objection to this districtwide program by any parents other than the couple before us here* - even though, as we have described, a public meeting was held to obtain parents' views. We find insufficient basis to contradict the judgment of Vernonia's parents, its school board, and the District Court, as to what was reasonably in the interest of these children under the circumstances." (Emphasis added) Likewise, in *Earls*, the Court refused to require a school district to show that a drug problem exists before implementing testing because,

> "Among other problems, it would be *difficult* to administer such a test. As we *cannot* articulate a threshold level of drug use that would suffice to justify a drug testing program for schoolchildren, we *refuse* to fashion what would in effect be a constitutional quantum of drug use necessary to show a 'drug problem.'" (Emphasis added).

One wonders what the Court means. Is the *Vernonia* Court actually saying that the constitutional rights of the individual are meaningless if enough members of a local community agree with violating them? Is the *Earls* Court saying that it "cannot" articulate some reasonable standard to justify drug testing? It appears instead that the Court is saying that it simply *"refuses"* to develop a standard.

Please remember that professional educators need not intrude on the privacy expectations of students merely because the Court says they may do so. Teachers, administrators, and other school officials may limit their actions to a greater extent than required by the questionable rulings handed down in *T.L.O.*, in *Vernonia*, and in *Earls*. While these cases may free public school educators to ignore the "niceties" of probable cause, it is perhaps more in accord with the ethics of the profession to remember the more lofty notions expressed in the case *West Virginia Board of Education v. Barnette*, 319 U.S. 624 (1943):

> "Boards of Education [have] important, delicate, and highly discretionary functions, but none that they may not perform within the limits of the Bill of Rights. *That they are educating the young for citizenship is reason for scrupulous protection of Constitutional freedoms of the individual, if we are not to strangle the free mind at its source and teach youth to discount important principles of our government as mere platitudes.*" (Emphasis added)

III. The Family Education Rights and Privacy Act: Protection From Unauthorized Disclosure of Student Records

Student education records are official and confidential documents protected by the Family Educational Rights and Privacy Act (FERPA, also known as the Buckley Amendment). Pursuant to FERPA, districts may release information about students only for specific and legally defined purposes. Generally, in order for records to be disclosed, parents must consent to such disclosure. However, there are some exceptions:

1. Teachers and school officials who work with the students may usually have access to education records without prior consent of the parent;

2. Information from students' records may be reviewed by local, state, or federal officials conducting audits or reviewing compliance with laws;

3. Schools do not require the consent of parents in order to respond to subpoenas or court orders. (However, schools must make reasonable efforts to notify parents before complying with subpoenas unless the subpoena provides otherwise.)

4. Schools can provide information in emergencies in order to protect health or safety.

Note that parents have the right to review student records maintained by schools and maintained by state agencies. This right applies to custodial and to noncustodial parents (unless a court order or state law revokes this right, and in the case of a court order, a copy of the order must be provided to the school by the parent wishing to restrict the access of the other parent). Once a student reaches the age of 18, FERPA rights transfer to the student.

FERPA defines education records as almost any record, whether recorded in handwriting, print, computer media, video or audio tape, film, microfilm, and microfiche. Examples are as follows:

1. Date and place of birth, parent(s) and/or guardian addresses, and where parents can be contacted in emergencies;

2. Grades, test scores, courses taken, academic specializations and activities, and official letters regarding a student's status in school;

3. Special education records;

4. Disciplinary records (except that schools may share information about disciplinary actions with officials from other schools);

5. Medical and health records created, collected, or maintained by the school;

6. Records of attendance, schools attended, courses taken, awards, and degrees; and

7. Personal information (student identification code, social security number, picture, or other information assistive in identifying or locating students).

Three Notes Regarding FERPA

1. The Child Abuse Exception

As a professional educator, you are a *mandatory reporter* of suspected child abuse. In other words, the law requires you to report suspected child abuse. States can revoke professional licenses for failure to report and/or investigate suspected child abuse (and they have indeed done so). If you think a child is being abused, you must report it to the state department that handles child abuse cases, or to the police. For more information on this topic, see "A Note on Child Abuse" – Appendix B, below.

2. Personal Notes

Note that the personal notes of teachers, administrators, etc. are not considered educational records unless they are shared with others. Also note that FERPA applies to more than just schools. Its rules apply to records maintained by parties acting on behalf of schools, including state and local education agencies, specialists, researchers, psychologists, medical practitioners, and others who work for or are contracted by schools.

3. What Happens When FERPA is Violated?

As discussed above, student information records are protected under FERPA. However, courts interpret FERPA as providing no legal cause of action. In the case *Gonzaga University v. Doe,* US Supreme Court (2002), the court refused to let a school be sued on the basis of violating FERPA. In the *Gonzaga* case,

"[A] student . . . sue[d] a . . . university for damages . . . to enforce provisions of the Family Educational Rights and Privacy Act of 1974 (FERPA), which prohibit[s] the federal funding of educational institutions that have a policy or practice of releasing education records to unauthorized persons. . . .

John Doe is a former undergraduate in the School of Education at Gonzaga University, a private university in Spokane, Washington. He planned to graduate and teach at a Washington public elementary school. . . . At the time, [Washington] required all of its new teachers to obtain an affidavit of good moral character from a dean of their graduating college or university. In October 1993, Roberta League, Gonzaga's teacher certification specialist, overheard one student tell another that respondent engaged in acts of sexual misconduct against Jane Doe, a female undergraduate. League launched an investigation and contacted the state agency responsible for teacher certification, identifying respondent by name and discussing the allegations against him. [John Doe] did not learn of the investigation, or that information about him had been disclosed, until March 1994, when he was told by League and others that he would not receive the affidavit required for certification as a Washington schoolteacher.

[Doe] then sued Gonzaga and League (petitioners) in state court. He alleged violations . . . for the release of personal information to an unauthorized person in violation of FERPA. A jury found for [Doe] on all counts, awarding him $1,155,000, including $150,000 in compensatory damages and $300,000 in punitive damages on the FERPA claim.

[However,] FERPA itself does not give rise to a private cause of action. . . . Congress enacted FERPA under its spending power to condition the receipt of federal funds on certain requirements relating to the access and disclosure of student educational records. The Act directs the Secretary of Education to withhold federal funds from any public or private educational agency or institution that fails to comply with these conditions. As relevant here, the Act provides:

> No funds shall be made available under any applicable program to any educational agency or institution which has a policy or practice of permitting the release of education records (or personally identifiable information contained therein) of students without the written consent of their parents to any individual, agency, or organization. . . .

[Doe] contends that this statutory regime confers upon any student enrolled at a covered school or institution a federal right . . . not to have education records disclosed to unauthorized persons without the students express written consent. But . . . spending legislation drafted in terms resembling those of FERPA [does not] confer enforceable rights. . . . In legislation enacted pursuant to the spending power, the typical remedy for . . . noncompliance with federally imposed conditions is not a private cause of action for noncompliance but rather action by the Federal Government to terminate funds to the [university]. . . . Since the Act conferred no specific, individually enforceable rights, there was no basis for private enforcement. . . . "

The Court held that because FERPA's nondisclosure provisions fail to confer enforceable rights, the student could not sue the university. Rather, the only way FERPA violations are addressed is through oversight by the US Department of Education, which can withhold federal funds if violations are intentional, ongoing, or remain uncorrected. (But consider the next chapter's discussion of tort claims – especially a claim based on the tort of "invasion of privacy.")

IV. Cases for Chapter Eight

Please read the edited versions of the following Supreme Court cases, which are found in Appendix A.

New Jersey v. T.L.O.
Vernonia School District v. Acton
Board of Education v. Earls

V. Discussion Item for Chapter Nine

Justice Sandra Day O'Connor dissented in the *Vernonia* case. In her dissenting opinion (in which she was joined by Justices Stevens and Souter) she analyzed the search issue in a manner providing an excellent example of the need to remember that neither safety nor freedom necessarily "comes first." Rather, we must always endeavor to come to an appropriate balance between individual and state interests, remembering that we set aside individual rights only when the state interest compels us to do so – and only to the extent required by such compelling interest.

Here is what Justice O'Connor had to say (note that Justice O'Connor believed that the facts of the *Vernonia* case did *not* support the suspicionless search in that particular case):

> "For most of our constitutional history, mass, suspicionless searches have been generally considered per se unreasonable within the meaning of the Fourth Amendment. . . . [W]e allow[] exceptions . . . only where it has been clear that a suspicion-based regime would be ineffectual. . . .
>
> That blanket searches are "intolerable and unreasonable" is well grounded in history. . . . [W]hat the Framers of the Fourth Amendment most strongly opposed, with limited exceptions . . ., were general searches . . . . Perhaps most telling of all, as reflected in the text of the Warrant Clause, the particular way the Framers chose to curb the abuses of general warrants – and by implication, all general searches – was not to impose a novel "evenhandedness" requirement; it was to retain the individualized suspicion requirement contained in the typical general warrant, but to make that requirement meaningful and enforceable . . . by

raising the required level of individualized suspicion to objective probable cause. . . .

In limited circumstances, where the privacy interests implicated by the search are minimal, and where an important governmental interest furthered by the intrusion would be placed in jeopardy by a requirement of individualized suspicion, a search may be reasonable despite the absence of such suspicion. The obvious negative implication of this reasoning is that, if such an individualized suspicion requirement would not place the government's objective in jeopardy, the requirement should not be forsaken. . . .

It cannot be stated too often that the greatest threats to our constitutional freedoms come in times of crisis. But we must also stay mindful that not all government responses to such times are hysterical overreactions; some crises are quite real, and when they are, they serve precisely as the compelling state interest that we have said may justify a measured intrusion on constitutional rights. The only way for judges to mediate these conflicting impulses is to do what they should do anyway: stay close to the record in each case that appears before them, and make their judgements based on that alone."

Please discuss your view of Justice O'Connor's opinion. What does she mean that "too often . . . the greatest threats to our constitutional freedoms come in times of crisis?"

Chapter Nine

Negligence and Tort Liability

I. Introduction

The goal of this chapter is to address the issues of negligence and tort liability. First, these issues are defined. Then, the chapter presents a brief discussion of the aspects typically of concern in the area of professional education.

II. What is a Tort?

According to Black's Law Dictionary, a tort is

> "A private or civil wrong or injury, . . . for which the court will provide a remedy in the form of an action for damages."

In other words, if you engage in tortious conduct towards another person, then that person can sue you and hold you personally liable for the damage you cause. There are three types of torts that are of primary concern to professional educators.

1. Negligence;
2. Intentional Torts; and
3. Constitutional Torts.

Before moving on to the discussion of negligence, we should first consider intentional and constitutional torts.

Intentional torts are *intended* acts of wrong-doing towards another. For the most part, intentional torts are fairly obvious. Two common intentional torts in the area of education are assault and battery. School personnel, whether in public or private schools, who engage in such behavior towards students may find themselves on the wrong end of a tort suit. Assault and battery are defined as follows:

> **Assault** - intentionally placing someone in fear of imminent bodily harm (for example, raising your hand as if to strike a student).
>
> **Battery** - an offensive touching of another person (in other words, touching another person without that person's consent).

Sexual Harassment is another type of conduct of great concern in the area of education. It is closely related to the traditional intentional torts. Sexual Harassment is defined as sexual advances, requests for sexual favors, and other verbal or physical behavior of a sexual nature. Note that the standard for determining whether behavior represents sexual harassment involves determining whether one's actions create what a reasonable person would consider a sexually hostile environment (so, for example, if the actions are against a woman, the question is whether a reasonable woman would consider the actions to create a sexually hostile environment).

Note that many actions constituting intentional torts are also illegal. Assault, battery, and harassment are not just torts; they are criminal offenses. Additionally, sexual harassment is a form of discrimination under federal law.

Constitutional torts are actions by state actors in violation of federal law or constitutional rights of citizens. Thus, when a school employee engages in discrimination or violates students' constitutional rights, that employee runs the risk of being sued and being found personally liable for the damage resulting from such discrimination or violation.

III. Negligence

A. Elements

We sometimes cause injury to others not as a result of an intent to do so, but by letting our behavior fall below a reasonable standard of care. Such behavior is called negligence. In order for behavior to be considered negligent, it must meet the following criteria, or "elements:"

1. **Duty:** One must have a duty towards another;

2. **Breach:** One's actions must fall below a reasonable or legal standard of care;

3. **Injury:** The victim must experience injury; and

4. **Causation:** The injury must be caused by the actor's unreasonable or illegal behavior.

One common type of negligence is professional malpractice. This is the basis for many suits against medical professionals. Such claims generally assert that a doctor has a duty to perform proper medical treatment on a patient, that the doctor failed to meet the reasonable standards of the medical profession, and that as a result of the doctor's actions, the patient suffered injury. Fortunately for educators, courts have so far been reluctant to adopt a tort of educational malpractice. Rather, courts have adopted the notion that educational decisions are best made by educators, not by judges.

Notwithstanding court resistance to malpractice in the field of education, educators can, and do, commit numerous other torts of negligence. Whether a student is physically injured is a relatively simple question of fact. However, whether an educator will be held liable for such injury due to negligence requires considering the remaining three elements of negligence:

1. **Duty** - There can be no question that educators have a duty towards students. Educators have the duty to look out for their students and to protect them from injury.

2. **Breach of Reasonable Care** - Educators must behave reasonably with regard to their duty. They must make sure that students obey safety rules; they must properly supervise students; etc.

3. **Cause** - The injury must have been a result of the actions of the educator in order for the educator to be liable. For example, consider the case of a student hurt in a chemistry lab. What caused the injury? If it was because the teacher failed to properly set up the equipment, then the teacher *caused* the injury. On the other hand, if the student came to class after taking LSD, thought her lab partner was a wicked warlock mixing a potion that would turn her into a frog, fought off the teacher's attempts to control her, and jumped screaming from the second story window suffering two broken legs, then the student is the *cause* of her own injury.

B. Defenses

There are defenses to a claim of negligence. If a defendant can prove a defense, that defendant will not be found liable, or may at least be found to have a lesser degree of liability. Some common defenses are as follow:

One's Actions Were Within the Scope on One's Duties: Consider whether the educator followed all school rules; whether all actions required by school procedure been appropriately taken; whether the necessary forms, equipment, instruction, etc. had been implemented; whether there appropriate supervision, etc.?

Contributory Negligence: If a student engages in actions that in some way contribute to the injury sustained, such as ignoring rules, engaging in negligent behavior on the student's own part, etc., and if such actions are the cause or a portion of the cause of the student's injuries, then the student's own behavior is considered a contributing factor and may relieve or reduce the liability of the educator. Note that in some states, if a victim causes any part of their own injury, then the other party is completely relieved of liability. However, in other states, courts apportion liability based on the extent to which various persons negligently contributed to the injury. Also note that the younger the student, the lower the standard applied in evaluating the student's own behavior.

Assumption of Risk: Certain activities are inherently dangerous, such as contact sports. One "assumes" the risk of typical injuries associated with such activities.

Self Defense: This is a defense commonly misunderstood by students. The privilege of self-defense enables persons to use reasonable force to defend oneself against unprivileged battery (or other bodily harm, including reasonably anticipated imminent harm). However, the privilege is limited to defense alone; it ceases when an attacker is disarmed, withdraws, or gives up. In other words, self-defense does not provide leeway to engage in retaliation; retaliation is not self-defense. Likewise, persons may engage in self-defense only against an unprivileged use of force.

C. Examples

The following situations are examples of cases in which courts have found educators liable for negligence:

1. An educator left a number of students with mental retardation unsupervised for approximately 30 minutes. One student injured another. *Gonzalez v. Mackler*, 241 N.Y.S.2d 254 (App. Div. 1963).

2. A nine-year-old student arrived at school early one morning. As he was parking his bicycle, he was injured by a paperclip shot with a rubber band by a second boy. The second boy was not a student at the school, but was waiting for his bus to arrive. It was normal for students to arrive early, the principal sometimes provided some degree of supervision for such students, the principal was aware of the second boy having engaged in similar "pranks" in the past, no rules had been announced regarding student behavior before school, and no teachers were assigned by the principal to supervise the area before school began. The principal was held liable for the injury. *Titus v. Lindberg*, 49 N.J. 66, 228 A.2d 65 (1967).

3. A boy suffered serious injury on school grounds when he fell into a hole filled with various types of debris (trash, etc. – including glass). The student had not been warned of the danger by school officials. *Dean v. Town of Waterford*, 523 A.2d 1059 (Md. App. 1987).

4. Students informed two school counselors that a friend intended to commit suicide. The friend did indeed commit suicide. The court held that the counselors had a duty to take reasonable steps to prevent the suicide and a duty to warn the parents of the student. The court held the counselors liable for breach of these duties. *Eisel v. Board of Education of Montgomery County*, 597 A.2d 447 (Md. 1991).

5. A student was participating in a class activity in a park. The park happened to be near her home. Upon obtaining permission from school personnel to do so, the student left the park to buy lunch at a nearby restaurant. When the student returned to the park, she was unable to find her class. She walked home alone. On the way home she was attacked and raped. *Bell v. Board of Education of New York*, 687 N.E.2d 1325 (N.Y. 1997).

IV. School District Liability

Note that injuries can occur even though an educator is properly acting within the scope of his or her employment and where all appropriate procedural safeguards required by a school or district have been followed. In such cases, the question often focuses on whether the rules, safeguards, and procedures themselves were sufficient. If the district's rules are not sufficient, it is possible for the school district, rather than the individual educator, to be found negligent (and held liable for damages).

Likewise, discrimination against students or violation of student rights can result from school district policies and procedures that are themselves discriminatory or otherwise violative of student rights. In such cases, the district, rather than the teacher who follows such policies and procedures, will be held liable (for committing a constitutional tort). In other words, districts cannot escape liability for their own actions, policies, etc. by trying to pin blame on the teachers, administrators, and other personnel who must follow such actions and policies.

V. A Brief Note About Invasion of Privacy

As discussed in the previous chapter, student information records are protected under FERPA. However, remember that FERPA alone does not provide a basis for people to file suit in court. Therefore, in the school context, the unauthorized disclosing of confidential student information is normally addressed through a tort suit. The tort is called invasion of privacy.

VI. "Section 1983" of the Civil Rights Act of 1871 (42 U.S.C. Section 1983)

Section 1983 of the Civil Rights Act of 1871 provides citizens with a means of obtaining a remedy for violations of their civil rights by state actors. In education, it provides students with the ability to obtain money damages from school officials, as well as from members of school boards, for bad faith violations of students' constitutional or statutory rights. It is important to note that the legal question is not whether a school official is aware of a violation of a student's rights; rather, the question is whether a reasonable person in the official's position would have been aware of a violation.

Specifically, Section 1983 states:

> "Every person who, under color of any statute, ordinance, regulation, custom, or usage of any state or territory, subjects or causes to be subjected, any citizen of the United States or other person within the jurisdiction thereof to the deprivation of any rights, privileges, or immunities secured by the Constitution and laws, shall be liable to the party injured in any

> action at law, suit in equity, or other proper proceeding for redress."

Note that Section 1983 creates a procedural right to damages; it does not create any specific substantive rights. Therefore, in order to file a suit under Section 1983, a person must be able to claim that a state actor (which includes professional educators in the public schools) violated a particular right of the injured person under the Constitution or statutory law. Therefore, for example, if professional educators in the public schools violate federal anti-discrimination statutes, or if they violate any of the constitutional protections discussed in the previous chapters of this book, such educators may be liable for monetary damages in a lawsuit through the provisions of Section 1983.

VII. Discussion Item for Chapter Nine

As discussed above, professional malpractice is the failure of a professional to act in accord with the standards of his or her profession such that this failure causes harm to another. Courts hold professionals who commit malpractice liable for the damage that results from their behavior. But teachers are lucky (so far); in general, courts have been reluctant to adopt a tort of educational malpractice. Rather, courts take the position that educators are experts who must be trusted to set their own standards and to judge performance within the profession. However, courts do sometimes find that school districts have not provided sufficient education to students - primarily in the area of special education. In such instances liability is usually limited to the school district paying the costs of the student's remediation to make up for what was not taught.

Part of the difficulty with a tort of educational malpractice is identification: How do we identify specifically what should be taught? What was or was not taught? What damage is a direct result of not being taught? If a teacher does not sufficiently teach an 8th grade language arts objective, so what? How can we identify a specific problem that results from such failure? Does a band teacher's failure to correct his tuba player's improper embouchure result in liability for the student's inability to realize her dreams of being the principal tubist in the New York Philharmonic? If so, how do we identify the monetary damages?

There is one area, however, in which more specificity is possible. This is the area of reading. Believe it or not, for years a vigorous debate raged over whether the "proper" method for teaching reading should be a phonics-oriented approach or a whole-language approach. Those favoring one side or the other quickly formed into camps, each camp launching vehement criticism at the other. The situation was as disastrous as it was senseless. Rather than implementing a well-rounded approach to teaching reading – one that used a variety of techniques depending on individual student needs – classroom instruction often focused exclusively on either one method or the other. As you can imagine, if a student did not benefit from the strict application of the particular method to which she was exposed, she simply fell through the cracks. Even worse, entire departments and schools of education adopted "our way only" stances resulting in hundreds, perhaps thousands, of teachers who now lack competence in the method in which they received no instruction as part of their particular teacher preparatory programs.

Gradually the situation has been improving. As sanity has returned to the area of reading, scholars and professionals have begun to acknowledge the obvious – that different approaches work with different students; that the proper focus is on the student, not the method. Identifying processing ability and other differences among individual students is how to determine what will work best for specific individuals.

Additionally, research gradually made it clear that neither method of teaching reading is effective for students who do not possess phonemic awareness. (Do not be misled by the use of the term "phonemic." This is not related to a phonics oriented teaching approach. Phonemic awareness is exactly what it sounds like (pardon the pun) – an ability to distinguish differences in sounds (i.e., phonemes)). In fact, current literature suggests that it is so important for students to be able to distinguish phonemes that failure to identify students who lack phonemic awareness in the primary grades should indeed be considered educational malpractice.

Please consider the following questions:

Given what the current literature tells us about learning reading, do you feel that we should consider either of the following to be educational malpractice? If we should consider either of these to be malpractice, how do you think courts should assess damages?

1. An elementary school teacher has a background in only one type of reading instruction (it does not matter whether it is whole language or phonics based) and limits instruction to that particular method.

2. Failure to evaluate the phonemic awareness of students at the primary grade levels.

Chapter Ten

A Basic Introduction to Employment Issues

I. Introduction

This chapter presents a *basic* introduction to the realm of the rights of professional educators. While the primary focus of this text has been to provide professional educators with an overview of the legal principles affecting actions towards students, it is nevertheless important for educators to understand that there is much more to learn about the relationship between law and professional education. However, it will be obvious to the reader that this chapter presents only the most basic, introductory information. Items not covered in the scope of this chapter, but which will be addressed forthcoming volumes of this series, include:

1. The full scope of the constitutional and statutory rights of professional educators in the workplace, including, but not limited to, political activity, privacy, academic freedom, and discrimination.

2. A detailed analysis of the legal and professional issues surrounding the education of exceptional students.

3. Employment issues and procedures affecting professional educators, including, but not limited to, evaluation procedures, hiring and transfers, collective bargaining and unions, grievance procedures and other contractual procedures, and general employment contract interpretation.

4. Tortious actions against teachers, such as defamation and discrimination.

II. Basic Constitutional Protection for Professional Educators

Educators in the public sector, including teachers, administrators, counselors, and other school personnel, are protected from unconstitutional actions by local, state, and federal school officials. Just as educators must respect the rights of students, so must supervisors, school boards, and other governmental authorities respect the rights of employees. The basic rule is the same as we have learned with regard to infringing upon student rights; namely, in order to justify infringing upon the rights of professional educators, school authorities must have a sufficient interest (usually a compelling interest). While the basic rights of professional educators are the same as the student rights discussed previously in this text, it is crucial that educators remember two points:

1. The rights of students almost always trump the rights of school personnel (thus protection of student rights usually constitutes an interest sufficient to justify infringement of staff rights); and

2. Just as the Constitution does not control the actions of private school authorities with regard to students, the Constitution does not control the actions of private school authorities with regard to employees.

III. An Introduction to Discrimination Against Professional Educators

Unlike the Constitution, federal and state legislation generally applies to all school authorities - public and private. As such, statutory law protects almost all professional educators from discrimination, whether the educators work in public schools or private schools. As discussed earlier in this text, such protection generally prohibits discrimination on seven bases: race, religion, gender, national origin, disability, marital status, and age. Additionally, some states prohibit discrimination on the basis of sexual orientation. (As of January 2000, ten states and the District of Columbia have statutes prohibiting discrimination on the basis of sexual orientation. The states are California, Connecticut, Hawaii, Massachusetts, Minnesota, New Hampshire, New Jersey, Rhode Island, Vermont, and Wisconsin. Several other states, including Oregon, have court cases requiring that insurance and other benefits apply equally to spouses and same-sex partners.)

Two things to remember about discrimination:

1. Private institutions may sometimes discriminate legally on the basis of religion. For example, parochial schools may exclusively hire members of the religion with which they are affiliated.

2. There is sometimes a difference between violating the Constitution and discriminating. Under the Constitution, officials may infringe upon the rights of educators if necessary in order to protect the rights of students. (For example, a teacher's Freedom of Expression may be limited in order to assure the consistency and quality of the educational curriculum. Likewise, as we have seen, public school personnel are significantly limited with regard to the free exercise of religion.) However, anti-discrimination statutes require that school officials implement such infringements in a non-discriminatory manner. For example, limitations on expression, if required to protect the rights of students, must apply to all educators alike, regardless of their race, religion, gender, etc. Likewise, limitations on religious exercise must apply equally to educators of all religions.

IV. A Special Note Regarding Procedural Due Process

A public school district violates an educator's procedural due process rights when it fails to follow proper disciplinary procedures. These procedures are usually found in the collective bargaining agreement (the "contract") in existence between the district and the local union (for teachers, counselors, and classified staff) or the local administrator's association (for administrators). In general, such contracts, if ethically, and professionally negotiated, provide for two essential rights: "progressive discipline" and "just cause."

"Progressive discipline" requires an employer to address an employee's misconduct, if any, in a progressive manner. The employer must give the employee appropriate and useful evaluative feedback about job performance and must also provide an appropriate opportunity for the employee to remedy deficiencies, to improve job performance, or both. In other words, the employer is expected to engage in documented "discipline" aimed at helping the employee, rather than moving prematurely to "termination" of employment. The specific procedures in any given school district are either explicit in the contract, or have been established by the past practices of the district with regard to discipline.

The other essential component of a proper collective bargaining agreement is a **"just cause"** provision. "Just cause" prohibits an employer from terminating an educator's employment unless there is an actual showing that the employee is unfit for his or her position.

Taken together with "progressive discipline," the protection provided by a "just cause" clause assures that educators do not lose their jobs unless employers document specific issues of concern about an employee's performance, that they inform the employee of such concerns, and that they give the employee ample opportunity to improve. Thus "just cause" for termination can only arise after following "progressive discipline" procedures.

Four Final Notes of Great Importance

1. **Insubordination** - Some behavior is held to be so egregious as to merit "just cause" for termination immediately upon its occurrence, thus no "progressive discipline" would be required. Such behavior includes, but is not limited to, immorality, criminal and/or highly dangerous conduct, and "insubordination."

2. **Right to Representation** - Member of unions have the right to have a union representative present with them when they feel any conversation between the union member and a supervisor may result in disciplinary action. *NLRB v. Weingarten, Inc.,* 420 U.S. 251 (1975). Union members may feel uncomfortable making this request of a supervisor, but most supervisors have been trained regarding this right to representation and should stop the meeting immediately to permit the union member to contact his or her building or district representative. It is a violation of the rights of a union employee for a supervisor to deny an assertion of the Weingarten right.

3. **Possible Bad Faith** - Educators should be concerned if any school district (or private school employer) seeks to negotiate an employment contract without "just cause" and "progressive discipline" provisions. An employer's (or an employer bargaining team's) act of seeking to omit such provisions is an indication that the employer may not be acting in good faith. A professional educator, whether teacher, administrator, specialist, or counselor, should not accept a contract that does not provide for "progressive discipline" and "just cause."

4. **Obey Now, Grieve Later** - Finally, avoid a charge of insubordination by always remembering and adhering to the following basic rule: OBEY NOW, GRIEVE LATER. Even if you believe that a school district or private employer is violating your contractual rights, you must comply with the employer's directive. Failure to comply is insubordination. Once you have complied, you may address you concerns via the proper procedures - file a grievance (for contractual issues) or file suit in court (for other issues).

V. Discussion Item for Chapter Ten

For your information, note that *the following is based on an actual occurrence.*

Teacher is a witch. She is a member of a small, but growing, religious sect that engages in a variety of non-traditional activities in its worship/veneration of entities it deems holy or otherwise important. Teacher has been a member of the religion for over 20 years and has been a teacher in School District for 12 of those 20 years. While Teacher has never kept the affiliation "secret," she has never discussed it in school in any way. Indeed, it was not widely known by students, parents, and other staff members until a few months ago when a state senator invited Teacher to give the invocation for a session of the state senate.

Teacher's professional and academic backgrounds are exemplary. Teacher has been recognized repeatedly as an outstanding professional and has never received anything but glowing professional evaluations. Teacher possesses several graduate degrees from highly respected institutions. Students, parents, and colleagues have historically lavished great praise on Teacher.

Nevertheless, after Teacher's religious affiliation became "public," at least one student expressly objected to Teacher teaching at the school because of Teacher's affiliation. Additionally, three fellow teachers object to Teacher remaining on the teaching staff, saying that it is objectionable to them as teachers and as parents. The vice-principal and the principal, as well as the retired superintendent of instruction, feel that Teacher's presence on the faculty may create problems. It has been suggested that retention of Teacher by School District could be interpreted as indicating to students that School District approves of the religion and the religious practices engaged in by Teacher and Teacher's fellow witches.

School District, after considering the above, has terminated Teacher's employment. School District explained that the termination was justified because "the conduct of Teacher may reasonably be expected to interfere with the ability of Teacher's fitness in Teacher's job and may interfere with Teacher's ability to discharge Teacher's responsibilities."

Discuss whether the termination is legally appropriate.

To the Reader:

Thank you for your patience. Your comments, questions, concerns, and suggestions will be greatly appreciated. Please contact the author via email at the following address:

Isaac@Ersoff.com

Appendix A

Cases

Case Titles **Page**

Case for Chapter Two

Pierce v. Society of Sisters 124

Cases for Chapter Three

Goss v. Lopez 129

Brown v. Board of Education . . . 139

Romer v. Evans 144

Lau v. Nichols 151

Tinker v. Des Moines School District . . 155

San Antonio School District v. Rodriguez . . 163

Hazelwood School District v. Kuhlmeier . . 173

Cases for Chapter Five

Lee v. Weisman 183

Newdow v. US Congress 200

Santa Fe Independent School District v. Doe. . 214

Cases for Chapter Six

Brown v. Board of Education . . . 139

Romer v. Evans 144

Zelman v. Simmons-Harris . . . 231

Cases for Chapter Eight

New Jersey v. T.L.O. 245

Vernonia School District v. Acton . . . 257

Board of Education v. Earls . . . 271

PIERCE v. SOCIETY OF SISTERS
U.S. Supreme Court, 268 U.S. 510 (1925)

Mr. Justice McREYNOLDS delivered the opinion of the Court.

These appeals are from decrees, based upon undenied allegations, which granted preliminary orders restraining appellants from threatening or attempting to enforce the Compulsory Education Act1 adopted November 7, 1922 (Laws Or. 1923, p. 9), under the initiative provision of her Constitution by the voters of Oregon. Judicial Code, 266 (Comp. St. 1243). They present the same points of law; there are no controverted questions of fact. Rights said to be guaranteed by the federal Constitution were specially set up, and appropriate prayers asked for their protection.

The challenged act, effective September 1, 1926, requires every parent, guardian, or other person having control or charge or custody of a child between 8 and 16 years to send him 'to a public school for the period of time a public school shall be held during the current year' in the district where the child resides; and failure so to do is declared a misdemeanor. There are exemptions-not specially important here-for children who are not normal, or who have completed the eighth grade, or whose parents or private teachers reside at considerable distances from any public school, or who hold special permits from the county superintendent. The manifest purpose is to compel general attendance at public schools by normal children, between 8 and 16, who have not completed the eight grade. And without doubt enforcement of the statute would seriously impair, perhaps destroy, the profitable features of appellees' business and greatly diminish the value of their property.

Appellee the Society of Sisters is an Oregon corporation, organized in 1880, with power to care for orphans, educate and instruct the youth, establish and maintain academies or schools, and acquire necessary real and personal property. It has long devoted its property and effort to the secular and religious education and care of children, and has acquired the valuable good will of many parents and guardians. It conducts interdependent primary and high schools and junior colleges, and maintains orphanages for the custody and control of children between 8 and 16. In its primary schools many children between those ages are taught the subjects usually pursued in Oregon public schools during the first eight years. Systematic religious instruction and moral training according to the tenets of the Roman Catholic Church are also regularly provided. All courses of study, both temporal and religious, contemplate continuity of training under appellee's charge; the primary schools are essential to the system and the most profitable. It owns valuable buildings, especially constructed and equipped for school purposes. The business is remunerative-the annual income from primary schools exceeds $30,000-and the successful conduct of this requires long time contracts with teachers and parents. The Compulsory Education Act of 1922 has already caused the withdrawal from its schools of children who would otherwise continue, and their income has steadily declined. The appellants, public officers, have proclaimed their purpose strictly to enforce the statute.

After setting out the above facts, the Society's bill alleges that the enactment conflicts with the right of parents to choose schools where their children will receive appropriate mental and religious training, the right of the child to influence the parents' choice of a school, the right of schools and teachers therein to engage in a useful business or profession, and is accordingly repugnant to the Constitution and void. And, further, that unless enforcement of lthe measure is enjoined the corporation's business and property will suffer irreparable injury.

Appellee Hill Military Academy is a private corporation organized in 1908 under the laws of Oregon, engaged in owning, operating, and conducting for profit an elementary, college preparatory, and military training school for boys between the ages of 5 and 21 years. The average attendance is 100, and the annual fees received for each student amount to some $800. The elementary department is divided into eight grades, as in the public schools; the college preparatory department has four grades, similar to those of the public high schools; the courses of study conform to the requirements of the state board of education. Military instruction and training are also given, under the supervision of an army officer. It owns considerable real and personal property, some useful only for school purposes. The business and incident good will are very valuable. In order to conduct its affairs, long time contracts must be made for supplies, equipment, teachers, and pupils. Appellants, law officers of the state and county, have publicly announced that the Act of November 7, 1922, is valid and have declared their intention to enforce it. By reason of the statute and threat of enforcement appellee's business is being destroyed and its property depreciated; parents and guardians are refusing to make contracts for the future instruction of their sons, and some are being withdrawn.

The Academy's bill states the foregoing facts and then alleges that the challenged act contravenes the corporation's rights guaranteed by the Fourteenth Amendment and that unless appellants are restrained from proclaiming its validity and threatening to enforce it irreparable injury will result. The prayer is for an appropriate injunction.

No answer was interposed in either cause, and after proper notices they were heard by three judges (Judicial Code, 266) on motions for preliminary injunctions upon the specifically alleged facts. The court ruled that the Fourteenth Amendment guaranteed appellees against the deprivation of their property without due process of law consequent upon the unlawful interference by appellants with the free choice of patrons, present and prospective. It declared the right to conduct schools was property and that parents and guardians, as a part of their liberty, might direct the education of children by selecting reputable teachers and places. Also, that appellees' schools were not unfit or harmful to the public, and that enforcement of the challenged statute would unlawfully deprive them of patronage and thereby destroy appellees' business and property. Finally, that the threats to enforce the act would continue to cause irreparable injury; and the suits were not premature.

No question is raised concerning the power of the state reasonably to regulate all schools, to inspect, supervise and examine them, their teachers and pupils; to require that all children of proper age attend some school, that teachers shall be of good moral character and patriotic disposition, that certain studies plainly essential to good citizenship must be taught, and that nothing be taught which is manifestly inimical to the public welfare.

The inevitable practical result of enforcing the act under consideration would be destruction of appellees' primary schools, and perhaps all other private primary schools for normal children within the state of Oregon. Appellees are engaged in a kind of undertaking not inherently harmful, but long regarded as useful and meritorious. Certainly there is nothing in the present records to indicate that they have failed to discharge their obligations to patrons, students, or the state. And there are no peculiar circumstances or present emergencies which demand extraordinary measures relative to primary education.

Under the doctrine of Meyer v. Nebraska, 262 U.S. 390, 43 S. Ct. 625, 29 A. L. R. 1146, we think it entirely plain that the Act of 1922 unreasonably interferes with the liberty of parents and guardians to direct the upbringing and education of children under their control. As often heretofore pointed out, rights guaranteed by the Constitution may not be abridged by legislation which has no reasonable relation to some purpose within the competency of the state. The fundamental theory of liberty upon which all governments in this Union repose excludes any general power of the state to standardize its children by forcing them to accept instruction from public teachers only. The child is not the mere creature of the state; those who nurture him and direct his destiny have the right, coupled with the high duty, to recognize and prepare him for additional obligations.

Appellees are corporations, and therefore, it is said, they cannot claim for themselves the liberty which the Fourteenth Amendment guarantees. Accepted in the proper sense, this is true. Northwestern Life Ins. Co. v. Riggs, 203 U.S. 243, 255, 27 S. Ct. 126, 7 Ann. Cas. 1104; Western Turf Association v. Greenberg, 204 U.S. 359, 363, 27 S. Ct. 384. But they have business and property for which they claim protection. These are threatened with destruction through the unwarranted compulsion which appellants are exercising over present and prospective patrons of their schools. And this court has gone very far to protect against loss threatened by such action. Truax v. Raich, 239 U.S. 33, 36 S. Ct. 7, L. R. A. 1916D, 543, Ann. Cas. 1917B, 283; Truax v. Corrigan, 257 U.S. 312, 42 S. Ct. 124, 27 A. L. R. 375; Terrace v. Thompson, 263 U.S. 197, 44 S. Ct. 15.

The courts of the state have not construed the act, and we must determine its meaning for ourselves. Evidently it was expected to have general application and cannot be construed as though merely intended to amend the charters of certain private corporations, as in Berea College v. Kentucky, 211 U.S. 45, 29 S. Ct. 33. No argument in favor of such view has been advanced.

Generally, it is entirely true, as urged by counsel, that no person in any business has such an interest in possible customers as to enable him to restrain exercise of proper power of the state upon the ground that he will be de prived of patronage. But the injunctions here sought are not against the exercise of any proper power. Appellees asked protection against arbitrary, unreasonable, and unlawful interference with their patrons and the consequent destruction of their business and property. Their interest is clear and immediate, within the rule approved in Truax v. Raich, Truax v. Corrigan, and Terrace v. Thompson, supra, and many other cases where injunctions have issued to protect business enterprises against interference with the freedom of patrons or customers. Hitchman Coal & Coke Co. v. Mitchell, 245 U.S. 229, 38 S. Ct. 65, L. R. A. 1918C, 497, Ann. Cas. 1918B, 461; Duplex Printing Press Co. v. Deering, 254 U.S. 443, 41 S. Ct. 172, 16 A. L. R. 196; American Steel Foundries v. Tri-City Central Trades Council, 257 U.S. 184, 42 S. Ct. 72, 27 A. L. R. 360; Nebraska District, etc., v. McKelvie, 262 U.S. 404, 43 S. Ct. 628; Truax v. Corrigan, supra, and cases there cited.

The suits were not premature. The injury to appellees was present and very real, not a mere possibility in the remote future. If no relief had been possible prior to the effective date of the act, the injury would have become irreparable. Prevention of impending injury by unlawful action is a well-recognized function of courts of equity.

The decrees below are affirmed.

GOSS v. LOPEZ
U.S. Supreme Court, 419 U.S. 565 (1975)

MR. JUSTICE WHITE delivered the opinion of the Court.

This appeal by various administrators of the Columbus, Ohio, Public School System (CPSS) challenges the judgment of a three-judge federal court, declaring that appellees - various high school students in the CPSS - were denied due process of law contrary to the command of the Fourteenth Amendment in that they were temporarily suspended from their high schools without a hearing either prior to suspension or within a reasonable time thereafter, and enjoining the administrators to remove all references to such suspensions from the students' records.

I

Ohio law, Rev. Code Ann. 3313.64 (1972), provides for free education to all children between the ages of six and 21. Section 3313.66 of the Code empowers the principal of an Ohio public school to suspend a pupil for misconduct for up to 10 days or to expel him. In either case, he must notify the student's parents within 24 hours and state the reasons for his action. A pupil who is expelled, or his parents, may appeal the decision to the Board of Education and in connection therewith shall be permitted to be heard at the board meeting. The Board may reinstate the pupil following the hearing. No similar procedure is provided in 3313.66 or any other provision of state law for a suspended student. Aside from a regulation tracking the statute, at the time of the imposition of the suspensions in this case the CPSS itself had not issued any written procedure applicable to suspensions. Nor, so far as the record reflects, had any of the individual high schools involved in this case. Each, however, had formally or informally described the conduct for which suspension could be imposed.

The nine named appellees, each of whom alleged that he or she had been suspended from public high school in Columbus for up to 10 days without a hearing pursuant to 3313.66, filed an action under 42 U.S.C. 1983 against the Columbus Board of Education and various administrators of the CPSS. The complaint sought a declaration that 3313.66 was unconstitutional in that it permitted public school administrators to deprive plaintiffs of their rights to an education without a hearing of any kind, in violation of the procedural due process component of the Fourteenth Amendment. It also sought to enjoin the public school officials from issuing future suspensions pursuant to 3313.66 and to require them to remove references to the past suspensions from the records of the students in question.

The proof below established that the suspensions arose out of a period of widespread student unrest in the CPSS during February and March 1971. Six of the named plaintiffs, Rudolph Sutton, Tyrone Washington, Susan Cooper, Deborah Fox, Clarence Byars, and Bruce Harris, were students at the Marion-Franklin High School and were each suspended for 10 days on account of disruptive or disobedient conduct committed in the presence of the school administrator who ordered the suspension. One of these, Tyrone Washington, was among a group of students demonstrating in the school auditorium while a class was being conducted there. He was ordered by the school principal to leave, refused to do so, and was suspended. Rudolph Sutton, in the presence of the principal, physically attacked a police officer who was attempting to remove Tyrone Washington from the auditorium. He was immediately suspended. The other four Marion-Franklin students were suspended for similar conduct. None was given a hearing to determine the operative facts underlying the suspension, but each, together with his or her parents, was offered the opportunity to attend a conference, subsequent to the effective date of the suspension, to discuss the student's future.

* * *

On the basis of this evidence, the three-judge court declared that plaintiffs were denied due process of law because they were "suspended without hearing prior to suspension or within a reasonable time thereafter," and that Ohio Rev. Code Ann. 3313.66 (1972) and regulations issued pursuant thereto were unconstitutional in permitting such suspensions. It was ordered that all references to plaintiffs' suspensions be removed from school files.

. . . We affirm.

II

At the outset, appellants contend that because there is no constitutional right to an education at public expense, the Due Process Clause does not protect against expulsions from the public school system. This position misconceives the nature of the issue and is refuted by prior decisions. The Fourteenth Amendment forbids the State to deprive any person of life, liberty, or property without due process of law. Protected interests in property are normally "not created by the Constitution. Rather, they are created and their dimensions are defined" by an independent source such as state statutes or rules entitling the citizen to certain benefits. Board of Regents v. Roth, 408 U.S. 564, 577 (1972).

Accordingly, a state employee who under state law, or rules promulgated by state officials, has a legitimate claim of entitlement to continued employment absent sufficient cause for discharge may demand the procedural protections of due process. Connell v. Higginbotham, 403 U.S. 207 (1971); Wieman v. Updegraff, 344 U.S. 183, 191-192 (1952); Arnett v. Kennedy, 416 U.S. 134, 164 (POWELL, J., concurring), 171 (WHITE, J., concurring and dissenting) (1974). So may welfare recipients who have statutory rights to welfare as long as they maintain the specified qualifications. Goldberg v. Kelly, 397 U.S. 254 (1970). Morrissey v. Brewer, 408 U.S. 471 (1972), applied the limitations of the Due Process Clause to governmental decisions to revoke parole, although a parolee has no constitutional right to that status. In like vein was Wolff v. McDonnell, 418 U.S. 539 (1974), where the procedural protections of the Due Process Clause were triggered by official cancellation of a prisoner's good-time credits accumulated under state law, although those benefits were not mandated by the Constitution.

Here, on the basis of state law, appellees plainly had legitimate claims of entitlement to a public education. Ohio Rev. Code Ann. 3313.48 and 3313.64 (1972 and Supp. 1973) direct local authorities to provide a free education to all residents between five and 21 years of age, and a compulsory-attendance law requires attendance for a school year of not less than 32 weeks. Ohio Rev. Code Ann. 3321.04 (1972). It is true that 3313.66 of the Code permits school principals to suspend students for up to 10 days; but suspensions may not be imposed without any grounds whatsoever. All of the schools had their own rules specifying the grounds for expulsion or suspension. Having chosen to extend the right to an education to people of appellees' class generally, Ohio may not withdraw that right on grounds of misconduct, absent fundamentally fair procedures to determine whether the misconduct has occurred. Arnett v. Kennedy, supra, at 164 (POWELL, J., concurring), 171 (WHITE, J., concurring and dissenting), 206 (MARSHALL, J., dissenting).

Although Ohio may not be constitutionally obligated to establish and maintain a public school system, it has nevertheless done so and has required its children to attend. Those young people do not "shed their constitutional rights" at the schoolhouse door. Tinker v. Des Moines School Dist., 393 U.S. 503, 506 (1969). "The Fourteenth Amendment, as now applied to the States, protects the citizen against the State itself and all of its creatures - Boards of Education not excepted." West Virginia Board of Education v. Barnette, 319 U.S. 624, 637 (1943). The authority possessed by the State to prescribe and enforce standards of conduct in its schools although concededly very broad, must be exercised consistently with constitutional safeguards. Among other things, the State is constrained to recognize a student's legitimate entitlement to a public education as a property interest which is protected by the Due Process Clause and which may not be taken away for misconduct without adherence to the minimum procedures required by that Clause.

The Due Process Clause also forbids arbitrary deprivations of liberty. "Where a person's good name, reputation, honor, or integrity is at stake because of what the government is doing to him," the minimal requirements of the Clause must be satisfied. Wisconsin v. Constantineau, 400 U.S. 433, 437 (1971); Board of Regents v. Roth, supra, at 573. School authorities here suspended appellees from school for periods of up to 10 days [419 U.S. 565, 575] based on charges of misconduct.

If sustained and recorded, those charges could seriously damage the students' standing with their fellow pupils and their teachers as well as interfere with later opportunities for higher education and employment. It is apparent that the claimed right of the State to determine unilaterally and without process whether that misconduct has occurred immediately collides with the requirements of the Constitution.

Appellants proceed to argue that even if there is a right to a public education protected by the Due Process Clause generally, the Clause comes into play only when the State subjects a student to a "severe detriment or grievous loss." The loss of 10 days, it is said, is neither severe nor grievous and the Due Process Clause is therefore of no relevance. Appellants' argument is again refuted by our prior decisions; for in determining "whether due process requirements apply in the first place, we must look not to the `weight' but to the nature of the interest at stake." Board of Regents v. Roth, supra, at 570-571. Appellees were excluded from school only temporarily, it is true, but the length and consequent severity of a deprivation, while another factor to weigh in determining the appropriate form of hearing, "is not decisive of the basic right" to a hearing of some kind. Fuentes v. Shevin, 407 U.S. 67, 86 (1972). The Court's view has been that as long as a property deprivation is not de minimis, its gravity is irrelevant to the question whether account must be taken of the Due Process Clause. Sniadach v. Family Finance Corp., 395 U.S. 337, 342 (1969) (Harlan, J., concurring); Boddie v. Connecticut, 401 U.S. 371, 378-379 (1971); Board of Regents v. Roth, supra, at 570 n. 8. A 10-day suspension from school is not de minimis in our view and may not be imposed in complete disregard of the Due Process Clause.

A short suspension is, of course, a far milder deprivation than expulsion. But, "education is perhaps the most important function of state and local governments," Brown v. Board of Education, 347 U.S. 483, 493 (1954), and the total exclusion from the educational process for more than a trivial period, and certainly if the suspension is for 10 days, is a serious event in the life of the suspended child. Neither the property interest in educational benefits temporarily denied nor the liberty interest in reputation, which is also implicated, is so insubstantial that suspensions may constitutionally be imposed by any procedure the school chooses, no matter how arbitrary.

III

"Once it is determined that due process applies, the question remains what process is due." Morrissey v. Brewer, 408 U.S., at 481. We turn to that question, fully realizing as our cases regularly do that the interpretation and application of the Due Process Clause are intensely practical matters and that "[t]he very nature of due process negates any concept of inflexible procedures universally applicable to every imaginable situation." Cafeteria Workers v. McElroy, 367 U.S. 886, 895 (1961). We are also mindful of our own admonition:

"Judicial interposition in the operation of the public school system of the Nation raises problems requiring care and restraint. . . . By and large, public education in our Nation is committed to the control of state and local authorities." Epperson v. Arkansas, 393 U.S. 97, 104 (1968).

There are certain benchmarks to guide us, however. Mullane v. Central Hanover Trust Co., 339 U.S. 306 (1950), a case often invoked by later opinions, said that "[m]any controversies have raged about the cryptic and abstract words of the Due Process Clause but there can be no doubt that at a minimum they require that deprivation of life, liberty or property by adjudication be preceded by notice and opportunity for hearing appropriate to the nature of the case." Id., at 313. "The fundamental requisite of due process of law is the opportunity to be heard," Grannis v. Ordean, 234 U.S. 385, 394 (1914), a right that "has little reality or worth unless one is informed that the matter is pending and can choose for himself whether to . . . contest." Mullane v. Central Hanover Trust Co., supra, at 314. See also Armstrong v. Manzo, 380 U.S. 545, 550 (1965); Anti-Fascist Committee v. McGrath, 341 U.S. 123, 168-169 (1951) (Frankfurter, J., concurring). At the very minimum, therefore, students facing suspension and the consequent interference with a protected property interest must be given some kind of notice and afforded some kind of hearing. "Parties whose rights are to be affected are entitled to be heard; and in order that they may enjoy that right they must first be notified." Baldwin v. Hale, 1 Wall. 223, 233 (1864).

It also appears from our cases that the timing and content of the notice and the nature of the hearing will depend on appropriate accommodation of the competing interests involved. Cafeteria Workers v. McElroy, supra, at 895; Morrissey v. Brewer, supra, at 481. The student's interest is to avoid unfair or mistaken exclusion from the educational process, with all of its unfortunate consequences. The Due Process Clause will not shield him from suspensions properly imposed, but it disserves both his interest and the interest of the State if his suspension is in fact unwarranted. The concern would be mostly academic if the disciplinary process were a totally accurate, unerring process, never mistaken and never unfair. Unfortunately, that is not the case, and no one suggests that it is. Disciplinarians, although proceeding in utmost good faith, frequently act on the reports and advice of others; and the controlling facts and the nature of the conduct under challenge are often disputed. The risk of error is not at all trivial, and it should be guarded against if that may be done without prohibitive cost or interference with the educational process.

The difficulty is that our schools are vast and complex. Some modicum of discipline and order is essential if the educational function is to be performed. Events calling for discipline are frequent occurrences and sometimes require immediate, effective action. Suspension is considered not only to be a necessary tool to maintain order but a valuable educational device. The prospect of imposing elaborate hearing requirements in every suspension case is viewed with great concern, and many school authorities may well prefer the untrammeled power to act unilaterally, unhampered by rules about notice and hearing. But it would be a strange disciplinary system in an educational institution if no communication was sought by the disciplinarian with the student in an effort to inform him of his dereliction and to let him tell his side of the story in order to make sure that an injustice is not done. "[F]airness can rarely be obtained by secret, onesided determination of facts decisive of rights. . . ." "Secrecy is not congenial to truth-seeking and self-righteousness gives too slender an assurance of rightness. No better instrument has been devised for arriving at truth than to give a person in jeopardy of serious loss notice of the case against him and opportunity to meet it." Anti-Fascist Committee v. McGrath, supra, at 170, 171-172 (Frankfurter, J., concurring).

We do not believe that school authorities must be totally free from notice and hearing requirements if their schools are to operate with acceptable efficiency. Students facing temporary suspension have interests qualifying for protection of the Due Process Clause, and due process requires, in connection with a suspension of 10 days or less, that the student be given oral or written notice of the charges against him and, if he denies them, an explanation of the evidence the authorities have and an opportunity to present his side of the story. The Clause requires at least these rudimentary precautions against unfair or mistaken findings of misconduct and arbitrary exclusion from school.

There need be no delay between the time "notice" is given and the time of the hearing. In the great majority of cases the disciplinarian may informally discuss the alleged misconduct with the student minutes after it has occurred. We hold only that, in being given an opportunity to explain his version of the facts at this discussion, the student first be told what he is accused of doing and what the basis of the accusation is. Lower courts which have addressed the question of the nature of the procedures required in short suspension cases have reached the same conclusion. Tate v. Board of Education, 453 F.2d 975, 979 (CA8 1972); Vail v. Board of Education, 354 F. Supp. 592, 603 (NH 1973). Since the hearing may occur almost immediately following the misconduct, it follows that as a general rule notice and hearing should precede removal of the student from school. We agree with the District Court, however, that there are recurring situations in which prior notice and hearing cannot be insisted upon. Students whose presence poses a continuing danger to persons or property or an ongoing threat of disrupting the academic process may be immediately removed from school. In such cases, the necessary notice and rudimentary hearing should follow as soon as practicable, as the District Court indicated.

In holding as we do, we do not believe that we have imposed procedures on school disciplinarians which are inappropriate in a classroom setting. Instead we have imposed requirements which are, if anything, less than a fair-minded school principal would impose upon himself in order to avoid unfair suspensions. Indeed, according to the testimony of the principal of Marion-Franklin High School, that school had an informal procedure, remarkably similar to that which we now require, applicable to suspensions generally but which was not followed in this case. Similarly, according to the most recent memorandum applicable to the entire CPSS, see n. 1, supra, school principals in the CPSS are now required by local rule to provide at least as much as the constitutional minimum which we have described.

We stop short of construing the Due Process Clause to require, countrywide, that hearings in connection with short suspensions must afford the student the opportunity to secure counsel, to confront and cross-examine witnesses supporting the charge, or to call his own witnesses to verify his version of the incident. Brief disciplinary suspensions are almost countless. To impose in each such case even truncated trial-type procedures might well overwhelm administrative facilities in many places and, by diverting resources, cost more than it would save in educational effectiveness. Moreover, further formalizing the suspension process and escalating its formality and adversary nature may not only make it too costly as a regular disciplinary tool but also destroy its effectiveness as part of the teaching process.

On the other hand, requiring effective notice and informal hearing permitting the student to give his version of the events will provide a meaningful hedge against erroneous action. At least the disciplinarian will be alerted to the existence of disputes about facts and arguments about cause and effect. He may then determine himself to summon the accuser, permit cross-examination, and allow the student to present his own witnesses. In more difficult cases, he may permit counsel. In any event, his discretion will be more informed and we think the risk of error substantially reduced.

Requiring that there be at least an informal give-and-take between student and disciplinarian, preferably prior to the suspension, will add little to the factfinding function where the disciplinarian himself has witnessed the conduct forming the basis for the charge. But things are not always as they seem to be, and the student will at least have the opportunity to characterize his conduct and put it in what he deems the proper context.

We should also make it clear that we have addressed ourselves solely to the short suspension, not exceeding 10 days. Longer suspensions or expulsions for the remainder of the school term, or permanently, may require more formal procedures. Nor do we put aside the possibility that in unusual situations, although involving only a short suspension, something more than the rudimentary procedures will be required.

IV

The District Court found each of the suspensions involved here to have occurred without a hearing, either before or after the suspension, and that each suspension was therefore invalid and the statute unconstitutional insofar as it permits such suspensions without notice or hearing. Accordingly, the judgment is

Affirmed.

BROWN v. BOARD OF EDUCATION
U.S. Supreme Court, 347 U.S. 483 (1954)

MR. CHIEF JUSTICE WARREN delivered the opinion of the Court.

These cases come to us from the States of Kansas, South Carolina, Virginia, and Delaware. They are premised on different facts and different local conditions, but a common legal question justifies their consideration together in this consolidated opinion.

In each of the cases, minors of the Negro race, through their legal representatives, seek the aid of the courts in obtaining admission to the public schools of their community on a nonsegregated basis. In each instance, they had been denied admission to schools attended by white children under laws requiring or permitting segregation according to race. This segregation was alleged to deprive the plaintiffs of the equal protection of the laws under the Fourteenth Amendment. In each of he cases other than the Delaware case, a three-judge federal district court denied relief to the plaintiffs on so-called "separate but equal" doctrine announced by this Court in Plessy v. Ferguson, 163 U.S. 537. Under that doctrine, equality of treatment is accorded when the races are provided substantially equal facilities, even though these facilities be separate. In the Delaware case, the Supreme Court of Delaware adhered to that doctrine, but ordered that the plaintiffs be admitted to the white schools because of their superiority to the Negro schools.

The plaintiffs contend that segregated public schools are not "equal" and cannot be made "equal," and that hence they are deprived of the equal protection of the laws. Because of the obvious importance of the question presented, the Court took jurisdiction. Argument was heard in the 1952 Term, and reargument was heard this Term on certain questions propounded by the Court.

Reargument was largely devoted to the circumstances surrounding the adoption of the Fourteenth Amendment in 1868. It covered exhaustively consideration of the Amendment in Congress, ratification by the states, then existing practices in racial segregation, and the views of proponents and opponents of the Amendment. This discussion and our own investigation convince us that, although these sources cast some light, it is not enough to resolve the problem with which we are faced. At best, they are inconclusive. The most avid proponents of the post-War Amendments undoubtedly intended them to remove all legal distinctions among "all persons born or naturalized in the United States." Their opponents, just as certainly, were antagonistic to both the letter and the spirit of the Amendments and wished them to have the most limited effect. What others in Congress and the state legislatures had in mind cannot be determined with any degree of certainty.

An additional reason for the inconclusive nature of the Amendment's history, with respect to segregated schools, is the status of public education at that time. In the South, the movement toward free common schools, supported by general taxation, had not yet taken hold. Education of white children was largely in the hands of private groups. Education of Negroes was almost nonexistent, and practically all of the race were illiterate. In fact, any education of Negroes was forbidden by law in some states. Today, in contrast, many Negroes have achieved outstanding success in the arts and sciences as well as in the business and professional world. It is true that public school education at the time of the Amendment had advanced further in the North, but the effect of the Amendment on Northern States was generally ignored in the congressional debates. Even in the North, the conditions of public education did not approximate those existing today. The curriculum was usually rudimentary; ungraded schools were common in rural areas; the school term was but three months a year in many states; and compulsory school attendance was virtually unknown. As a consequence, it is not surprising that there should be so little in the history of the Fourteenth Amendment relating to its intended effect on public education.

In the first cases in this Court construing the Fourteenth Amendment, decided shortly after its adoption, the Court interpreted it as proscribing all state-imposed discriminations against the Negro race. The doctrine of "separate but equal" did not make its appearance in this Court until 1896 in the case of Plessy v. Ferguson, supra, involving not education but transportation. American courts have since labored with the doctrine for over half a century. In this Court, there have been six cases involving the "separate but equal" doctrine in the field of public education. In Cumming v. County Board of Education, 175 U.S. 528, and Gong Lum v. Rice, 275 U.S. 78, the validity of the doctrine itself was not challenged.8 In more recent cases, all on the graduate school level, inequality was found in that specific benefits enjoyed by white students were denied to Negro students of the same educational qualifications. Missouri ex rel. Gaines v. Canada, 305 U.S. 337; Sipuel v. Oklahoma, 332 U.S. 631; Sweatt v. Painter, 339 U.S. 629; McLaurin v. Oklahoma State Regents, 339 U.S. 637. In none of these cases was it necessary to re-examine the doctrine to grant relief to the Negro plaintiff. And in Sweatt v. Painter, supra, the Court expressly reserved decision on the question whether Plessy v. Ferguson should be held inapplicable to public education.

In the instant cases, that question is directly presented. Here, unlike Sweatt v. Painter, there are findings below that the Negro and white schools involved have been equalized, or are being equalized, with respect to buildings, curricula, qualifications and salaries of teachers, and other "tangible" factors. Our decision, therefore, cannot turn on merely a comparison of these tangible factors in the Negro and white schools involved in each of the cases. We must look instead to the effect of segregation itself on public education.

In approaching this problem, we cannot turn the clock back to 1868 when the Amendment was adopted, or even to 1896 when Plessy v. Ferguson was written. We must consider public education in the light of its full development and its present place in American life throughout the Nation. Only in this way can it be determined if segregation in public schools deprives these plaintiffs of the equal protection of the laws.

Today, education is perhaps the most important function of state and local governments. Compulsory school attendance laws and the great expenditures for education both demonstrate our recognition of the importance of education to our democratic society. It is required in the performance of our most basic public responsibilities, even service in the armed forces. It is the very foundation of good citizenship. Today it is a principal instrument in awakening the child to cultural values, in preparing him for later professional training, and in helping him to adjust normally to his environment. In these days, it is doubtful that any child may reasonably be expected to succeed in life if he is denied the opportunity of an education. Such an opportunity, where the state has undertaken to provide it, is a right which must be made available to all on equal terms.

We come then to the question presented: Does segregation of children in public schools solely on the basis of race, even though the physical facilities and other "tangible" factors may be equal, deprive the children of the minority group of equal educational opportunities? We believe that it does.

In Sweatt v. Painter, supra, in finding that a segregated law school for Negroes could not provide them equal educational opportunities, this Court relied in large part on "those qualities which are incapable of objective measurement but which make for greatness in a law school." In McLaurin v. Oklahoma State Regents, supra, the Court, in requiring that a Negro admitted to a white graduate school be treated like all other students, again resorted to intangible considerations: ". . . his ability to study, to engage in discussions and exchange views with other students, and, in general, to learn his profession." Such considerations apply with added force to children in grade and high schools. To separate them from others of similar age and qualifications solely because of their race generates a feeling of inferiority as to their status in the community that may affect their hearts and minds in a way unlikely ever to be undone. The effect of this separation on their educational opportunities was well stated by a finding in the Kansas case by a court which nevertheless felt compelled to rule against the Negro plaintiffs:

"Segregation of white and colored children in public schools has a detrimental effect upon the colored children. The impact is greater when it has the sanction of the law; for the policy of separating the races is usually interpreted as denoting the inferiority of the negro group. A sense of inferiority affects the motivation of a child to learn. Segregation with the sanction of law, therefore, has a tendency to [retard] the educational and mental development of negro children and to deprive them of some of the benefits they would receive in a racial[ly] integrated school system."

Whatever may have been the extent of psychological knowledge at the time of Plessy v. Ferguson, this finding is amply supported by modern authority.Any language in Plessy v. Ferguson contrary to this finding is rejected.

We conclude that in the field of public education the doctrine of "separate but equal" has no place. Separate educational facilities are inherently unequal. Therefore, we hold that the plaintiffs and others similarly situated for whom the actions have been brought are, by reason of the segregation complained of, deprived of the equal protection of the laws guaranteed by the Fourteenth Amendment. This disposition makes unnecessary any discussion whether such segregation also violates the Due Process Clause of the Fourteenth Amendment.

Because these are class actions, because of the wide applicability of this decision, and because of the great variety of local conditions, the formulation of decrees in these cases presents problems of considerable complexity. On reargument, the consideration of appropriate relief was necessarily subordinated to the primary question - the constitutionality of segregation in public education. We have now announced that such segregation is a denial of the equal protection of the laws. In order that we may have the full assistance of the parties in formulating decrees, the cases will be restored to the docket, and the parties are requested to present further argument on Questions 4 and 5 previously propounded by the Court for the reargument this Term.13 The Attorney General of the United States is again invited to participate. The Attorneys General of the states requiring or permitting segregation in public education will also be permitted to appear as amici curiae upon request to do so by September 15, 1954, and submission of briefs by October 1, 1954.

It is so ordered.

ROMER v. EVANS
U.S. Supreme Court, 1996

JUSTICE KENNEDY delivered the opinion of the Court.

One century ago, the first Justice Harlan admonished this Court that the Constitution "neither knows nor tolerates classes among citizens." Plessy v. Ferguson, 163 U.S. 537, 559 (1896) (dissenting opinion). Unheeded then, those words now are understood to state a commitment to the law's neutrality where the rights of persons are at stake. The Equal Protection Clause enforces this principle and today requires us to hold invalid a provision of Colorado's Constitution.

I

The enactment challenged in this case is an amendment to the Constitution of the State of Colorado, adopted in a 1992 statewide referendum. The parties and the state courts refer to it as "Amendment 2," its designation when submitted to the voters. The impetus for the amendment and the contentious campaign that preceded its adoption came in large part from ordinances that had been passed in various Colorado municipalities. For example, the cities of Aspen and Boulder and the City and County of Denver each had enacted ordinances which banned discrimination in many transactions and activities, including housing, employment, education, public accommodations, and health and welfare services. What gave rise to the statewide controversy was the protection the ordinances afforded to persons discriminated against by reason of their sexual orientation. Amendment 2 repeals these ordinances to the extent they prohibit discrimination on the basis of "homosexual, lesbian or bisexual orientation, conduct, practices or relationships."

Yet Amendment 2, in explicit terms, does more than repeal or rescind these provisions. It prohibits all legislative, executive or judicial action at any level of state or local government designed to protect the named class, a class we shall refer to as homosexual persons or gays and lesbians. The amendment reads:

"No Protected Status Based on Homosexual, Lesbian, or Bisexual Orientation. Neither the State of Colorado, through any of its branches or departments, nor any of its agencies, political subdivisions, municipalities or school districts, shall enact, adopt or enforce any statute, regulation, ordinance or policy whereby homosexual, lesbian or bisexual orientation, conduct, practices or relationships shall constitute or otherwise be the basis of or entitle any person or class of persons to have or claim any minority status, quota preferences, protected status or claim of discrimination. This Section of the Constitution shall be in all respects self-executing."

II

The State's principal argument in defense of Amendment 2 is that it puts gays and lesbians in the same position as all other persons. So, the State says, the measure does no more than deny homosexuals special rights. This reading of the amendment's language is implausible. [Rather,] the ultimate effect of Amendment 2 is [that] homosexuals, by state decree, are put in a solitary class with respect to transactions and relations in both the private and governmental spheres. The amendment withdraws from homosexuals, but no others, specific legal protection from the injuries caused by discrimination, and it forbids reinstatement of these laws and policies.

[The Private Sphere:]

The change that Amendment 2 works in the legal status of gays and lesbians in the private sphere is far-reaching, both on its own terms and when considered in light of the structure and operation of modern anti-discrimination laws. That structure is well illustrated by contemporary statutes and ordinances prohibiting discrimination by providers of public accommodations. At common law, innkeepers, smiths, and others who made profession of a public employment, were prohibited from refusing, without good reason, to serve a customer. The duty was a general one and did not specify protection for particular groups. The common law rules, however, proved insufficient in many instances, and it was settled early that the Fourteenth Amendment did not give Congress a general power to prohibit discrimination in public accommodations, Civil Rights Cases, 109 U.S. 3, 25 (1883). In consequence, most States have chosen to counter discrimination by enacting detailed statutory schemes.

Colorado's state and municipal laws typify this emerging tradition of statutory protection and follow a consistent pattern. The laws first enumerate the persons or entities subject to a duty not to discriminate. The list goes well beyond the entities covered by the common law. The Boulder ordinance, for example, has a comprehensive definition of entities deemed places of "public accommodation." They include "any place of business engaged in any sales to the general public and any place that offers services, facilities, privileges, or advantages to the general public or that receives financial support through solicitation of the general public or through governmental subsidy of any kind." Boulder Rev. Code 12-1-1(j) (1987). The Denver ordinance is of similar breadth, applying, for example, to hotels, restaurants, hospitals, dental clinics, theaters, banks, common carriers, travel and insurance agencies, and "shops and stores dealing with goods or services of any kind," Denver Rev. Municipal Code, Art. IV, 28-92.

These statutes and ordinances also depart from the common law by enumerating the groups or persons within their ambit of protection. Enumeration is the essential device used to make the duty not to discriminate concrete and to provide guidance for those who must comply.

Amendment 2 bars homosexuals from securing protection against the injuries that these public-accommodations laws address. That in itself is a severe consequence, but there is more. Amendment 2, in addition, nullifies specific legal protections for this targeted class in all transactions in housing, sale of real estate, insurance, health and welfare services, private education, and employment.

[The Public Sphere:]

Not confined to the private sphere, Amendment 2 also operates to repeal and forbid all laws or policies providing specific protection for gays or lesbians from discrimination by every level of Colorado government. The State Supreme Court cited two examples of protections in the governmental sphere that are now rescinded and may not be reintroduced. The first is Colorado Executive Order D0035 (1990), which forbids employment discrimination against "`all state employees, classified and exempt' on the basis of sexual orientation." 854 P.2d, at 1284. Also repealed, and now forbidden, are "various provisions prohibiting discrimination based on sexual orientation at state colleges." Id., at 1284, 1285. The repeal of these measures and the prohibition against their future reenactment demonstrates that Amendment 2 has the same force and effect in Colorado's governmental sector as it does elsewhere and that it applies to policies as well as ordinary legislation.

Amendment 2's reach may not be limited to specific laws passed for the benefit of gays and lesbians. It is a fair, if not necessary, inference from the broad language of the amendment that it deprives gays and lesbians even of the protection of general laws and policies that prohibit arbitrary discrimination in governmental and private settings.

Even if, as we doubt, homosexuals could find some safe harbor in laws of general application, we cannot accept the view that Amendment 2's prohibition on specific legal protections does no more than deprive homosexuals of special rights. To the contrary, the amendment imposes a special disability upon those persons alone. Homosexuals are forbidden the safeguards that others enjoy or may seek without constraint. . . . This is so no matter how local or discrete the harm, no matter how public and widespread the injury. We find nothing special in the protections Amendment 2 withholds. These are protections taken for granted by most people either because they already have them or do not need them; these are protections against exclusion from an almost limitless number of transactions and endeavors that constitute ordinary civic life in a free society.

III

Even in the ordinary equal protection case calling for the most deferential of standards, we insist on knowing the relation between the classification adopted and the object to be attained.

The search for the link between classification and objective gives substance to the Equal Protection Clause; it provides guidance and discipline for the legislature, which is entitled to know what sorts of laws it can pass; and it marks the limits of our own authority. In the ordinary case, a law will be sustained if it can be said to advance a legitimate government interest, even if the law seems unwise or works to the disadvantage of a particular group, or if the rationale for it seems tenuous. By requiring that the classification bear a rational relationship to an independent and legitimate legislative end, we ensure that classifications are not drawn for the purpose of disadvantaging the group burdened by the law.

Amendment 2 confounds this normal process of judicial review. It is at once too narrow and too broad. It identifies persons by a single trait and then denies them protection across the board. The resulting disqualification of a class of persons from the right to seek specific protection from the law is unprecedented in our jurisprudence. The absence of precedent for Amendment 2 is itself instructive; "[d]iscriminations of an unusual character especially suggest careful consideration to determine whether they are obnoxious to the constitutional provision." Louisville Gas & Elec. Co. v. Coleman, 277 U.S. 32, 37-38 (1928).

It is not within our constitutional tradition to enact laws of this sort. Central both to the idea of the rule of law and to our own Constitution's guarantee of equal protection is the principle that government and each of its parts remain open on impartial terms to all who seek its assistance. "`Equal protection of the laws is not achieved through indiscriminate imposition of inequalities.'" Sweatt v. Painter, 339 U.S. 629, 635 (1950) (quoting Shelley v. Kraemer, 334 U.S. 1, 22 (1948)). Respect for this principle explains why laws singling out a certain class of citizens for disfavored legal status or general hardships are rare. A law declaring that in general it shall be more difficult for one group of citizens than for all others to seek aid from the government is itself a denial of equal protection of the laws in the most literal sense. "The guaranty of `equal protection of the laws is a pledge of the protection of equal laws.'" Skinner v. Oklahoma ex rel. Williamson, 316 U.S. 535, 541 (1942) (quoting Yick Wo v. Hopkins, 118 U.S. 356, 369 (1886)).

A second and related point is that laws of the kind now before us raise the inevitable inference that the imposed is born of animosity toward the class of persons affected. "[I]f the constitutional conception of `equal protection of the laws' means anything, it must at the very least mean that a bare . . . desire to harm a politically unpopular group constitute a legitimate governmental interest." Department of Agriculture v. Moreno, 413 U.S. 528, 534 (1973). Even laws enacted for broad and ambitious purposes often can be explained by reference to legitimate public policies which justify the incidental disadvantages they impose on certain persons. Amendment 2, however, in making a general announcement that gays and lesbians shall not have any particular protections from the law, inflicts on them immediate, continuing, and real injuries that outrun and belie any legitimate justifications that may be claimed for it. We conclude that, in addition to the far-reaching deficiencies of Amendment 2 that we have noted, the principles it offends, in another sense, are conventional and venerable; a law must bear a rational relationship to a legitimate governmental purpose, Kadrmas v. Dickinson Public Schools, 487 U.S. 450, 462 (1988), and Amendment 2 does not.

The primary rationale the State offers for Amendment 2 is respect for other citizens' freedom of association, and in particular the liberties of landlords or employers who have personal or religious objections to homosexuality. Colorado also cites its interest in conserving resources to fight discrimination against other groups. The breadth of the Amendment is so far removed from these particular justifications that we find it impossible to credit them. We cannot say that Amendment 2 is directed to any identifiable legitimate purpose or discrete objective. It is a status-based enactment divorced from any factual context from which we could discern a relationship to legitimate state interests; it is a classification of persons undertaken for its own sake, something the Equal Protection Clause does not permit. "[C]lass legislation . . . [is] obnoxious to the prohibitions of the Fourteenth Amendment . . . ." Civil Rights Cases, 109 U.S., at 24.

We must conclude that Amendment 2 classifies homosexuals not to further a proper legislative end but to make them unequal to everyone else. This Colorado cannot do. A State cannot so deem a class of persons a stranger to its laws. Amendment 2 violates the Equal Protection Clause, and the judgment of the Supreme Court of Colorado is affirmed.

LAU v. NICHOLS
U.S. Supreme Court, 414 U.S. 563 (1974)

MR. JUSTICE DOUGLAS delivered the opinion of the Court.

The San Francisco, California, school system was integrated in 1971 as a result of a federal court decree, 339 F. Supp. 1315. See Lee v. Johnson, 404 U.S. 1215. The District Court found that there are 2,856 students of Chinese ancestry in the school system who do not speak English. Of those who have that language deficiency, about 1,000 are given supplemental courses in the English language. About 1,800, however, do not receive that instruction.

This class suit brought by non-English-speaking Chinese students against officials responsible for the operation of the San Francisco Unified School District seeks relief against the unequal educational opportunities, which are alleged to violate, inter alia, the Fourteenth Amendment. No specific remedy is urged upon us. Teaching English to the students of Chinese ancestry who do not speak the language is one choice. Giving instructions to this group in Chinese is another. There may be others. Petitioners ask only that the Board of Education be directed to apply its expertise to the problem and rectify the situation.

The District Court denied relief. The Court of Appeals affirmed, holding that there was no violation of the Equal Protection Clause of the Fourteenth Amendment or of 601 of the Civil Rights Act of 1964, 78 Stat. 252, 42 U.S.C. 2000d, which excludes from participation in federal financial assistance, recipients of aid which discriminate against racial groups, 483 F.2d 791. One judge dissented. A hearing en banc was denied, two judges dissenting. Id., at 805.

We granted the petition for certiorari because of the public importance of the question presented, 412 U.S. 938.

The Court of Appeals reasoned that "[e]very student brings to the starting line of his educational career different advantages and disadvantages caused in part by social, economic and cultural background, created and continued completely apart from any contribution by the school system," 483 F.2d, at 797. Yet in our view the case may not be so easily decided. This is a public school system of California and 71 of the California Education Code states that "English shall be the basic language of instruction in all schools." That section permits a school district to determine "when and under what circumstances instruction may be given bilingually." That section also states as "the policy of the state" to insure "the mastery of English by all pupils in the schools." And bilingual instruction is authorized "to the extent that it does not interfere with the systematic, sequential, and regular instruction of all pupils in the English language."

Moreover, 8573 of the Education Code provides that no pupil shall receive a diploma of graduation from grade 12 who has not met the standards of proficiency in "English," as well as other prescribed subjects. Moreover, by 12101 of the Education Code (Supp. 1973) children between the ages of six and 16 years are (with exceptions not material here) "subject to compulsory full-time education."

Under these state-imposed standards there is no equality of treatment merely by providing students with the same facilities, textbooks, teachers, and curriculum; for students who do not understand English are effectively foreclosed from any meaningful education.

Basic English skills are at the very core of what these public schools teach. Imposition of a requirement that, before a child can effectively participate in the educational program, he must already have acquired those basic skills is to make a mockery of public education. We know that those who do not understand English are certain to find their classroom experiences wholly incomprehensible and in no way meaningful.

We do not reach the Equal Protection Clause argument which has been advanced but rely solely on 601 of the Civil Rights Act of 1964, 42 U.S.C. 2000d, to reverse the Court of Appeals. That section bans discrimination based "on the ground of race, color, or national origin," in "any program or activity receiving Federal financial assistance." The school district involved in this litigation receives large amounts of federal financial assistance. The Department of Health, Education, and Welfare (HEW), which has authority to promulgate regulations prohibiting discrimination in federally assisted school systems, 42 U.S.C. 2000d-1, in 1968 issued one guideline that "[s]chool systems are responsible for assuring that students of a particular race, color, or national origin are not denied the opportunity to obtain the education generally obtained by other students in the system." 33 Fed. Reg. 4956. In 1970 HEW made the guidelines more specific, requiring school districts that were federally funded "to rectify the language deficiency in order to open" the instruction to students who had "linguistic deficiencies," 35 Fed. Reg. 11595.

By 602 of the Act HEW is authorized to issue rules, regulations, and orders to make sure that recipients of federal aid under its jurisdiction conduct any federally financed projects consistently with 601. HEW's regulations, 45 CFR 80.3 (b) (1), specify that the recipients may not

"(ii) Provide any service, financial aid, or other benefit to an individual which is different, or is provided in a different manner, from that provided to others under the program; . . . . .

"(iv) Restrict an individual in any way in the enjoyment of any advantage or privilege enjoyed by others receiving any service, financial aid, or other benefit under the program."

Discrimination among students on account of race or national origin that is prohibited includes "discrimination . . . in the availability or use of any academic . . . or other facilities of the grantee or other recipient." Id., 80.5 (b).

Discrimination is barred which has that effect even though no purposeful design is present: a recipient "may not . . . utilize criteria or methods of administration which have the effect of subjecting individuals to discrimination" or have "the effect of defeating or substantially impairing accomplishment of the objectives of the program as respect individuals of a particular race, color, or national origin." Id., 80.3 (b) (2).

It seems obvious that the Chinese-speaking minority receive fewer benefits than the English-speaking majority from respondents' school system which denies them a meaningful opportunity to participate in the educational program - all earmarks of the discrimination banned by the regulations. In 1970 HEW issued clarifying guidelines, 35 Fed. Reg. 11595, which include the following:

"Where inability to speak and understand the English language excludes national origin-minority group children from effective participation in the educational program offered by a school district, the district must take affirmative steps to rectify the language deficiency in order to open its instructional program to these students."

"Any ability grouping or tracking system employed by the school system to deal with the special language skill needs of national origin-minority group children must be designed to meet such language skill needs as soon as possible and must not operate as an educational deadend or permanent track."

Respondent school district contractually agreed to "comply with title VI of the Civil Rights Act of 1964 . . . and all requirements imposed by or pursuant to the Regulation" of HEW (45 CFR pt. 80) which are "issued pursuant to that title . . ." and also immediately to "take any measures necessary to effectuate this agreement." The Federal Government has power to fix the terms on which its money allotments to the States shall be disbursed. Oklahoma v. CSC, 330 U.S. 127, 142-143. Whatever may be the limits of that power, Steward Machine Co. v. Davis, 301 U.S. 548, 590 et seq., they have not been reached here. Senator Humphrey, during the floor debates on the Civil Rights Act of 1964, said:

"Simple justice requires that public funds, to which all taxpayers of all races contribute, not be spent in any fashion which encourages, entrenches, subsidizes, or results in racial discrimination."

We accordingly reverse the judgment of the Court of Appeals and remand the case for the fashioning of appropriate relief.

Reversed and remanded.

TINKER v. DES MOINES SCHOOL DIST.
U.S. Supreme Court, 393 U.S. 503 (1969)

MR. JUSTICE FORTAS delivered the opinion of the Court.

Petitioner John F. Tinker, 15 years old, and petitioner Christopher Eckhardt, 16 years old, attended high schools in Des Moines, Iowa. Petitioner Mary Beth Tinker, John's sister, was a 13-year-old student in junior high school.

In December 1965, a group of adults and students in Des Moines held a meeting at the Eckhardt home. The group determined to publicize their objections to the hostilities in Vietnam and their support for a truce by wearing black armbands during the holiday season and by fasting on December 16 and New Year's Eve. Petitioners and their parents had previously engaged in similar activities, and they decided to participate in the program.

The principals of the Des Moines schools became aware of the plan to wear armbands. On December 14, 1965, they met and adopted a policy that any student wearing an armband to school would be asked to remove it, and if he refused he would be suspended until he returned without the armband. Petitioners were aware of the regulation that the school authorities adopted.

On December 16, Mary Beth and Christopher wore black armbands to their schools. John Tinker wore his armband the next day. They were all sent home and suspended from school until they would come back without their armbands. They did not return to school until after the planned period for wearing armbands had expired - that is, until after New Year's Day.

* * *

I

The District Court recognized that the wearing of an armband for the purpose of expressing certain views is the type of symbolic act that is within the Free Speech Clause of the First Amendment. See West Virginia v. Barnette, 319 U.S. 624 (1943); Stromberg v. California, 283 U.S. 359 (1931). Cf. Thornhill v. Alabama, 310 U.S. 88 (1940); Edwards v. South Carolina, 372 U.S.

229 (1963); Brown v. Louisiana, 383 U.S. 131 (1966). As we shall discuss, the wearing of armbands in the circumstances of this case was entirely divorced from actually or potentially disruptive conduct by those participating in it. It was closely akin to "pure speech" which, we have repeatedly held, is entitled to comprehensive protection under the First Amendment. Cf. Cox v. Louisiana, 379 U.S. 536, 555 (1965); Adderley v. Florida, 385 U.S. 39 (1966).

First Amendment rights, applied in light of the special characteristics of the school environment, are available to teachers and students. It can hardly be argued that either students or teachers shed their constitutional rights to freedom of speech or expression at the schoolhouse gate. This has been the unmistakable holding of this Court for almost 50 years. In Meyer v. Nebraska, 262 U.S. 390 (1923), and Bartels v. Iowa, 262 U.S. 404 (1923), this Court, in opinions by Mr. Justice McReynolds, held that the Due Process Clause of the Fourteenth Amendment prevents States from forbidding the teaching of a foreign language to young students. Statutes to this effect, the Court held, unconstitutionally interfere with the liberty of teacher, student, and parent.2 See also Pierce v. Society of Sisters, 268 U.S. 510 (1925); West Virginia v. Barnette, 319 U.S. 624 (1943); McCollum v. Board of Education, 333 U.S. 203 (1948); Wieman v. Updegraff, 344 U.S. 183, 195 (1952) (concurring opinion); Sweezy v. New Hampshire, 354 U.S. 234 (1957); Shelton v. Tucker, 364 U.S. 479, 487 (1960); Engel v. Vitale, 370 U.S. 421 (1962); Keyishian v. Board of Regents, 385 U.S. 589, 603 (1967); Epperson v. Arkansas, ante, p. 97 (1968).

In West Virginia v. Barnette, supra, this Court held that under the First Amendment, the student in public school may not be compelled to salute the flag. Speaking through Mr. Justice Jackson, the Court said:

"The Fourteenth Amendment, as now applied to the States, protects the citizen against the State itself and all of its creatures - Boards of Education not excepted. These have, of course, important, delicate, and highly discretionary functions, but none that they may not perform within the limits of the Bill of Rights. That they are educating the young for citizenship is reason for scrupulous protection of Constitutional freedoms of the individual, if we are not to strangle the free mind at its source and teach youth to discount important principles of our government as mere platitudes." 319 U.S., at 637.

On the other hand, the Court has repeatedly emphasized the need for affirming the comprehensive authority of the States and of school officials, consistent with fundamental constitutional safeguards, to prescribe and control conduct in the schools. See Epperson v. Arkansas, supra, at 104; Meyer v. Nebraska, supra, at 402. Our problem lies in the area where students in the exercise of First Amendment rights collide with the rules of the school authorities.

II

The problem posed by the present case does not relate to regulation of the length of skirts or the type of clothing, to hair style, or deportment. Cf. Ferrell v. Dallas Independent School District, 392 F.2d 697 (1968); Pugsley v. Sellmeyer, 158 Ark. 247, 250 S. W. 538 (1923). It does not concern aggressive, disruptive action or even group demonstrations. Our problem involves direct, primary First Amendment rights akin to "pure speech."

The school officials banned and sought to punish petitioners for a silent, passive expression of opinion, unaccompanied by any disorder or disturbance on the part of petitioners. There is here no evidence whatever of petitioners' interference, actual or nascent, with the schools' work or of collision with the rights of other students to be secure and to be let alone. Accordingly, this case does not concern speech or action that intrudes upon the work of the schools or the rights of other students.

Only a few of the 18,000 students in the school system wore the black armbands. Only five students were suspended for wearing them. There is no indication that the work of the schools or any class was disrupted. Outside the classrooms, a few students made hostile remarks to the children wearing armbands, but there were no threats or acts of violence on school premises.

The District Court concluded that the action of the school authorities was reasonable because it was based upon their fear of a disturbance from the wearing of the armbands. But, in our system, undifferentiated fear or apprehension of disturbance is not enough to overcome the right to freedom of expression. Any departure from absolute regimentation may cause trouble. Any variation from the majority's opinion may inspire fear. Any word spoken, in class, in the lunchroom, or on the campus, that deviates from the views of another person may start an argument or cause a disturbance. But our Constitution says we must take this risk, Terminiello v. Chicago, 337 U.S. 1 (1949); and our history says that it is this sort of hazardous freedom – this kind of openness - that is the basis of our national strength and of the independence and vigor of Americans who grow up and live in this relatively permissive, often disputatious, society.

In order for the State in the person of school officials to justify prohibition of a particular expression of opinion, it must be able to show that its action was caused by something more than a mere desire to avoid the discomfort and unpleasantness that always accompany an unpopular viewpoint. Certainly where there is no finding and no showing that engaging in the forbidden conduct would "materially and substantially interfere with the requirements of appropriate discipline in the operation of the school," the prohibition cannot be sustained. Burnside v. Byars, supra, at 749.

In the present case, the District Court made no such finding, and our independent examination of the record fails to yield evidence that the school authorities had reason to anticipate that the wearing of the armbands would substantially interfere with the work of the school or impinge upon the rights of other students. Even an official memorandum prepared after the suspension that listed the reasons for the ban on wearing the armbands made no reference to the anticipation of such disruption.

On the contrary, the action of the school authorities appears to have been based upon an urgent wish to avoid the controversy which might result from the expression, even by the silent symbol of armbands, of opposition to this Nation's part in the conflagration in Vietnam. It is revealing, in this respect, that the meeting at which the school principals decided to issue the contested regulation was called in response to a student's statement to the journalism teacher in one of the schools that he wanted to write an article on Vietnam and have it published in the school paper. (The student was dissuaded.)

It is also relevant that the school authorities did not purport to prohibit the wearing of all symbols of political or controversial significance. The record shows that students in some of the schools wore buttons relating to national political campaigns, and some even wore the Iron Cross, traditionally a symbol of Nazism. The order prohibiting the wearing of armbands did not extend to these. Instead, a particular symbol - black armbands worn to exhibit opposition to this Nation's involvement in Vietnam - was singled out for prohibition. Clearly, the prohibition of expression of one particular opinion, at least without evidence that it is necessary to avoid material and substantial interference with schoolwork or discipline, is not constitutionally permissible.

In our system, state-operated schools may not be enclaves of totalitarianism. School officials do not possess absolute authority over their students. Students in school as well as out of school are "persons" under our Constitution. They are possessed of fundamental rights which the State must respect, just as they themselves must respect their obligations to the State. In our system, students may not be regarded as closed-circuit recipients of only that which the State chooses to communicate. They may not be confined to the expression of those sentiments that are officially approved. In the absence of a specific showing of constitutionally valid reasons to regulate their speech, students are entitled to freedom of expression of their views. As Judge Gewin, speaking for the Fifth Circuit, said, school officials cannot suppress "expressions of feelings with which they do not wish to contend." Burnside v. Byars, supra, at 749.

In Meyer v. Nebraska, supra, at 402, Mr. Justice McReynolds expressed this Nation's repudiation of the principle that a State might so conduct its schools as to "foster a homogeneous people." He said:

"In order to submerge the individual and develop ideal citizens, Sparta assembled the males at seven into barracks and intrusted their subsequent education and training to official guardians. Although such measures have been deliberately approved by men of great genius, their ideas touching the relation between individual and State were wholly different from those upon which our institutions rest; and it hardly will be affirmed that any legislature could impose such restrictions upon the people of a State without doing violence to both letter and spirit of the Constitution."

This principle has been repeated by this Court on numerous occasions during the intervening years. In Keyishian v. Board of Regents, 385 U.S. 589, 603, MR. JUSTICE BRENNAN, speaking for the Court, said:

"'The vigilant protection of constitutional freedoms is nowhere more vital than in the community of American schools.' Shelton v. Tucker, at 487. The classroom is peculiarly the `marketplace of ideas.' The Nation's future depends upon leaders trained through wide exposure to that robust exchange of ideas which discovers truth `out of a multitude of tongues, [rather] than through any kind of authoritative selection.'"

The principle of these cases is not confined to the supervised and ordained discussion which takes place in the classroom. The principal use to which the schools are dedicated is to accommodate students during prescribed hours for the purpose of certain types of activities. Among those activities is personal intercommunication among the students.6 This is not only an inevitable part of the process of attending school; it is also an important part of the educational process. A student's rights, therefore, do not embrace merely the classroom hours. When he is in the cafeteria, or on the playing field, or on the campus during the authorized hours, he may express his opinions, even on controversial subjects like the conflict in Vietnam, if he does so without "materially and substantially interfer[ing] with the requirements of appropriate discipline in the operation of the school" and without colliding with the rights of others. Burnside v. Byars, supra, at 749. But conduct by the student, in class or out of it, which for any reason - whether it stems from time, place, or type of behavior - materially disrupts classwork or involves substantial disorder or invasion of the rights of others is, of course, not immunized by the constitutional guarantee of freedom of speech. Cf. Blackwell v. Issaquena County Board of Education, 363 F.2d 749 (C. A. 5th Cir. 1966).

Under our Constitution, free speech is not a right that is given only to be so circumscribed that it exists in principle but not in fact. Freedom of expression would not truly exist if the right could be exercised only in an area that a benevolent government has provided as a safe haven for crackpots. The Constitution says that Congress (and the States) may not abridge the right to free speech. This provision means what it says. We properly read it to permit reasonable regulation of speech-connected activities in carefully restricted circumstances. But we do not confine the permissible exercise of First Amendment rights to a telephone booth or the four corners of a pamphlet, or to supervised and ordained discussion in a school classroom.

If a regulation were adopted by school officials forbidding discussion of the Vietnam conflict, or the expression by any student of opposition to it anywhere on school property except as part of a prescribed classroom exercise, it would be obvious that the regulation would violate the constitutional rights of students, at least if it could not be justified by a showing that the students' activities would materially and substantially disrupt the work and discipline of the school. Cf. Hammond v. South Carolina State College, 272 F. Supp. 947 (D.C. S. C. 1967) (orderly protest meeting on state college campus); Dickey v. Alabama State Board of Education, 273 F. Supp. 613 (D.C. M. D. Ala. 1967) (expulsion of student editor of college newspaper). In the circumstances of the present case, the prohibition of the silent, passive "witness of the armbands," as one of the children called it, is no less offensive to the Constitution's guarantees.

As we have discussed, the record does not demonstrate any facts which might reasonably have led school authorities to forecast substantial disruption of or material interference with school activities, and no disturbances or disorders on the school premises in fact occurred. These petitioners merely went about their ordained rounds in school. Their deviation consisted only in wearing on their sleeve a band of black cloth, not more than two inches wide. They wore it to exhibit their disapproval of the Vietnam hostilities and their advocacy of a truce, to make their views known, and, by their example, to influence others to adopt them. They neither interrupted school activities nor sought to intrude in the school affairs or the lives of others. They caused discussion outside of the classrooms, but no interference with work and no disorder. In the circumstances, our Constitution does not permit officials of the State to deny their form of expression.

We express no opinion as to the form of relief which should be granted, this being a matter for the lower courts to determine. We reverse and remand for further proceedings consistent with this opinion.

Reversed and remanded.

SAN ANTONIO SCHOOL DISTRICT v. RODRIGUEZ
U.S. Supreme Court, 411 U.S. 1 (1973)

MR. JUSTICE POWELL delivered the opinion of the Court.

This suit attacking the Texas system of financing public education was initiated by Mexican-American parents whose children attend the elementary and secondary schools in the Edgewood Independent School District, an urban school district in San Antonio, Texas. They brought a class action on behalf of schoolchildren throughout the State who are members of minority groups or who are poor and reside in school districts having a low property tax base.

* * *

Until recent times, Texas was a predominantly rural State and its population and property wealth were spread relatively evenly across the State. Sizable differences in the value of assessable property between local school districts became increasingly evident as the State became more industrialized and as rural-to-urban population shifts became more pronounced.

* * *

Recognizing the need for increased state funding to help offset disparities in local spending and to meet Texas' changing educational requirements, the state legislature * * * [developed a funding program calling] for state and local contributions to a fund earmarked specifically for teacher salaries, operating expenses, and transportation costs. The State, supplying funds from its general revenues, finances approximately 80% of the Program, and the school districts are responsible - as a unit - for providing the remaining 20%.

* * *

The design of this . . . system was twofold. First, it was an attempt to assure that the . . . Program would have an equalizing influence on expenditure levels between school districts by placing the heaviest burden on the school districts most capable of paying. Second, the Program's architects sought to establish a Local Fund Assignment that would force every school district to contribute to the education of its children24 but that would not by itself exhaust any district's resources.

* * *

Today every school district does impose a property tax from which it derives locally expendable funds in excess of the amount necessary to satisfy its Local Fund Assignment under the Foundation Program.

The school district in which appellees reside, the Edgewood Independent School District, has been compared throughout this litigation with the Alamo Heights Independent School District. This comparison between the least and most affluent districts in the San Antonio area serves to illustrate the manner in which the dual system of finance operates and to indicate the extent to which substantial disparities exist despite the State's impressive progress in recent years. Edgewood is one of seven public school districts in the metropolitan area. Approximately 22,000 students are enrolled in its 25 elementary and secondary schools. The district is situated in the core-city sector of San Antonio in a residential neighborhood that has little commercial or industrial property. The residents are predominantly of Mexican-American descent: approximately 90% of the student population is Mexican-American and over 6% is Negro. The average assessed property value per pupil is $5,960 – the lowest in the metropolitan area - and the median family income ($4,686) is also the lowest.30 At an equalized tax rate of $1.05 per $100 of assessed property - the highest in the metropolitan area - the district contributed $26 to the education of each child for the 1967-1968 school year above its Local Fund Assignment for the Minimum Foundation Program. The Foundation Program contributed $222 per pupil for a state-local total of $248.31 Federal funds added another $108 for a total of $356 per pupil.

Alamo Heights is the most affluent school district in San Antonio. Its six schools, housing approximately 5,000 students, are situated in a residential community quite unlike the Edgewood District. The school population is predominantly "Anglo," having only 18% Mexican-Americans and less than 1% Negroes. The assessed property value per pupil exceeds $49,000,33 and the median family income is $8,001. In 1967-1968 the local tax rate of $.85 per $100 of valuation yielded $333 per pupil over and above its contribution to the Foundation Program. Coupled with the $225 provided from that Program, the district was able to supply $558 per student. Supplemented by a $36 per-pupil grant from federal sources, Alamo Heights spent $594 per pupil.

* * *

[S]ubstantial interdistrict disparities in school expenditures found by the District Court to prevail in San Antonio and in varying degrees throughout the State still exist. And it was [411 U.S. 1, 16] these disparities, largely attributable to differences in the amounts of money collected through local property taxation, that led the District Court to conclude that Texas' dual system of public school financing violated the Equal Protection Clause. The District Court held that the Texas system discriminates on the basis of wealth in the manner in which education is provided for its people. 337 F. Supp., at 282. Finding that wealth is a "suspect" classification and that education is a "fundamental" interest, the District Court held that the Texas system could be sustained only if the State could show that it was premised upon some compelling state interest. Id., at 282-284. On this issue the court concluded that "[n]ot only are defendants unable to demonstrate compelling state interests . . . they fail even to establish a reasonable basis for these classifications." Id., at 284.

Texas virtually concedes that its historically rooted dual system of financing education could not withstand the strict judicial scrutiny that this Court has found appropriate in reviewing legislative judgments that interfere with fundamental constitutional rights or that involve suspect classifications. If, as previous decisions have indicated, strict scrutiny means that the State's system is not entitled to the usual presumption of validity, that the State rather than the complainants must carry a "heavy burden of justification," that the State must demonstrate that its educational system has been structured with "precision," and is "tailored" narrowly to serve legitimate objectives and that it has selected the "less drastic means" for effectuating its objectives, the Texas financing system and its counterpart in virtually every other State will not pass muster. The State candidly admits that "[n]o one familiar with the Texas system would contend that it has yet achieved perfection."42 Apart from its concession that educational financing in Texas has "defects"43 and "imperfections,"44 the State defends the system's rationality with vigor and disputes the District Court's finding that it lacks a "reasonable basis."

This, then, establishes the framework for our analysis. We must decide, first, whether the Texas system of financing public education operates to the disadvantage of some suspect class or impinges upon a fundamental right explicitly or implicitly protected by the Constitution, thereby requiring strict judicial scrutiny. If so, the judgment of the District Court should be affirmed. If not, the Texas scheme must still be examined to determine whether it rationally furthers some legitimate, articulated state purpose and therefore does not constitute an invidious discrimination in violation of the Equal Protection Clause of the Fourteenth Amendment.

* * *

The wealth discrimination discovered by the District Court in this case, and by several other courts that have recently struck down school-financing laws in other States, is quite unlike any of the forms of wealth discrimination heretofore reviewed by this Court. Rather than focusing on the unique features of the alleged discrimination, the courts in these cases have virtually assumed their findings of a suspect classification through a simplistic process of analysis: since, under the traditional systems of financing public schools, some poorer people receive less expensive educations than other more affluent people, these systems discriminate on the basis of wealth. This approach largely ignores the hard threshold questions, including whether it makes a difference for purposes of consideration under the Constitution that the class of disadvantaged "poor" cannot be identified or defined in customary equal protection terms, and whether the relative - rather than absolute - nature of the asserted deprivation is of significant consequence. Before a State's laws and the justifications for the classifications they create are subjected to strict judicial scrutiny, we think these threshold considerations must be analyzed more closely than they were in the court below.

The case comes to us with no definitive description of the classifying facts or delineation of the disfavored class. Examination of the District Court's opinion and of appellees' complaint, briefs, and contentions at oral argument suggests, however, at least three ways in which the discrimination claimed here might be described. The Texas system of school financing might be regarded as discriminating (1) against "poor" persons whose incomes fall below some identifiable level of poverty or who might be characterized as functionally "indigent," or (2) against those who are relatively poorer than others, or (3) against all those who, irrespective of their personal incomes, happen to reside in relatively poorer school districts.51 Our task must be to ascertain whether, in fact, the Texas system has been shown to discriminate on any of these possible bases and, if so, whether the resulting classification may be regarded as suspect.

The precedents of this Court provide the proper starting point. The individuals, or groups of individuals, who constituted the class discriminated against in our prior cases shared two distinguishing characteristics: because of their impecunity they were completely unable to pay for some desired benefit, and as a consequence, they sustained an absolute deprivation of a meaningful opportunity to enjoy that benefit.

* * *

Even a cursory Examination . . . demonstrates that neither of the two distinguishing characteristics of wealth classifications can be found here. First, in support of their charge that the system discriminates against the "poor," appellees have made no effort to demonstrate that it operates to the peculiar disadvantage of any class fairly definable as indigent, or as composed of persons whose incomes are beneath any designated poverty level. Indeed, there is reason to believe that the poorest families are not necessarily clustered in the poorest property districts. A recent and exhaustive study of school districts in Connecticut concluded that "[i]t is clearly incorrect . . . to contend that the `poor' live in `poor' districts . . . . Thus, the major factual assumption of Serrano - that the educational financing system discriminates against the `poor' - is simply false in Connecticut." Defining "poor" families as those below the Bureau of the Census "poverty level," the Connecticut study found, not surprisingly, that the poor were clustered around commercial and industrial areas - those same areas that provide the most attractive sources of property tax income for school districts.55 Whether a similar pattern would be discovered in Texas is not known, but there is no basis on the record in this case for assuming that the poorest people - defined by reference to any level of absolute impecunity - are concentrated in the poorest districts.

Second, neither appellees nor the District Court addressed the fact that, unlike each of the foregoing cases, lack of personal resources has not occasioned an absolute deprivation of the desired benefit. The argument here is not that the children in districts having relatively low assessable property values are receiving no public education; rather, it is that they are receiving a poorer quality education than that available to children in districts having more assessable wealth. Apart from the unsettled and disputed question whether the quality of education may be determined by the amount of money expended for it, a sufficient answer to appellees' argument is that, at least where wealth is involved, the Equal Protection Clause does not require absolute equality or precisely equal advantages. Nor, indeed, in view of the infinite variables affecting the educational process, can any system assure equal quality of education except in the most relative sense. Texas asserts that the Minimum Foundation Program provides an "adequate" education for all children in the State. By providing 12 years of free public-school education, and by assuring teachers, books, transportation, and operating funds, the Texas Legislature has endeavored to "guarantee, for the welfare of the state as a whole, that all people shall have at least an adequate program of education. This is what is meant by `A Minimum Foundation Program of Education.'" The State repeatedly asserted in its briefs in this Court that it has fulfilled this desire and that it now assures "every child in every school district an adequate education."59 No proof was offered at trial persuasively discrediting or refuting the State's assertion.

For these two reasons - the absence of any evidence that the financing system discriminates against any definable category of "poor" people or that it results in the absolute deprivation of education - the disadvantaged class is not susceptible of identification in traditional terms.

* * *

We thus conclude that the Texas system does not operate to the peculiar disadvantage of any suspect class. But in recognition of the fact that this Court has never heretofore held that wealth discrimination alone provides an adequate basis for invoking strict scrutiny, appellees have not relied solely on this contention. They also assert that the State's system impermissibly interferes with the exercise of a "fundamental" right and that accordingly the prior decisions of this Court require the application of the strict standard of judicial review. Graham v. Richardson, 403 U.S. 365, 375-376 (1971); Kramer v. Union School District, 395 U.S. 621 (1969); Shapiro v. Thompson, 394 U.S. 618 (1969). It is this question – whether education is a fundamental right, in the sense that it is among the rights and liberties protected by the Constitution - which has so consumed the attention of courts and commentators in recent years.

* * *

In Brown v. Board of Education, 347 U.S. 483 (1954), a unanimous Court recognized that "education is perhaps the most important function of state and local governments." Id., at 493. What was said there in the context of racial discrimination has lost none of its vitality with the passage of time:

"Compulsory school attendance laws and the great expenditures for education both demonstrate our recognition of the importance of education to our democratic society. It is required in the performance of our most basic public responsibilities, even service in the armed forces. It is the very foundation of good citizenship. Today it is a principal instrument in awakening the child to cultural values, in preparing him for later professional training, and in helping him to adjust normally to his environment. In these days, it is doubtful that any child may reasonably be expected to succeed in life if he is denied the opportunity of an education. Such an opportunity, where the state has undertaken to provide it, is a right which must be made available to all on equal terms." Ibid.

This theme, expressing an abiding respect for the vital role of education in a free society, may be found in numerous opinions of Justices of this Court writing both before and after Brown was decided.

* * *

Nothing this Court holds today in any way detracts from our historic dedication to public education. We are in complete agreement with the conclusion of the three-judge panel below that "the grave significance of education both to the individual and to our society" cannot be doubted. But the importance of a service performed by the State does not determine whether it must be regarded as fundamental for purposes of examination under the Equal Protection Clause.

* * *

It is not the province of this Court to create substantive constitutional rights in the name of guaranteeing equal protection of the laws. Thus, the key to discovering whether education is "fundamental" is not to be found in comparisons of the relative societal significance of education as opposed to subsistence or housing. Nor is it to be found by weighing whether education is as important as the right to travel. Rather, the answer lies in assessing whether there is a right to education explicitly or implicitly guaranteed by the Constitution.

* * *

Education, of course, is not among the rights afforded explicit protection under our Federal Constitution. Nor do we find any basis for saying it is implicitly so protected. As we have said, the undisputed importance of education will not alone cause this Court to depart from the usual standard for reviewing a State's social and economic legislation. It is appellees' contention, however, that education is distinguishable from other services and benefits provided by the State because it bears a peculiarly close relationship to other rights and liberties accorded protection under the Constitution. Specifically, they insist that education is itself a fundamental personal right because it is essential to the effective exercise of First Amendment freedoms and to intelligent utilization of the right to vote. In asserting a nexus between speech and education, appellees urge that the right to speak is meaningless unless the speaker is capable of articulating his thoughts intelligently and persuasively. The "marketplace of ideas" is an empty forum for those lacking basic communicative tools. Likewise, they argue that the corollary right to receive information becomes little more than a hollow privilege when the recipient has not been taught to read, assimilate, and utilize available knowledge.

* * *

We need not dispute any of these propositions. The Court has long afforded zealous protection against unjustifiable governmental interference with the individual's rights to speak and to vote. Yet we have never presumed to possess either the ability or the authority to guarantee to the citizenry the most effective speech or the most informed electoral choice. That these may be desirable goals of a system of freedom of expression and of a representative form of government is not to be doubted. These are indeed goals to be pursued by a people whose thoughts and beliefs are freed from governmental interference. But they are not values to be pursued by a implemented by judicial intrusion into otherwise legitimate state activities.

Even if it were conceded that some identifiable quantum of education is a constitutionally protected prerequisite to the meaningful exercise of either right, we have no indication that the present levels of educational expenditures in
Texas provide an education that falls short. Whatever merit appellees' argument might have if a State's financing system occasioned an absolute denial of educational opportunities to

any of its children, that argument provides no basis for finding an interference with fundamental rights where only relative differences in spending levels are involved and where - as is true in the present case - no charge fairly could be made that the system fails to provide each child with an opportunity to acquire the basic minimal skills necessary for the enjoyment of the rights of speech and of full participation in the political process.

* * *

It should be clear, for the reasons stated above and in accord with the prior decisions of this Court, that this is not a case in which the challenged state action must be subjected to the searching judicial scrutiny reserved for laws that create suspect classifications or impinge upon constitutionally protected rights.

* * *

Reversed.

HAZELWOOD SCHOOL DIST. v. KUHLMEIER
U.S. Supreme Court, 484 U.S. 260 (1988)

JUSTICE WHITE delivered the opinion of the Court.

This case concerns the extent to which educators may exercise editorial control over the contents of a high school newspaper produced as part of the school's journalism curriculum.

I

Petitioners are the Hazelwood School District in St. Louis County, Missouri; various school officials; Robert Eugene Reynolds, the principal of Hazelwood East High School; and Howard Emerson, a teacher in the school district. Respondents are three former Hazelwood East students who were staff members of Spectrum, the school newspaper. They contend that school officials violated their First Amendment rights by deleting two pages of articles from the May 13, 1983, issue of Spectrum.

Spectrum was written and edited by the Journalism II class at Hazelwood East. The newspaper was published every three weeks or so during the 1982-1983 school year. More than 4,500 copies of the newspaper were distributed during that year to students, school personnel, and members of the community.

The Board of Education allocated funds from its annual budget for the printing of Spectrum. These funds were supplemented by proceeds from sales of the newspaper. The printing expenses during the 1982-1983 school year totaled $4,668.50; revenue from sales was $1,166.84. The other costs associated with the newspaper - such as supplies, textbooks, and a portion of the journalism teacher's salary - were borne entirely by the Board.

The Journalism II course was taught by Robert Stergos for most of the 1982-1983 academic year. Stergos left Hazelwood East to take a job in private industry on April 29, 1983, when the May 13 edition of Spectrum was nearing completion, and petitioner Emerson took his place as newspaper adviser for the remaining weeks of the term.

The practice at Hazelwood East during the spring 1983 semester was for the journalism teacher to submit page proofs of each Spectrum issue to Principal Reynolds for his review prior to publication. On May 10, Emerson delivered the proofs of the May 13 edition to Reynolds, who objected to two of the articles scheduled to appear in that edition. One of the stories described three Hazelwood East students' experiences with pregnancy; the other discussed the impact of divorce on students at the school.

Reynolds was concerned that, although the pregnancy story used false names "to keep the identity of these girls a secret," the pregnant students still might be identifiable from the text. He also believed that the article's references to sexual activity and birth control were inappropriate for some of the younger students at the school. In addition, Reynolds was concerned that a student identified by name in the divorce story had complained that her father "wasn't spending enough time with my mom, my sister and I" prior to the divorce, "was always out of town on business or out late playing cards with the guys," and "always argued about everything" with her mother. App. to Pet. for Cert. 38. Reynolds believed that the student's parents should have been given an opportunity to respond to these remarks or to consent to their publication. He was unaware that Emerson had deleted the student's name from the final version of the article.

Reynolds believed that there was no time to make the necessary changes in the stories before the scheduled press run and that the newspaper would not appear before the end of the school year if printing were delayed to any significant extent. He concluded that his only options under the circumstances were to publish a four-page newspaper instead of the planned six-page newspaper, eliminating the two pages on which the offending stories appeared, or to publish no newspaper at all. Accordingly, he directed Emerson to withhold from publication the two pages containing the stories on pregnancy and divorce. He informed his superiors of the decision, and they concurred.

II

Students in the public schools do not "shed their constitutional rights to freedom of speech or expression at the schoolhouse gate." Tinker, supra, at 506. They cannot be punished merely for expressing their personal views on the school premises - whether "in the cafeteria, or on the playing field, or on the campus during the authorized hours," 393 U.S., at 512-513 - unless school authorities have reason to believe that such expression will "substantially interfere with the work of the school or impinge upon the rights of other students." Id., at 509.

We have nonetheless recognized that the First Amendment rights of students in the public schools "are not automatically coextensive with the rights of adults in other settings," Bethel School District No. 403 v. Fraser, 478 U.S. 675, 682 (1986), and must be "applied in light of the special characteristics of the school environment." Tinker, supra, at 506; cf. New Jersey v. T. L. O., 469 U.S. 325, 341-343 (1985). A school need not tolerate student speech that is inconsistent with its "basic educational mission," Fraser, supra, at 685, even though the government could not censor similar speech outside the school. Accordingly, we held in Fraser that a student could be disciplined for having delivered a speech that was "sexually explicit" but not legally obscene at an official school assembly, because the school was entitled to "disassociate itself" from the speech in a manner that would demonstrate to others that such vulgarity is "wholly inconsistent with the `fundamental values' of public school education." 478 U.S., at 685-686. We thus recognized that "[t]he determination of what manner of speech in the classroom or in school assembly is inappropriate properly rests with the school board," id., at 683, rather than with the federal courts. It is in this context that respondents' First Amendment claims must be considered.

A

We deal first with the question whether Spectrum may appropriately be characterized as a forum for public expression. The public schools do not possess all of the attributes of streets, parks, and other traditional public forums that "time out of mind, have been used for purposes of assembly, communicating thoughts between citizens, and discussing public questions." Hague v. CIO, 307 U.S. 496, 515 (1939). Cf. Widmar v. Vincent, 454 U.S. 263, 267-268, n. 5 (1981). Hence, school facilities may be deemed to be public forums only if school authorities have "by policy or by practice" opened those facilities "for indiscriminate use by the general public," Perry Education Assn. v. Perry Local Educators' Assn., 460 U.S. 37, 47 (1983), or by some segment of the public, such as student organizations. Id., at 46, n. 7 (citing Widmar v. Vincent). If the facilities have instead been reserved for other intended purposes, "communicative or otherwise," then no public forum has been created, and school officials may impose reasonable restrictions on the speech of students, teachers, and other members of the school community. 460 U.S., at 46, n. 7. "The government does not create a public forum by inaction or by permitting limited discourse, but only by intentionally opening a nontraditional forum for public discourse." Cornelius v. NAACP Legal Defense & Educational Fund, Inc., 473 U.S. 788, 802 (1985).

The policy of school officials toward Spectrum was reflected in Hazelwood School Board Policy 348.51 and the Hazelwood East Curriculum Guide. Board Policy 348.51 provided that "[s]chool sponsored publications are developed within the adopted curriculum and its educational implications in regular classroom activities." App. 22. The Hazelwood East Curriculum Guide described the Journalism II course as a "laboratory situation in which the students publish the school newspaper applying skills they have learned in Journalism I." Id., at 11. The lessons that were to be learned from the Journalism II course, according to the Curriculum Guide, included development of journalistic skills under deadline pressure, "the legal, moral, and ethical restrictions imposed upon journalists within the school community," and "responsibility and acceptance of criticism for articles of opinion." Ibid. Journalism II was taught by a faculty member during regular class hours. Students received grades and academic credit for their performance in the course.

School officials did not deviate in practice from their policy that production of Spectrum was to be part of the educational curriculum and a "regular classroom activit[y]." The District Court found that Robert Stergos, the journalism teacher during most of the 1982-1983 school year, "both had the authority to exercise and in fact exercised a great deal of control over Spectrum." 607 F. Supp., at 1453. For example, Stergos selected the editors of the newspaper, scheduled publication dates, decided the number of pages for each issue, assigned story ideas to class members, advised students on the development of their stories, reviewed the use of quotations, edited stories, selected and edited the letters to the editor, and dealt with the printing company. Many of these decisions were made without consultation with the Journalism II students. The District Court thus found it "clear that Mr. Stergos was the final authority with respect to almost every aspect of the production and publication of Spectrum, including its content." Ibid. Moreover, after [484 U.S. 260, 269] each Spectrum issue had been finally approved by Stergos or his successor, the issue still had to be reviewed by Principal Reynolds prior to publication. Respondents' assertion that they had believed that they could publish "practically anything" in Spectrum was therefore dismissed by the District Court as simply "not credible." Id., at 1456. These factual findings are amply supported by the record, and were not rejected as clearly erroneous by the Court of Appeals.

The evidence relied upon by the Court of Appeals in finding Spectrum to be a public forum, see 795 F.2d, at 1372-1373, is equivocal at best. For example, Board Policy 348.51, which stated in part that "[s]chool sponsored student publications will not restrict free expression or diverse viewpoints within the rules of responsible journalism," also stated that such publications were "developed within the adopted curriculum and its educational implications." App. 22. One might reasonably infer from the full text of Policy 348.51 that school officials retained ultimate control over what constituted "responsible journalism" in a school-sponsored newspaper. Although the Statement of Policy published in the September 14, 1982, issue of Spectrum declared that "Spectrum, as a student-press publication, accepts all rights implied by the First Amendment," this statement, understood in the context of the paper's role in the school's curriculum, suggests at most that the administration will not interfere with the students' exercise of those First Amendment rights that attend the publication of a school-sponsored newspaper. It does not reflect an intent to expand those rights by converting a curricular newspaper into a public forum.

Finally, that students were permitted to exercise some authority over the contents of Spectrum was fully consistent with the Curriculum Guide objective of teaching the Journalism II students "leadership responsibilities as issue and page editors." App. 11. A decision to teach leadership skills in the context of a classroom activity hardly implies a decision to relinquish school control over that activity. In sum, the evidence relied upon by the Court of Appeals fails to demonstrate the "clear intent to create a public forum," Cornelius, 473 U.S., at 802, that existed in cases in which we found public forums to have been created. See id., at 802-803 (citing Widmar v. Vincent, 454 U.S., at 267; Madison School District v. Wisconsin Employment Relations Comm'n, 429 U.S. 167, 174, n. 6 (1976); Southeastern Promotions, Ltd. v. Conrad, 420 U.S. 546, 555 (1975)). School officials did not evince either "by policy or by practice," Perry Education Assn., 460 U.S., at 47, any intent to open the pages of Spectrum to "indiscriminate use," ibid, by its student reporters and editors, or by the student body generally. Instead, they "reserve[d] the forum for its intended purpos[e]," id., at 46, as a supervised learning experience for journalism students. Accordingly, school officials were entitled to regulate the contents of Spectrum in any reasonable manner. Ibid. It is this standard, rather than our decision in Tinker, that governs this case.

B

The question whether the First Amendment requires a school to tolerate particular student speech - the question that we addressed in Tinker - is different from the question whether the First Amendment requires a school affirmatively to promote particular student speech. The former question addresses educators' ability to silence a student's personal expression that happens to occur on the school premises. The latter question concerns educators' authority over school-sponsored publications, theatrical productions, and other expressive activities that students, parents, and members of the public might reasonably perceive to bear the imprimatur of the school. These activities may fairly be characterized as part of the school curriculum, whether or not they occur in a traditional classroom setting, so long as they are supervised by faculty members and designed to impart particular knowledge or skills to student participants and audiences.

Educators are entitled to exercise greater control over this second form of student expression to assure that participants learn whatever lessons the activity is designed to teach, that readers or listeners are not exposed to material that may be inappropriate for their level of maturity, and that the views of the individual speaker are not erroneously attributed to the school. Hence, a school may in its capacity as publisher of a school newspaper or producer of a school play "disassociate itself," Fraser, 478 U.S., at 685, not only from speech that would "substantially interfere with [its] work . . . or impinge upon the rights of other students," Tinker, 393 U.S., at 509, but also from speech that is, for example, ungrammatical, poorly written, inadequately researched, biased or prejudiced, vulgar or profane, or unsuitable for immature audiences.4 A school must be able to set high standards for the student speech that is disseminated under its auspices - standards that may be higher than those demanded by some newspaper publishers or theatrical producers in the "real" world - and may refuse to disseminate student speech that does not meet those standards. In addition, a school must be able to take into account the emotional maturity of the intended audience in determining whether to disseminate student speech on potentially sensitive topics, which might range from the existence of Santa Claus in an elementary school setting to the particulars of teenage sexual activity in a high school setting. A school must also retain the authority to refuse to sponsor student speech that might reasonably be perceived to advocate drug or alcohol use, irresponsible sex, or conduct otherwise inconsistent with "the shared values of a civilized social order," Fraser, supra, at 683, or to associate the school with any position other than neutrality on matters of political controversy. Otherwise, the schools would be unduly constrained from fulfilling their role as "a principal instrument in awakening the child to cultural values, in preparing him for later professional training, and in helping him to adjust normally to his environment." Brown v. Board of Education, 347 U.S. 483, 493 (1954).

Accordingly, we conclude that the standard articulated in Tinker for determining when a school may punish student expression need not also be the standard for determining when a school may refuse to lend its name and resources to the dissemination of student expression.5 Instead, we hold that educators do not offend the First Amendment by exercising editorial control over the style and content of student speech in school-sponsored expressive activities so long as their actions are reasonably related to legitimate pedagogical concerns.

This standard is consistent with our oft-expressed view that the education of the Nation's youth is primarily the responsibility of parents, teachers, and state and local school officials, and not of federal judges. See, e. g., Board of Education of Hendrick Hudson Central School Dist. v. Rowley, 458 U.S. 176, 208 (1982); Wood v. Strickland, 420 U.S. 308, 326 (1975); Epperson v. Arkansas, 393 U.S. 97, 104 (1968). It is only when the decision to censor a school-sponsored publication, theatrical production, or other vehicle of student expression has no valid educational purpose that the First Amendment is so "directly and sharply implicate[d]," ibid., as to require judicial intervention to protect students' constitutional rights.

III

We also conclude that Principal Reynolds acted reasonably in requiring the deletion from the May 13 issue of Spectrum of the pregnancy article, the divorce article, and the remaining articles that were to appear on the same pages of the newspaper.

The initial paragraph of the pregnancy article declared that "[a]ll names have been changed to keep the identity of these girls a secret." The principal concluded that the students' anonymity was not adequately protected, however, given the other identifying information in the article and the small number of pregnant students at the school. Indeed, a teacher at the school credibly testified that she could positively identify at least one of the girls and possibly all three. It is likely that many students at Hazelwood East would have been at least as successful in identifying the girls. Reynolds therefore could reasonably have feared that the article violated whatever pledge of anonymity had been given to the pregnant students. In addition, he could reasonably have been concerned that the article was not sufficiently sensitive to the privacy interests of the students' boyfriends and parents, who were discussed in the article but who were given no opportunity to consent to its publication or to offer a response. The article did not contain graphic accounts of sexual activity. The girls did comment in the article, however, concerning their sexual histories and their use or nonuse of birth control. It was not unreasonable for the principal to have concluded that such frank talk was inappropriate in a school-sponsored publication distributed to 14-year-old freshmen [484 U.S. 260, 275] and presumably taken home to be read by students' even younger brothers and sisters.

The student who was quoted by name in the version of the divorce article seen by Principal Reynolds made comments sharply critical of her father. The principal could reasonably have concluded that an individual publicly identified as an inattentive parent - indeed, as one who chose "playing cards with the guys" over home and family - was entitled to an opportunity to defend himself as a matter of journalistic fairness. These concerns were shared by both of Spectrum's faculty advisers for the 1982-1983 school year, who testified that they would not have allowed the article to be printed without deletion of the student's name.

Principal Reynolds testified credibly at trial that, at the time that he reviewed the proofs of the May 13 issue during an extended telephone conversation with Emerson, he believed that there was no time to make any changes in the articles, and that the newspaper had to be printed immediately or not at all. It is true that Reynolds did not verify whether the necessary modifications could still have been made in the articles, and that Emerson did not volunteer the information that printing could be delayed until the changes were made. We nonetheless agree with the District Court that the decision to excise the two pages containing the problematic articles was reasonable given the particular circumstances of this case. These circumstances included the very recent replacement of Stergos by Emerson, who may not have been entirely familiar with Spectrum editorial and production procedures, and the pressure felt by Reynolds to make an immediate decision so that students would not be deprived of the newspaper altogether.

In sum, we cannot reject as unreasonable Principal Reynolds' conclusion that neither the pregnancy article nor the divorce article was suitable for publication in Spectrum. Reynolds could reasonably have concluded that the students who had written and edited these articles had not sufficiently mastered those portions of the Journalism II curriculum that pertained to the treatment of controversial issues and personal attacks, the need to protect the privacy of individuals whose most intimate concerns are to be revealed in the newspaper, and "the legal, moral, and ethical restrictions imposed upon journalists within [a] school community" that includes adolescent subjects and readers. Finally, we conclude that the principal's decision to delete two pages of Spectrum, rather than to delete only the offending articles or to require that they be modified, was reasonable under the circumstances as he understood them. Accordingly, no violation of First Amendment rights occurred.

The judgment of the Court of Appeals for the Eighth Circuit is therefore

Reversed.

LEE v. WEISMAN
U. S. Supreme Court, 505 U.S. 577 (1992)

JUSTICE KENNEDY delivered the opinion of the Court.

School principals in the public school system of the city of Providence, Rhode Island, are permitted to invite members of the clergy to offer invocation and benediction prayers as part of the formal graduation ceremonies for middle schools and for high schools. The question before us is whether including clerical members who offer prayers as part of the official school graduation ceremony is consistent with the Religion Clauses of the First Amendment, provisions the Fourteenth Amendment makes applicable with full force to the States and their school districts.

I

A

Deborah Weisman graduated from Nathan Bishop Middle School, a public school in Providence, at a formal ceremony in June, 1989. She was about 14 years old. For many years, it has been the policy of the Providence School Committee and the Superintendent of Schools to permit principals to invite members of the clergy to give invocations and benedictions at middle school and high school graduations. Many, but not all, of the principals elected to include prayers as part of the graduation ceremonies. Acting for himself and his daughter, Deborah's father, Daniel Weisman, objected to any prayers at Deborah's middle school graduation, but to no avail. The school principal, petitioner Robert E. Lee, invited a rabbi to deliver prayers at the graduation exercises for Deborah's class. Rabbi Leslie Gutterman, of the Temple Beth El in Providence, accepted.

It has been the custom of Providence school officials to provide invited clergy with a pamphlet entitled "Guidelines for Civic Occasions," prepared by the National Conference of Christians and Jews. The Guidelines recommend that public prayers at nonsectarian civic ceremonies be composed with "inclusiveness and sensitivity," though they acknowledge that "[p]rayer of any kind may be inappropriate on some civic occasions." App. 20-21. The principal gave Rabbi Gutterman the pamphlet before the graduation, and advised him the invocation and benediction should be nonsectarian. Agreed Statement of Facts 7, id., at 13.

Rabbi Gutterman's prayers were as follows:

INVOCATION

"God of the Free, Hope of the Brave:

"For the legacy of America where diversity is celebrated and the rights of minorities are protected, we thank You. May these young men and women grow up to enrich it.

"For the liberty of America, we thank You. May these new graduates grow up to guard it.

"For the political process of America in which all its citizens may participate, for its court system where all may seek justice, we thank You. May those we honor this morning always turn to it in trust.

"For the destiny of America, we thank You. May the graduates of Nathan Bishop Middle School so live that they might help to share it.

"May our aspirations for our country and for these young people, who are our hope for the future, be richly fulfilled.

AMEN"

BENEDICTION

"O God, we are grateful to You for having endowed us with the capacity for learning which we have celebrated on this joyous commencement.

"Happy families give thanks for seeing their children achieve an important milestone. Send Your blessings upon the teachers and administrators who helped prepare them.

"The graduates now need strength and guidance for the future; help them to understand that we are not complete with academic knowledge alone. We must each strive to fulfill what You require of us all: to do justly, to love mercy, to walk humbly.

"We give thanks to You, Lord, for keeping us alive, sustaining us, and allowing us to reach this special, happy occasion.

AMEN"

Id., at 22-23.

The record in this case is sparse in many respects, and we are unfamiliar with any fixed custom or practice at middle school graduations, referred to by the school district as "promotional exercises." We are not so constrained with reference to high schools, however. High school graduations are such an integral part of American cultural life that we can with confidence describe their customary features, confirmed by aspects of the record and by the parties' representations at oral argument. In the Providence school system, most high school graduation ceremonies are conducted away from the school, while most middle school ceremonies are held on school premises. Classical High School, which Deborah now attends, has conducted its graduation ceremonies on school premises. Agreed Statement of Facts 37, id., at 17. The parties stipulate that attendance at graduation ceremonies is voluntary. Agreed Statement of Facts 41, id., at 18. The graduating students enter as a group in a processional, subject to the direction of teachers and school officials, and sit together, apart from their families. We assume the clergy's participation in any high school graduation exercise would be about what it was at Deborah's middle school ceremony. There the students stood for the Pledge of Allegiance and remained standing during the rabbi's prayers. Tr. of Oral Arg. 38. Even on the assumption that there was a respectful moment of silence both before and after the prayers, the rabbi's two presentations must not have extended much beyond a minute each, if that. We do not know whether he remained on stage during the whole ceremony, or whether the students received individual diplomas on stage, or if he helped to congratulate them.

The school board (and the United States, which supports it as amicus curie) argued that these short prayers and others like them at graduation exercises are of profound meaning to many students and parents throughout this country who consider that due respect and acknowledgment for divine guidance and for the deepest spiritual aspirations of our people ought to be expressed at an event as important in life as a graduation. We assume this to be so in addressing the difficult case now before us, for the significance of the prayers lies also at the heart of Daniel and Deborah Weisman's case.

B

Deborah's graduation was held on the premises of Nathan Bishop Middle School on June 29, 1989. Four days before the ceremony, Daniel Weisman, in his individual capacity as a Providence taxpayer and as next friend of Deborah, sought a temporary restraining order in the United States District Court for the District of Rhode Island to prohibit school officials from including an invocation or benediction in the graduation ceremony. The court denied the motion for lack of adequate time to consider it. Deborah and her family attended the graduation, where the prayers were recited. In July, 1989, Daniel Weisman filed an amended complaint seeking a permanent injunction barring petitioners, various officials of the Providence public schools, from inviting the clergy to deliver invocations and benedictions at future graduations. We find it unnecessary to address Daniel Weisman's taxpayer standing, for a live and justiciable controversy is before us. Deborah Weisman is enrolled as a student at Classical High School in Providence and from the record it appears likely, if not certain, that an invocation and benediction will be conducted at her high school graduation. Agreed Statement of Facts 38, App. at 17.

The case was submitted on stipulated facts. The District Court held that petitioners' practice of including invocations and benedictions in public school graduations violated the Establishment Clause of the First Amendment, and it enjoined petitioners from continuing the practice. 728 F.Supp. 68 (RI 1990). The court applied the three-part Establishment Clause test set forth in Lemon v. Kurtzman, 403 U.S. 602 (1971). Under that test as described in our past cases, to satisfy the Establishment Clause, a governmental practice must (1) reflect a clearly secular purpose; (2) have a primary effect that neither advances nor inhibits religion; and (3) avoid excessive government entanglement with religion. Committee for Public Ed. & Religious Liberty v. Nyquist, 413 U.S. 756, 773 (1973). The District Court held that petitioners' actions violated the second part of the test, and so did not address either the first or the third. The court decided, based on its reading of our precedents, that the effects test of Lemon is violated whenever government action "creates an identification of the state with a religion, or with religion in general," 728 F.Supp., at 71, or when "the effect of the governmental action is to endorse one religion over another, or to endorse religion in general." Id., at 72. The court determined that the practice of including invocations and benedictions, even so-called nonsectarian ones, in public school graduations creates an identification of governmental power with religious practice, endorses religion, and violates the Establishment Clause. In so holding, the court expressed the determination not to follow Stein v. Plainwell Community Schools, 822 F.2d 1406 (1987), in which the Court of Appeals for the Sixth Circuit, relying on our decision in Marsh v. Chambers, 463 U.S. 783 (1983), held that benedictions and invocations at public school graduations are not always unconstitutional. In Marsh, we upheld the constitutionality of the Nebraska State Legislature's practice of opening each of its sessions with a prayer offered by a chaplain paid out of public funds. The District Court in this case disagreed with the Sixth Circuit's reasoning because it believed that Marsh was a narrow decision, "limited to the unique situation of legislative prayer," and did not have any relevance to school prayer cases. 728 F.Supp., at 74.

On appeal, the United States Court of Appeals for the First Circuit affirmed. The majority opinion by Judge Torruella adopted the opinion of the District Court. 908 F.2d 1090 (1990). Judge Bownes joined the majority, but wrote a separate concurring opinion in which he decided that the practices challenged here violated all three parts of the Lemon test. Judge Bownes went on to agree with the District Court that Marsh had no application to school prayer cases, and that the Stein decision was flawed. He concluded by suggesting that, under Establishment Clause rules, no prayer, even one excluding any mention of the Deity, could be offered at a public school graduation ceremony. 908 F.2d, at 1090-1097. Judge Campbell dissented, on the basis of Marsh and Stein. He reasoned that, if the prayers delivered were nonsectarian, and if school officials ensured that persons representing a variety of beliefs and ethical systems were invited to present invocations and benedictions, there was no violation of the Establishment Clause. 908 F.2d, at 1099. We granted certiorari, 499 U.S. 918 (1991), and now affirm.

II

These dominant facts mark and control the confines of our decision: State officials direct the performance of a formal religious exercise at promotional and graduation ceremonies for secondary schools. Even for those students who object to the religious exercise, their attendance and participation in the state-sponsored religious activity are, in a fair and real sense, obligatory, though the school district does not require attendance as a condition for receipt of the diploma.

This case does not require us to revisit the difficult questions dividing us in recent cases, questions of the definition and full scope of the principles governing the extent of permitted accommodation by the State for the religious beliefs and practices of many of its citizens. See County of Allegheny v. American Civil Liberties Union, Greater Pittsburgh Chapter, 492 U.S. 573 (1989); Wallace v. Jaffree, 472 U.S. 38 (1985); Lynch v. Donnelly, 465 U.S. 668 (1984). For without reference to those principles in other contexts, the controlling precedents as they relate to prayer and religious exercise in primary and secondary public schools compel the holding here that the policy of the city of Providence is an unconstitutional one. We can decide the case without reconsidering the general constitutional framework by which public schools' efforts to accommodate religion are measured. Thus, we do not accept the invitation of petitioners and amicus the United States to reconsider our decision in Lemon v. Kurtzman, supra. The government involvement with religious activity in this case is pervasive, to the point of creating a state-sponsored and state-directed religious exercise in a public school. Conducting this formal religious observance conflicts with settled rules pertaining to prayer exercises for students, and that suffices to determine the question before us.

The principle that government may accommodate the free exercise of religion does not supersede the fundamental limitations imposed by the Establishment Clause. It is beyond dispute that, at a minimum, the Constitution guarantees that government may not coerce anyone to support or participate in religion or its exercise, or otherwise act in a way which "establishes a [state] religion or religious faith, or tends to do so." Lynch, supra, at 678; see also County of Allegheny, supra, at 591, quoting Everson v. Board of Ed. of Ewing, 330 U.S. 1, 15 -16 (1947). The State's involvement in the school prayers challenged today violates these central principles.

That involvement is as troubling as it is undenied. A school official, the principal, decided that an invocation and a benediction should be given; this is a choice attributable to the State, and, from a constitutional perspective, it is as if a state statute decreed that the prayers must occur. The principal chose the religious participant, here a rabbi, and that choice is also attributable to the State. The reason for the choice of a rabbi is not disclosed by the record, but the potential for divisiveness over the choice of a particular member of the clergy to conduct the ceremony is apparent.

Divisiveness, of course, can attend any state decision respecting religions, and neither its existence nor its potential necessarily invalidates the State's attempts to accommodate religion in all cases. The potential for divisiveness is of particular relevance here, though, because it centers around an overt religious exercise in a secondary school environment where, as we discuss below, see infra, at 593-594, subtle coercive pressures exist, and where the student had no real alternative which would have allowed her to avoid the fact or appearance of participation.

The State's role did not end with the decision to include a prayer and with the choice of clergyman. Principal Lee provided Rabbi Gutterman with a copy of the "Guidelines for Civic Occasions" and advised him that his prayers should be nonsectarian. Through these means, the principal directed and controlled the content of the prayers. Even if the only sanction for ignoring the instructions were that the rabbi would not be invited back, we think no religious representative who valued his or her continued reputation and effectiveness in the community would incur the State's displeasure in this regard. It is a cornerstone principle of our Establishment Clause jurisprudence that it is no part of the business of government to compose official prayers for any group of the American people to recite as a part of a religious program carried on by government, Engel v. Vitale, 370 U.S. 421, 425 (1962), and that is what the school officials attempted to do.

Petitioners argue, and we find nothing in the case to refute it, that the directions for the content of the prayers were a good-faith attempt by the school to ensure that the sectarianism which is so often the flashpoint for religious animosity be removed from the graduation ceremony. The concern is understandable, as a prayer which uses ideas or images identified with a particular religion may foster a different sort of sectarian rivalry than an invocation or benediction in terms more neutral. The school's explanation, however, does not resolve the dilemma caused by its participation. The question is not the good faith of the school in attempting to make the prayer acceptable to most persons, but the legitimacy of its undertaking that enterprise at all when the object is to produce a prayer to be used in a formal religious exercise which students, for all practical purposes are obliged to attend.

We are asked to recognize the existence of a practice of nonsectarian prayer, prayer within the embrace of what is known as the Judeo-Christian tradition, prayer which is more acceptable than one which, for example, makes explicit references to the God of Israel, or to Jesus Christ, or to a patron saint. There may be some support, as an empirical observation, to the statement of the Court of Appeals for the Sixth Circuit, picked up by Judge Campbell's dissent in the Court of Appeals in this case, that there has emerged in this country a civic religion, one which is tolerated when sectarian exercises are not. Stein, 822 F.2d, at 1409; 908 F.2d 1090, 1098-1099 (CA1 1990) (Campbell, J., dissenting) (case below); see also Note, Civil Religion and the Establishment Clause, 95 Yale L.J. 1237 (1986). If common ground can be defined which permits once conflicting faiths to express the shared conviction that there is an ethic and a morality which transcend human invention, the sense of community and purpose sought by all decent societies might be advanced. But though the First Amendment does not allow the government to stifle prayers which aspire to these ends, neither does it permit the government to undertake that task for itself.

The First Amendment's Religion Clauses mean that religious beliefs and religious expression are too precious to be either proscribed or prescribed by the State. The design of the Constitution is that preservation and transmission of religious beliefs and worship is a responsibility and a choice committed to the private sphere, which itself is promised freedom to pursue that mission. It must not be forgotten, then, that, while concern must be given to define the protection granted to an objector or a dissenting nonbeliever, these same Clauses exist to protect religion from government interference. James Madison, the principal author of the Bill of Rights, did not rest his opposition to a religious establishment on the sole ground of its effect on the minority. A principal ground for his view was: [E]xperience witnesseth that ecclesiastical establishments, instead of maintaining the purity and efficacy of Religion, have had a contrary operation. Memorial and Remonstrance Against Religious Assessments (1785), in 8 Papers of James Madison 301 (W. Rachal, R. Rutland, B. Ripel, & F. Teute eds. 1973).

These concerns have particular application in the case of school officials, whose effort to monitor prayer will be perceived by the students as inducing a participation they might otherwise reject. Though the efforts of the school officials in this case to find common ground appear to have been a good faith attempt to recognize the common aspects of religions, and not the divisive ones, our precedents do not permit school officials to assist in composing prayers as an incident to a formal exercise for their students. Engel v. Vitale, supra, at 425. And these same precedents caution us to measure the idea of a civic religion against the central meaning of the Religion Clauses of the First Amendment, which is that all creeds must be tolerated, and none favored. The suggestion that government may establish an official or civic religion as a means of avoiding the establishment of a religion with more specific creeds strikes us as a contradiction that cannot be accepted.

The degree of school involvement here made it clear that the graduation prayers bore the imprint of the State, and thus put school-age children who objected in an untenable position. We turn our attention now to consider the position of the students, both those who desired the prayer and she who did not.

To endure the speech of false ideas or offensive content and then to counter it is part of learning how to live in a pluralistic society, a society which insists upon open discourse towards the end of a tolerant citizenry. And tolerance presupposes some mutuality of obligation. It is argued that our constitutional vision of a free society requires confidence in our own ability to accept or reject ideas of which we do not approve, and that prayer at a high school graduation does nothing more than offer a choice. By the time they are seniors, high school students no doubt have been required to attend classes and assemblies and to complete assignments exposing them to ideas they find distasteful or immoral or absurd, or all of these. Against this background, students may consider it an odd measure of justice to be subjected during the course of their educations to ideas deemed offensive and irreligious, but to be denied a brief, formal prayer ceremony that the school offers in return. This argument cannot prevail, however. It overlooks a fundamental dynamic of the Constitution.

The First Amendment protects speech and religion by quite different mechanisms. Speech is protected by ensuring its full expression even when the government participates, for the very object of some of our most important speech is to persuade the government to adopt an idea as its own. Meese v. Keene, 481 U.S. 465, 480 -481 (1987); see also Keller v. State Bar of California, 496 U.S. 1, 10 -11 (1990); Abood v. Detroit Bd. of Ed., 431 U.S. 209 (1977). The method for protecting freedom of worship and freedom of conscience in religious matters is quite the reverse. In religious debate or expression, the government is not a prime participant, for the Framers deemed religious establishment antithetical to the freedom of all. The Free Exercise Clause embraces a freedom of conscience and worship that has close parallels in the speech provisions of the First Amendment, but the Establishment Clause is a specific prohibition on forms of state intervention in religious affairs, with no precise counterpart in the speech provisions. Buckley v. Valeo, 424 U.S. 1, 92 -93, and n. 127 (1976) (per curiam). The explanation lies in the lesson of history that was and is the inspiration for the Establishment Clause, the lesson that, in the hands of government, what might begin as a tolerant expression of religious views may end in a policy to indoctrinate and coerce. A state-created orthodoxy puts at grave risk that freedom of belief and conscience which are the sole assurance that religious faith is real, not imposed.

The lessons of the First Amendment are as urgent in the modern world as in the 18th century, when it was written. One timeless lesson is that, if citizens are subjected to state-sponsored religious exercises, the State disavows its own duty to guard and respect that sphere of inviolable conscience and belief which is the mark of a free people. To compromise that principle today would be to deny our own tradition and forfeit our standing to urge others to secure the protections of that tradition for themselves.

As we have observed before, there are heightened concerns with protecting freedom of conscience from subtle coercive pressure in the elementary and secondary public schools. See, e.g., School Dist. of Abington v. Schempp, 374 U.S. 203, 307 (1963) (Goldberg, J., concurring); Edward v. Aguillard, 482 U.S. 578, 584 (1987); Board of Ed. of Westside Community v. Mergens, 496 U.S. 226, 261 -262 (1990) (KENNEDY, J., concurring). Our decisions in Engel v. Vitale, 370 U.S. 421 (1962), and School Dist. of Abington, supra, recognize, among other things, that prayer exercises in public schools carry a particular risk of indirect coercion. The concern may not be limited to the context of schools, but it is most pronounced there. See County of Allegheny v. American Civil Liberties Union, Greater Pittsburgh Chapter, 492 U.S., at 661 (KENNEDY, J., concurring in judgment in part and dissenting in part). What to most believers may seem nothing more than a reasonable request that the nonbeliever respect their religious practices, in a school context may appear to the nonbeliever or dissenter to be an attempt to employ the machinery of the State to enforce a religious orthodoxy.

We need not look beyond the circumstances of this case to see the phenomenon at work. The undeniable fact is that the school district's supervision and control of a high school graduation ceremony places public pressure, as well as peer pressure, on attending students to stand as a group or, at least, maintain respectful silence during the invocation and benediction. This pressure, though subtle and indirect, can be as real as any overt compulsion. Of course, in our culture, standing or remaining silent can signify adherence to a view or simple respect for the views of others. And no doubt some persons who have no desire to join a prayer have little objection to standing as a sign of respect for those who do. But for the dissenter of high school age, who has a reasonable perception that she is being forced by the State to pray in a manner her conscience will not allow, the injury is no less real. There can be no doubt that for many, if not most, of the students at the graduation, the act of standing or remaining silent was an expression of participation in the rabbi's prayer. That was the very point of the religious exercise. It is of little comfort to a dissenter, then, to be told that, for her, the act of standing or remaining in silence signifies mere respect, rather than participation. What matters is that, given our social conventions, a reasonable dissenter in this milieu could believe that the group exercise signified her own participation or approval of it.

Finding no violation under these circumstances would place objectors in the dilemma of participating, with all that implies, or protesting. We do not address whether that choice is acceptable if the affected citizens are mature adults, but we think the State may not, consistent with the Establishment Clause, place primary and secondary school children in this position. Research in psychology supports the common assumption that adolescents are often susceptible to pressure from their peers towards conformity, and that the influence is strongest in matters of social convention. Brittain, Adolescent Choices and Parent-Peer Cross-Pressures, 28 Am. Sociological Rev. 385 (June 1963); Clasen & Brown, The Multidimensionality of Peer

Pressure in Adolescence, 14 J. of Youth and Adolescence 451 (Dec. 1985); Brown, Clasen, & Eicher, Perceptions of Peer Pressure, Peer Conformity Dispositions, and Self-Reported Behavior Among Adolescents, 22 Developmental Psychology 521 (July 1986). To recognize that the choice imposed by the State constitutes an unacceptable constraint only acknowledges that the government may no more use social pressure to enforce orthodoxy than it may use more direct means.

The injury caused by the government's action, and the reason why Daniel and Deborah Weisman object to it, is that the State, in a school setting, in effect required participation in a religious exercise. It is, we concede, a brief exercise during which the individual can concentrate on joining its message, meditate on her own religion, or let her mind wander. But the embarrassment and the intrusion of the religious exercise cannot be refuted by arguing that these prayers, and similar ones to be said in the future, are of a de minimis character. To do so would be an affront to the rabbi who offered them and to all those for whom the prayers were an essential and profound recognition of divine authority. And for the same reason, we think that the intrusion is greater than the two minutes or so of time consumed for prayers like these. Assuming, as we must, that the prayers were offensive to the student and the parent who now object, the intrusion was both real and, in the context of a secondary school, a violation of the objectors' rights. That the intrusion was in the course of promulgating religion that sought to be civic or nonsectarian, rather than pertaining to one sect, does not lessen the offense or isolation to the objectors. At best it narrows their number, at worst, increases their sense of isolation and affront. See supra, at 593.

There was a stipulation in the District Court that attendance at graduation and promotional ceremonies is voluntary. Statement of Agreed Facts 41, App. 18. Petitioners and the United States, as amicus, made this a center point of the case, arguing that the option of not attending the graduation excuses any inducement or coercion in the ceremony itself. The argument lacks all persuasion. Law reaches past formalism. And to say a teenage student has a real choice not to attend her high school graduation is formalistic in the extreme. True, Deborah could elect not to attend commencement without renouncing her diploma; but we shall not allow the case to turn on this point. Everyone knows that, in our society and in our culture, high school graduation is one of life's most significant occasions. A school rule which excuses attendance is beside the point. Attendance may not be required by official decree, yet it is apparent that a student is not free to absent herself from the graduation exercise in any real sense of the term "voluntary," for absence would require forfeiture of those intangible benefits which have motivated the student through youth and all her high school years. Graduation is a time for family and those closest to the student to celebrate success and express mutual wishes of gratitude and respect, all to the end of impressing upon the young person the role that it is his or her right and duty to assume in the community and all of its diverse parts.

The importance of the event is the point the school district and the United States rely upon to argue that a formal prayer ought to be permitted, but it becomes one of the principal reasons why their argument must fail. Their contention, one of considerable force were it not for the constitutional constraints applied to state action, is that the prayers are an essential part of these ceremonies because, for many persons, an occasion of this significance lacks meaning if there is no recognition, however brief, that human achievements cannot be understood apart from their spiritual essence. We think the Government's position that this interest suffices to force students to choose between compliance or forfeiture demonstrates fundamental inconsistency in its argumentation. It fails to acknowledge that what for many of Deborah's classmates and their parents was a spiritual imperative was, for Daniel and Deborah Weisman, religious conformance compelled by the State. While in some societies the wishes of the majority might prevail, the Establishment Clause of the First Amendment is addressed to this contingency, and rejects the balance urged upon us. The Constitution forbids the State to exact religious conformity from a student as the price of attending her own high school graduation. This is the calculus the Constitution commands.

The Government's argument gives insufficient recognition to the real conflict of conscience faced by the young student. The essence of the Government's position is that, with regard to a civic, social occasion of this importance, it is the objector, not the majority, who must take unilateral and private action to avoid compromising religious scruples, hereby electing to miss the graduation exercise. This turns conventional First Amendment analysis on its head. It is a tenet of the First Amendment that the State cannot require one of its citizens to forfeit his or her rights and benefits as the price of resisting conformance to state-sponsored religious practice. To say that a student must remain apart from the ceremony at the opening invocation and closing benediction is to risk compelling conformity in an environment analogous to the classroom setting, where we have said the risk of compulsion is especially high. See supra, at 593-594. Just as, in Engel v. Vitale, 370 U.S., at 430 , and School Dist. of Abington v. Schempp, 374 U.S., at 224 - 225, where we found that provisions within the challenged legislation permitting a student to be voluntarily excused from attendance or participation in the daily prayers did not shield those practices from invalidation, the fact that attendance at the graduation ceremonies is voluntary in a legal sense does not save the religious exercise.

Inherent differences between the public school system and a session of a state legislature distinguish this case from Marsh v. Chambers, 463 U.S. 783 (1983). The considerations we have raised in objection to the invocation and benediction are, in many respects, similar to the arguments we considered in Marsh. But there are also obvious differences. The atmosphere at the opening of a session of a state legislature, where adults are free to enter and leave with little comment and for any number of reasons, cannot compare with the constraining potential of the one school event most important for the student to attend. The influence and force of a formal exercise in a school graduation are far greater than the prayer exercise we condoned in Marsh. The Marsh majority in fact gave specific recognition to this distinction, and placed particular reliance on it in upholding the prayers at issue there. 463 U.S., at 792 . Today's case is different. At a high school graduation, teachers and principals must and do retain a high degree of control over the precise contents of the program, the speeches, the timing, the movements, the dress, and the decorum of the students. Bethel School Dist. No. 403 v. Fraser, 478 U.S. 675 (1986). In this atmosphere, the state-imposed character of an invocation and benediction by clergy selected by the school combine to make the prayer a state-sanctioned religious exercise in which the student was left with no alternative but to submit. This is different from Marsh, and suffices to make the religious exercise a First Amendment violation. Our Establishment Clause jurisprudence remains a delicate and fact-sensitive one, and we cannot accept the parallel relied upon by petitioners and the United States between the facts of Marsh and the case now before us. Our decisions in Engel v. Vitale, supra, and School Dist. of Abington v. Schempp, supra, require us to distinguish the public school context.

We do not hold that every state action implicating religion is invalid if one or a few citizens find it offensive. People may take offense at all manner of religious as well as nonreligious messages, but offense alone does not in every case show a violation. We know too that sometimes to endure social isolation or even anger may be the price of conscience or nonconformity. But, by any reading of our cases, the conformity required of the student in this case was too high an exaction to withstand the test of the Establishment Clause. The prayer exercises in this case are especially improper because the State has in every practical sense compelled attendance and participation in an explicit religious exercise at an event of singular importance to every student, one the objecting student had no real alternative to avoid.

Our jurisprudence in this area is of necessity one of line-drawing, of determining at what point a dissenter's rights of religious freedom are infringed by the State.

"The First Amendment does not prohibit practices which, by any realistic measure, create none of the dangers which it is designed to prevent, and which do not so directly or substantially involve the state in religious exercises or in the favoring of religion as to have meaningful and practical impact. It is, of course, true that great consequences can grow from small beginnings, but the measure of constitutional adjudication is the ability and willingness to distinguish between real threat and mere shadow. School Dist. of Abington v. Schempp, supra, at 308 (Goldberg, J., concurring).

\ Our society would be less than true to its heritage if it lacked abiding concern for the values of its young people, and we acknowledge the profound belief of adherents to many faiths that there must be a place in the student's life for precepts of a morality higher even than the law we today enforce. We express no hostility to those aspirations, nor would our oath permit us to do so. A relentless and all-pervasive attempt to exclude religion from every aspect of public life could itself become inconsistent with the Constitution. See School Dist. of Abington, supra, at 306 (Goldberg, J., concurring). We recognize that, at graduation time and throughout the course of the educational process, there will be instances when religious values, religious practices, and religious persons will have some interaction with the public schools and their students. See Board of Ed. of Westside Community Schools (Dist. 66) v. Mergens, 496 U.S. 226 (1990). But these matters, often questions of accommodation of religion, are not before us. The sole question presented is whether a religious exercise may be conducted at a graduation ceremony in circumstances where, as we have found, young graduates who object are induced to conform. No holding by this Court suggests that a school can persuade or compel a student to participate in a religious exercise. That is being done here, and it is forbidden by the Establishment Clause of the First Amendment.

For the reasons we have stated, the judgment of the Court of Appeals is Affirmed.

NEWDOW v. US CONGRESS
9th Circuit Court of Appeals (2002)

JUDGE GOODWIN delivered the opinion of the Court.

Michael Newdow . . . challenge[s] . . . the constitutionality of the words "under God" in the Pledge of Allegiance to the Flag. Newdow argues that the addition of these words by a 1954 federal statute to the previous version of the Pledge of Allegiance (which made no reference to God) and the daily recitation in the classroom of the Pledge of Allegiance, with the added words included, by his daughter's public school teacher are violations of the Establishment Clause of the First Amendment to the United States Constitution.

FACTUAL AND PROCEDURAL BACKGROUND

Newdow is an atheist whose daughter attends public elementary school in the Elk Grove Unified School District ("EGUSD") in California. In accordance with state law and a school district rule, EGUSD teachers begin each school day by leading their students in a recitation of the Pledge of Allegiance ("the Pledge"). The California Education Code requires that public schools begin each school day with "appropriate patriotic exercises" and that "[t]he giving of the Pledge of Allegiance to the Flag of the United States of America shall satisfy" this requirement. Cal. Educ. Code § 52720 (1989) (hereinafter "California statute").

To implement the California statute, the school district that Newdow's daughter attends has promulgated a policy that states, in pertinent part: "Each elementary school class [shall] recite the pledge of allegiance to the flag once each day."

The relevant portion of California Education Code § 52720 reads: In every public elementary school each day during the school year at the beginning of the first regularly scheduled class or activity period at which the majority of the pupils of the school normally begin the schoolday, there shall be conducted appropriate patriotic exercises. The giving of the Pledge of Allegiance to the Flag of the United States of America shall satisfy the requirements of this section.

* * *

The classmates of Newdow's daughter in the EGUSD are led by their teacher in reciting the Pledge codified in federal law. On June 22, 1942, Congress first codified the Pledge as "I pledge allegiance to the flag of the United States of America and to the Republic for which it stands, one Nation indivisible, with liberty and justice for all." Pub. L. No. 623, Ch. 435, § 7, 56 Stat. 380 (1942) (codified at 36 U.S.C. § 1972). On June 14, 1954, Congress amended Section 1972 to add the words "under God" after the word "Nation." Pub. L. No. 396, Ch. 297, 68 Stat. 249 (1954) ("1954 Act"). The Pledge is currently codified as "I pledge allegiance to the Flag of the United States of America, and to the Republic for which it stands, one nation under God, indivisible, with liberty and justice for all." 4 U.S.C. § 4 (1998) (Title 36 was revised and recodified by Pub. L. No. 105-225, § 2(a), 112 Stat. 1494 (1998). Section 172 was abolished, and the Pledge is now found in Title 4.)

Newdow does not allege that his daughter's teacher or school district requires his daughter to participate in reciting the Pledge. Rather, he claims that his daughter is injured when she is compelled to "watch and listen as her state-employed teacher in her state-run school leads her classmates in a ritual proclaiming that there is a God, and that our's [sic] is 'one nation under God.' " Newdow's complaint in the district court challenged the constitutionality, under the First Amendment, of the 1954 Act, the California statute, and the school district's policy requiring teachers to lead willing students in recitation of the Pledge.

Compelling students to recite the Pledge was held to be a First Amendment violation in West Virginia State Board of Education v. Barnette, 319 U.S. 624, 642 (1943) ("[T]he action of the local authorities in compelling the flag salute and pledge transcends constitutional limitations on their power and invades the sphere of intellect and spirit which it is the purpose of the First Amendment to our Constitution to reserve from all official control."). Barnette was decided before the 1954 Act added the words "under God" to the Pledge.

* * *

DISCUSSION

A. Jurisdiction

Newdow asks the district court to order the President of the United States ("the President") to "alter, modify or repeal" the Pledge by removing the words "under God"; and to order the United States Congress ("Congress") "immediately to act to remove the words 'under God' from the Pledge." The President, however, is not an appropriate defendant in an action challenging the constitutionality of a federal statute. See Franklin v. Massachusetts, 505 U.S. 788, 802-03 (1992) (plurality) (observing that a court of the United States " 'has no jurisdiction of a bill to enjoin the President in the performance of his official duties' ") (quoting Mississippi v. Johnson, 71 U.S. 475, 501 (1866)).

Similarly, in light of the Speech and Debate Clause of the Constitution, Art. I, § 6, cl. 1, the federal courts lack jurisdiction to issue orders directing Congress to enact or amend legislation. Because the words that amended the Pledge were enacted into law by statute, the district court may not direct Congress to delete those words any more than it may order the President to take such action. All this, of course, is aside from the fact that the President has no authority to amend a statute or declare a law unconstitutional, those functions being reserved to Congress and the federal judiciary respectively.

Newdow nevertheless argues that because the 1954 Act violates the Establishment Clause, Congress should not be protected by the Speech and Debate Clause. This argument misses the jurisdictional, or separation of powers, point. As the Court held in Eastland, in determining whether or not the acts of members of Congress are protected by the Speech and Debate Clause, the court looks solely to whether or not the acts fall within the legitimate legislative sphere; if they do, Congress is protected by the absolute prohibition of the Clause against being "questioned in any other Place." Id. at 501. "If the mere allegation that a valid legislative act was undertaken for an unworthy purpose would lift the protection of the Clause, then the Clause simply would not provide the protection historically undergirding it." Id. at 508-09.

Although the district court lacks jurisdiction over the President and the Congress, the question of the constitutionality of the 1954 Act remains before us.

* * *

D. Establishment Clause

[History of Supreme Court Analysis –
The Three Possible Tests]

The Establishment Clause of the First Amendment states that "Congress shall make no law respecting an establishment of religion," U.S. Const. amend. I, a provision that "the Fourteenth Amendment makes applicable with full force to the States and their school districts." Lee v. Weisman, 505 U.S. 577, 580 (1992). Over the last three decades, the Supreme Court has used three interrelated tests to analyze alleged violations of the Establishment Clause in the realm of public education: the three-prong test set forth in Lemon v. Kurtzman, 403 U.S. 602, 612-13 (1971); the "endorsement" test, first articulated by Justice O'Connor in her concurring opinion in Lynch, and later adopted by a majority of the Court in County of Allegheny v. ACLU, 492 U.S. 573 (1989); and the "coercion" test first used by the Court in Lee.

[The Lemon Test]

In 1971, in the context of unconstitutional state aid to nonpublic schools, the Supreme Court in Lemon set forth the following test for evaluating alleged Establishment Clause violations. To survive the "Lemon test," the government conduct in question (1) must have a secular purpose, (2) must have a principal or primary effect that neither advances nor inhibits religion, and (3) must not foster an excessive government entanglement with religion. Lemon, 403 U.S. at 612-13. The Supreme Court applied the Lemon test to every Establishment case it decided between 1971 and 1984, with the exception of Marsh v. Chambers, 463 U.S. 783 (1983), the case upholding legislative prayer. See Wallace, 472 U.S. at 63 (Powell, J., concurring).

[The "Endorsement" Test]

In the 1984 Lynch case, which upheld the inclusion of a nativity scene in a city's Christmas display, Justice O'Connor wrote a concurring opinion in order to suggest a "clarification" of Establishment Clause jurisprudence. 465 U.S. at 687. In Marsh, the Court "held that the Nebraska Legislature's practice of opening each day's session with a prayer by a chaplain paid by the State did not violate the Establishment Clause of the First Amendment. [The] holding was based upon the historical acceptance of the practice that had become 'part of the fabric of our society.'" Wallace, 472 U.S. at 63 n.4 (Powell, J., concurring) (quoting Marsh, 463 U.S. at 792) (O'Connor, J., concurring). Justice O'Connor's "endorsement" test effectively collapsed the first two prongs of the Lemon test:

The Establishment Clause prohibits government from making adherence to a religion relevant in any way to a person's standing in the political community. Government can run afoul of that prohibition in two principal ways. One is excessive entanglement with religious institutions . . . . The second and more direct infringement is government endorsement or disapproval of religion. Endorsement sends a message to nonadherents that they are outsiders, not full members of the political community, and an accompanying message to adherents that they are insiders, favored members of the political community. Id. at 687-88 (O'Connor, J., concurring).

[The Lee Test, or "Coercion", Test]

The Court formulated the "coercion test" when it held unconstitutional the practice of including invocations and benedictions in the form of "nonsectarian" prayers at public school graduation ceremonies. Lee, 505 U.S. at 599. Declining to reconsider the validity of the Lemon test, the Court in Lee found it unnecessary to apply the Lemon test to find the challenged practices unconstitutional. Id. at 587. Rather, it relied on the principle that "at a minimum, the Constitution guarantees that government may not coerce anyone to support or participate in religion or its exercise, or otherwise to act in a way which establishes a state religion or religious faith, or tends to do so." Id. (citations and internal quotation marks omitted).

The Court first examined the degree of school involvement in the prayer, and found that "the graduation prayers bore the imprint of the State and thus put school-age children who objected in an untenable position." Id. at 590. The next issue the Court considered was "the position of the students, both those who desired the prayer and she who did not." Id. Noting that "there are heightened concerns with protecting freedom of conscience from subtle coercive pressure in the elementary and secondary public schools," id. at 592, the Court held that the school district's supervision and control of the graduation ceremony put impermissible pressure on students to participate in, or at least show respect during, the prayer, id. at 593. The Court concluded that primary and secondary school children may not be placed in the dilemma of either participating in a religious ceremony or protesting. Id. at 594.

[Using All Three Tests in One Case]

Finally, in its most recent school prayer case, the Supreme Court applied the Lemon test, the endorsement test, and the coercion test to strike down a school district's policy of permitting student-led "invocations" before high school football games. See Santa Fe, 530 U.S. at 310-16. Citing Lee, the Court held that "the delivery of a pregame prayer has the improper effect of coercing those present to participate in an act of religious worship." Id. at 312. Applying the Lemon test, the Court found that the school district policy was facially unconstitutional because it did not have a secular purpose. Id. at 314-16. The Court also used language associated with the endorsement test. Id. at 315 ("[T]his policy was implemented with the purpose of endorsing school prayer."); id. at 317. "The Court has never relied on coercion alone as the touchstone of Establishment Clause analysis. To require a showing of coercion, even indirect coercion, as an essential element of an Establishment Clause violation would make the free Exercise Clause a redundancy." Allegheny, 492 U.S. at 628 (O'Connor, J., concurring). "Over the years, this Court has declared the invalidity of many noncoercive state laws and practices conveying a message of religious endorsement." Lee, 505 U.S. at 618 (Souter, J., concurring). ("Government efforts to endorse religion cannot evade constitutional reproach based solely on the remote possibility that those attempts may fail.").

We are free to apply any or all of the three tests, and to invalidate any measure that fails any one of them. The Supreme Court has not repudiated Lemon; in Santa Fe, it found that the application of each of the three tests provided an independent ground for invalidating the statute at issue in that case; and in Lee, the Court invalidated the policy solely on the basis of the coercion test. Although this court has typically applied the Lemon test to alleged Establishment Clause violations, see, e.g., Am. Family Ass'n, Inc. v. City and County of San Francisco, 277 F.3d 1114, 1120-21 (9th Cir. 2002), we are not required to apply it if a practice fails one of the other tests. Nevertheless, for purposes of completeness, we will analyze the school district policy and the 1954 Act under all three tests.

[ANALYSIS]

[The Pledge Violates the "Endorsement" Test.]

We first consider whether the 1954 Act and the EGUSD's policy of teacher-led Pledge recitation survive the endorsement test. The magistrate judge found that "the ceremonial reference to God in the pledge does not convey endorsement of particular religious beliefs." Supreme Court precedent does not support that conclusion.

In the context of the Pledge, the statement that the United States is a nation "under God" is an endorsement of religion. It is a profession of a religious belief, namely, a belief in monotheism. The recitation that ours is a nation "under God" is not a mere acknowledgment that many Americans believe in a deity. Nor is it merely descriptive of the undeniable historical significance of religion in the founding of the Republic. Rather, the phrase "one nation under God" in the context of the Pledge is normative. To recite the Pledge is not to describe the United States; instead, it is to swear allegiance to the values for which the flag stands: unity, indivisibility, liberty, justice, and – since 1954 – monotheism. The text of the official Pledge, codified in federal law, impermissibly takes a position with respect to the purely religious question of the existence and identity of God. A profession that we are a nation "under God" is identical, for Establishment Clause purposes, to a profession that we are a nation "under Jesus," a nation "under Vishnu," a nation "under Zeus," or a nation "under no god," because none of these professions can be neutral with respect to religion. "[T]he government must pursue a course of complete neutrality toward religion." Wallace, 472 U.S. at 60.

Furthermore, the school district's practice of teacher-led recitation of the Pledge aims to inculcate in students a respect for the ideals set forth in the Pledge, and thus amounts to state endorsement of these ideals. Although students cannot be forced to participate in recitation of the Pledge, the school district is nonetheless conveying a message of state endorsement of a religious belief when it requires public school teachers to recite, and lead the recitation of, the current form of the Pledge.

The Supreme Court recognized the normative and ideological nature of the Pledge in Barnette, 319 U.S. 624. There, the Court held unconstitutional a school district's wartime policy of punishing students who refused to recite the Pledge and salute the flag. Id. at 642. The Court noted that the school district was compelling the students "to declare a belief," id. at 631, and "requir[ing] the individual to communicate by word and sign his acceptance of the political ideas [the flag] . . . bespeaks," id. at 633. "[T]he compulsory flag salute and pledge requires affirmation of a belief and an attitude of mind." Id. The Court emphasized that the political concepts articulated in the Pledge were idealistic, not descriptive: "'[L]iberty and justice for all,' if it must be accepted as descriptive of the present order rather than an ideal, might to some seem an overstatement." Id. at 634 n.14. The Court concluded that: "If there is any fixed star in our constitutional constellation, it is that no official, high or petty, can prescribe what shall be orthodox in politics, nationalism, religion, or other matters of opinion or force citizens to confess by word or act their faith therein." Id. at 642.

The Pledge, as currently codified, is an impermissible government endorsement of religion because it sends a message to unbelievers "that they are outsiders, not full members of the political community, and an accompanying message to adherents that they are insiders, favored members of the political community." Lynch, 465 U.S. at 688 (O'Connor, J., concurring). Justice Kennedy, in his dissent in Allegheny, agreed: [B]y statute, the Pledge of Allegiance to the Flag describes the United States as 'one nation under God.' To be sure, no one is obligated to recite this phrase, . . . but it borders on sophistry to suggest that the reasonable atheist would not feel less than a full member of the political community every time his fellow Americans recited, as part of their expression of patriotism and love for country, a phrase he believed to be false. Allegheny, 492 U.S. at 672 (Kennedy, J., dissenting) (citations and internal quotation marks omitted). Consequently, the policy and the Act fail the endorsement test.

[The Pledge Violates the "Coercion" Test.]

Similarly, the policy and the Act fail the coercion test. Just as in Lee, the policy and the Act place students in the untenable position of choosing between participating in an exercise with religious content or protesting. As the Court observed with respect to the graduation prayer in that case:

"What to most believers may seem nothing more than a reasonable request that the nonbeliever respect their religious practices, in a school context may appear to the nonbeliever or dissenter to be an attempt to employ the machinery of the State to enforce a religious orthodoxy." Lee, 505 U.S. at 592.

Although the defendants argue that the religious content of "one nation under God" is minimal, to an atheist or a believer in certain non-Judeo-Christian religions or philosophies, it may reasonably appear to be an attempt to enforce a "religious orthodoxy" of monotheism, and is therefore impermissible.

The coercive effect of this policy is particularly pronounced in the school setting given the age and impressionability of schoolchildren, and their understanding that they are required to adhere to the norms set by their school, their teacher and their fellow students. Furthermore, under Lee, the fact that students are not required to participate is no basis for distinguishing Barnette from the case at bar because, even without a recitation requirement for each child, the mere fact that a pupil is required to listen every day to the statement "one nation under God" has a coercive effect. The coercive effect of the Act is apparent from its context and legislative history, which indicate that the Act was designed to result in the daily recitation of the words "under God" in school class-rooms. President Eisenhower, during the Act's signing ceremony, stated: "From this day forward, the millions of our school children will daily proclaim in every city and town, every village and rural schoolhouse, the dedication of our Nation and our people to the Almighty." 100 Cong. Rec. 8618 (1954) (statement of Sen. Ferguson incorporating signing statement of President Eisenhower). Therefore, the policy and the Act fail the coercion test.

[The Pledge Violates the Lemon Test.]

[A. The 1954 Act]

Finally we turn to the Lemon test, the first prong of which asks if the challenged policy has a secular purpose. Historically, the primary purpose of the 1954 Act was to advance religion, in conflict with the first prong of the Lemon test. The federal defendants "do not dispute that the words 'under God' were intended" "to recognize a Supreme Being," at a time when the government was publicly inveighing against atheistic communism. Nonetheless, the federal defendants argue that the Pledge must be considered as a whole when assessing whether it has a secular purpose. They claim that the Pledge has the secular purpose of "solemnizing public occasions, expressing confidence in the future, and encouraging the recognition of what is worthy of appreciation in society." Lynch, 465 U.S. at 693.

The flaw in defendants' argument is that it looks at the text of the Pledge "as a whole," and glosses over the 1954 Act. The problem with this approach is apparent when one considers the Court's analysis in Wallace. There, the Court struck down Alabama's statute mandating a moment of silence for "meditation or voluntary prayer" not because the final version "as a whole" lacked a primary secular purpose, but because the state legislature had amended the statute specifically and solely to add the words "or voluntary prayer." 472 U.S. at 59-60.

By analogy to Wallace, we apply the purpose prong of the Lemon test to the amendment that added the words "under God" to the Pledge, not to the Pledge in its final version. As was the case with the amendment to the Alabama statute in Wallace, the legislative history of the 1954 Act reveals that the Act's sole purpose was to advance religion, in order to differentiate the United States from nations under communist rule. "[T]he First Amendment requires that a statute must be invalidated if it is entirely motivated by a purpose to advance religion." Id. at 56 (citations omitted) (applying the Lemon test). As the legislative history of the 1954 Act sets forth:

At this moment of our history the principles underlying our American Government and the American way of life are under attack by a system whose philosophy is at direct odds with our own. Our American Government is founded on the concept of the individuality and the dignity of the human being. Underlying this concept is the belief that the human person is important because he was created by God and endowed by Him with certain inalienable rights which no civil authority may usurp. The inclusion of God in our pledge therefore would further acknowledge the dependence of our people and our Government upon the moral directions of the Creator. At the same time it would serve to deny the atheistic and materialistic concepts of communism with its attendant subservience of the individual. H.R. Rep. No. 83-1693, at 1-2 (1954), reprinted in 1954 U.S.C.C.A.N. 2339, 2340.

This language reveals that the purpose of the 1954 Act was to take a position on the question of theism, namely, to support the existence and moral authority of God, while "deny[ing] . . . atheistic and materialistic concepts." Id. Such a purpose runs counter to the Establishment Clause, which prohibits the government's endorsement or advancement not only of one particular religion at the expense of other religions, but also of religion at the expense of atheism.

[T]he Court has unambiguously concluded that the individual freedom of conscience protected by the First Amendment embraces the right to select any religious faith or none at all. This conclusion derives support not only from the interest in respecting the individual's freedom of conscience, but also from the conviction that religious beliefs worthy of respect are the product of a free and voluntary choice by the faithful, and from recognition of the fact that the political interest in forestalling intolerance extends beyond intolerance among Christian sects – or even intolerance among "religions" – to encompass intolerance of the disbeliever and the uncertain. Wallace, 472 U.S. at 52-54.

In language that attempts to prevent future constitutional challenges, the sponsors of the 1954 Act expressly disclaimed a religious purpose. "This is not an act establishing a religion . . . . A distinction must be made between the existence of a religion as an institution and a belief in the sovereignty of God. The phrase 'under God' recognizes only the guidance of God in our national affairs." H.R. Rep. No. 83-1693, at 3 (1954), reprinted in 1954 U.S.C.C.A.N. 2339, 2341-42. This alleged distinction is irrelevant for constitutional purposes. The Act's affirmation of "a belief in the sovereignty of God" and its recognition of "the guidance of God" are endorsements by the government of religious beliefs. The Establishment Clause is not limited to "religion as an institution"; this is clear from cases such as Santa Fe, where the Court struck down student-initiated and student-led prayer at high school football games. 530 U.S. 310-16. The Establishment Clause guards not only against the establishment of "religion as an institution," but also against the endorsement of religious ideology by the government. Because the Act fails the purpose prong of Lemon, we need not examine the other prongs. Lemon, 403 U.S. at 612-14.

[B. The School District Policy]

Similarly, the school district policy also fails the Lemon test. Although it survives the first prong of Lemon because, as even Newdow concedes, the school district had the secular purpose of fostering patriotism in enacting the policy, the policy fails the second prong. As explained by this court in Kreisner v. City of San Diego, 1 F. 3d 775, 782 (9th Cir. 1993), and by the Supreme Court in School District of Grand Rapids v. Ball, 473 U.S. 373, 390 (1985), the second Lemon prong asks whether the challenged government action is sufficiently likely to be perceived by adherents of the controlling denominations as an endorsement, and by the nonadherents as a disapproval, of their individual religious choices." Ball, 473 U.S. at 390. Given the age and impressionability of schoolchildren, as discussed above, particularly within the confined environment of the classroom, the policy is highly likely to convey an impermissible message of endorsement to some and disapproval to others of their beliefs regarding the existence of a monotheistic God. Therefore the policy fails the effects prong of Lemon, and fails the Lemon test.

[CONCLUSION]

In sum, both the policy and the Act fail the Lemon test as well as the endorsement and coercion tests. In conclusion, we hold that (1) the 1954 Act adding the words "under God" to the Pledge, and (2) EGUSD's policy and practice of teacher-led recitation of the Pledge, with the added words included, violate the Establishment Clause. The judgment of dismissal is vacated with respect to these two claims, and the cause is remanded for further proceedings consistent with our holding. Plaintiff is to recover costs on this appeal.

REVERSED AND REMANDED.

[FOOTNOTE by the Court Regarding
Previous Supreme Court Dicta
about the "under God" language]:

We recognize that the Supreme Court has occasionally commented in dicta that the presence of "one nation under God" in the Pledge of Allegiance is constitutional. See Allegheny, 492 U.S. at 602-03; Lynch, 465 U.S. at 676; id. at 693 (O'Connor, J., concurring); Abington Sch. Dist. v. Schempp, 374 U.S. 203, 303-04 (1963) (Brennan, J., concurring); id. at 306-08 (Goldberg, J., joined by Harlan, J., concurring); Engel, 370 U.S. at 435 n. 21. However, the Court has never been presented with the question directly, and has always clearly refrained from deciding it. Accordingly, it has never applied any of the three tests to the Act or to any school policy regarding the recitation of the Pledge. That task falls to us, although the final word, as always, remains with the Supreme Court. The only other United States Court of Appeals to consider the issue is the Seventh Circuit, which held in Sherman v. Community Consolidated School District 21, 980 F.2d 437 (7th Cir. 1992), that a policy similar to the one before us regarding the recitation of the Pledge of Allegiance containing the words "one nation under God" was constitutional. The Sherman court first stated that: If as Barnette holds no state may require anyone to recite the Pledge, and if as the prayer cases hold the recitation by a teacher or rabbi of unwelcome words is coercion, then the Pledge of Allegiance becomes unconstitutional under all circumstances, just as no school may read from a holy scripture at the start of class. 980 F.2d at 444. It then concludes, however, that this reasoning is flawed because the First Amendment "[does] not establish general rules about speech or schools; [it] call[s] for religion to be treated differently." Id. We have some difficulty understanding this statement; we do not believe that the Constitution prohibits compulsory patriotism as in Barnette, but permits compulsory religion as in this case. If government-endorsed religion is to be treated differently from government-endorsed patriotism, the treatment must be less favorable, not more.

The Seventh Circuit makes an even more serious error, however. It not only refuses to apply the Lemon test because of the Supreme Court's criticism of that test in Lee, but it also fails to apply the coercion test from Lee or the endorsement test from Lynch. Circuit courts are not free to ignore Supreme Court precedent in this manner.

SANTA FE INDEPENDENT SCHOOL DIST. v. DOE
U.S. Supreme Court, (2000)

JUSTICE STEVENS delivered the opinion of the Court.

Prior to 1995, the Santa Fe High School student who occupied the school's elective office of student council chaplain delivered a prayer over the public address system before each varsity football game for the entire season. This practice, along with others, was challenged in District Court as a violation of the Establishment Clause of the First Amendment. While these proceedings were pending in the District Court, the school district adopted a different policy that permits, but does not require, prayer initiated and led by a student at all home games. The District Court entered an order modifying that policy to permit only nonsectarian, nonproselytizing prayer. The Court of Appeals held that, even as modified by the District Court, the football prayer policy was invalid. We granted the school district's petition for certiorari to review that holding.

I

The Santa Fe Independent School District (District) is a political subdivision of the State of Texas, responsible for the education of more than 4,000 students in a small community in the southern part of the State. The District includes the Santa Fe High School, two primary schools, an intermediate school and the junior high school. Respondents are two sets of current or former students and their respective mothers. One family is Mormon and the other is Catholic. The District Court permitted respondents (Does) to litigate anonymously to protect them from intimidation or harassment.

Respondents commenced this action in April 1995 and moved for a temporary restraining order to prevent the District from violating the Establishment Clause at the imminent graduation exercises. In their complaint the Does alleged that the District had engaged in several proselytizing practices, such as promoting attendance at a Baptist revival meeting, encouraging membership in religious clubs, chastising children who held minority religious beliefs, and distributing Gideon Bibles on school premises. They also alleged that the District allowed students to read Christian invocations and benedictions from the stage at graduation ceremonies, and to deliver overtly Christian prayers over the public address system at home football games.

On May 10, 1995, the District Court entered an interim order addressing a number of different issues. With respect to the impending graduation, the order provided that "non-denominational prayer" consisting of "an invocation and/or benediction" could be presented by a senior student or students selected by members of the graduating class. The text of the prayer was to be determined by the students, without scrutiny or preapproval by school officials. References to particular religious figures "such as Mohammed, Jesus, Buddha, or the like" would be permitted "as long as the general thrust of the prayer is non-proselytizing." App. 32.

In response to that portion of the order, the District adopted a series of policies over several months dealing with prayer at school functions. The policies enacted in May and July for graduation ceremonies provided the format for the August and October policies for football games. The May policy provided:

"'The board has chosen to permit the graduating senior class, with the advice and counsel of the senior class principal or designee, to elect by secret ballot to choose whether an invocation and benediction shall be part of the graduation exercise. If so chosen the class shall elect by secret ballot, from a list of student volunteers, students to deliver nonsectarian, nonproselytizing invocations and benedictions for the purpose of solemnizing their graduation ceremonies.' " 168 F. 3d 806, 811 (CA5 1999) (emphasis deleted).

The parties stipulated that after this policy was adopted, "the senior class held an election to determine whether to have an invocation and benediction at the commencement [and that the] class voted, by secret ballot, to include prayer at the high school graduation." App. 52. In a second vote the class elected two seniors to deliver the invocation and benediction.

In July, the District enacted another policy eliminating the requirement that invocations and benedictions be "nonsectarian and nonproselytising," but also providing that if the District were to be enjoined from enforcing that policy, the May policy would automatically become effective.

The August policy, which was titled "Prayer at Football Games," was similar to the July policy for graduations. It also authorized two student elections, the first to determine whether "invocations" should be delivered, and the second to select the spokesperson to deliver them. Like the July policy, it contained two parts, an initial statement that omitted any requirement that the content of the invocation be "nonsectarian and nonproselytising," and a fallback provision that automatically added that limitation if the preferred policy should be enjoined. On August 31, 1995, according to the parties' stipulation, "the district's high school students voted to determine whether a student would deliver prayer at varsity football games... . The students chose to allow a student to say a prayer at football games." Id., at 65. A week later, in a separate election, they selected a student "to deliver the prayer at varsity football games." Id., at 66.

The final policy (October policy) is essentially the same as the August policy, though it omits the word "prayer" from its title, and refers to "messages" and "statements" as well as "invocations." It is the validity of that policy that is before us.

The District Court did enter an order precluding enforcement of the first, open-ended policy. Relying on our decision in Lee v. Weisman, 505 U. S. 577 (1992), it held that the school's "action must not `coerce anyone to support or participate in' a religious exercise." App. to Pet. for Cert. E7. Applying that test, it concluded that the graduation prayers appealed "to distinctively Christian beliefs," and that delivering a prayer "over the school's public address system prior to each football and baseball game coerces student participation in religious events." Both parties appealed, the District contending that the enjoined portion of the October policy was permissible and the Does contending that both alternatives violated the Establishment Clause. The Court of Appeals majority agreed with the Does.

The decision of the Court of Appeals followed Fifth Circuit precedent that had announced two rules. In Jones v. Clear Creek Independent School Dist., 977 F. 2d 963 (1992), that court held that student-led prayer that was approved by a vote of the students and was nonsectarian and nonproselytizing was permissible at high school graduation ceremonies. On the other hand, in later cases the Fifth Circuit made it clear that the Clear Creek rule applied only to high school graduations and that school-encouraged prayer was constitutionally impermissible at school-related sporting events. Thus, in Doe v. Duncanville Independent School Dist., 70 F. 3d 402 (1995), it had described a high school graduation as "a significant, once in-a-lifetime event" to be contrasted with athletic events in "a setting that is far less solemn and extraordinary." Id., at 406-407.

In its opinion in this case, the Court of Appeals explained:

"The controlling feature here is the same as in Duncanville: The prayers are to be delivered at football games--hardly the sober type of annual event that can be appropriately solemnized with prayer. The distinction to which [the District] points is simply one without difference. Regardless of whether the prayers are selected by vote or spontaneously initiated at these frequently-recurring, informal, school-sponsored events, school officials are present and have the authority to stop the prayers. Thus, as we indicated in Duncanville, our decision in Clear Creek II hinged on the singular context and singularly serious nature of a graduation ceremony. Outside that nurturing context, a Clear Creek Prayer Policy cannot survive. We therefore reverse the district court's holding that [the District's] alternative Clear Creek Prayer Policy can be extended to football games, irrespective of the presence of the nonsectarian, nonproselytizing restrictions." 168 F. 3d, at 823.

The dissenting judge rejected the majority's distinction between graduation ceremonies and football games. In his opinion the District's October policy created a limited public forum that had a secular purpose1 and provided neutral accommodation of noncoerced, private, religious speech.

We granted the District's petition for certiorari, limited to the following question: "Whether petitioner's policy permitting student-led, student-initiated prayer at football games violates the Establishment Clause." 528 U. S. 1002 (1999). We conclude, as did the Court of Appeals, that it does.

II

The first Clause in the First Amendment to the Federal Constitution provides that "Congress shall make no law respecting an establishment of religion, or prohibiting the free exercise thereof." The Fourteenth Amendment imposes those substantive limitations on the legislative power of the States and their political subdivisions. Wallace v. Jaffree, 472 U. S. 38, 49-50 (1985). In Lee v. Weisman, 505 U. S. 577 (1992), we held that a prayer delivered by a rabbi at a middle school graduation ceremony violated that Clause. Although this case involves student prayer at a different type of school function, our analysis is properly guided by the principles that we endorsed in Lee.

As we held in that case:

"The principle that government may accommodate the free exercise of religion does not supersede the fundamental limitations imposed by the Establishment Clause. It is beyond dispute that, at a minimum, the Constitution guarantees that government may not coerce anyone to support or participate in religion or its exercise, or otherwise act in a way which `establishes a [state] religion or religious faith, or tends to do so.' " Id., at 587 (citations omitted) (quoting Lynch v. Donnelly, 465 U. S. 668, 678 (1984)).

In this case the District first argues that this principle is inapplicable to its October policy because the messages are private student speech, not public speech. It reminds us that "there is a crucial difference between government speech endorsing religion, which the Establishment Clause forbids, and private speech endorsing religion, which the Free Speech and Free Exercise Clauses protect." Board of Ed. of Westside Community Schools (Dist. 66) v. Mergens, 496 U. S. 226, 250 (1990) (opinion of O'Connor, J.). We certainly agree with that distinction, but we are not persuaded that the pregame invocations should be regarded as "private speech."

These invocations are authorized by a government policy and take place on government property at government-sponsored school-related events. Of course, not every message delivered under such circumstances is the government's own. We have held, for example, that an individual's contribution to a government-created forum was not government speech. See Rosenberger v. Rector and Visitors of Univ. of Va., 515 U. S. 819

(1995). Although the District relies heavily on Rosenberger and similar cases involving such forums, it is clear that the pregame ceremony is not the type of forum discussed in those cases. The Santa Fe school officials simply do not "evince either `by policy or by practice,' any intent to open the [pregame ceremony] to `indiscriminate use,' . . . by the student body generally." Hazelwood School Dist. v. Kuhlmeier, 484 U. S. 260, 270 (1988) (quoting Perry Ed. Assn. v. Perry Local Educators' Assn., 460 U. S. 37, 47 (1983)). Rather, the school allows only one student, the same student for the entire season, to give the invocation. The statement or invocation, moreover, is subject to particular regulations that confine the content and topic of the student's message . . . . By comparison, in Perry we rejected a claim that the school had created a limited public forum in its school mail system despite the fact that it had allowed far more speakers to address a much broader range of topics than the policy at issue here. As we concluded in Perry, "selective access does not transform government property into a public forum." 460 U. S., at 47.

Granting only one student access to the stage at a time does not, of course, necessarily preclude a finding that a school has created a limited public forum. Here, however, Santa Fe's student election system ensures that only those messages deemed "appropriate" under the District's policy may be delivered. That is, the majoritarian process implemented by the District guarantees, by definition, that minority candidates will never prevail and that their views will be effectively silenced.

Recently, in Board of Regents of Univ. of Wis. System v. Southworth, 529 U. S. ___ (2000), we explained why student elections that determine, by majority vote, which expressive activities shall receive or not receive school benefits are constitutionally problematic:

"To the extent the referendum substitutes majority determinations for viewpoint neutrality it would undermine the constitutional protection the program requires. The whole theory of viewpoint neutrality is that minority views are treated with the same respect as are majority views. Access to a public forum, for instance, does not depend upon majoritarian consent. That principle is controlling here." Id., at __ (slip op., at 16-17).

Like the student referendum for funding in Southworth, this student election does nothing to protect minority views but rather places the students who hold such views at the mercy of the majority. Because "fundamental rights may not be submitted to vote; they depend on the outcome of no elections," West Virginia Bd. of Ed. v. Barnette, 319 U. S. 624, 638 (1943), the District's elections are insufficient safeguards of diverse student speech.

In Lee, the school district made the related argument that its policy of endorsing only "civic or nonsectarian" prayer was acceptable because it minimized the intrusion on the audience as a whole. We rejected that claim by explaining that such a majoritarian policy "does not lessen the offense or isolation to the objectors. At best it narrows their number, at worst increases their sense of isolation and affront." 505 U. S., at 594. Similarly, while Santa Fe's majoritarian election might ensure that most of the students are represented, it does nothing to protect the minority; indeed, it likely serves to intensify their offense.

Moreover, the District has failed to divorce itself from the religious content in the invocations. It has not succeeded in doing so, either by claiming that its policy is " `one of neutrality rather than endorsement'" or by characterizing the individual student as the "circuit-breaker" in the process. Contrary to the District's repeated assertions that it has adopted a "hands-off" approach to the pregame invocation, the realities of the situation plainly reveal that its policy involves both perceived and actual endorsement of religion. In this case, as we found in Lee, the "degree of school involvement" makes it clear that the pregame prayers bear "the imprint of the State and thus put school-age children who objected in an untenable position." 505 U. S., at 590.

The District has attempted to disentangle itself from the religious messages by developing the two-step student election process. The text of the October policy, however, exposes the extent of the school's entanglement. The elections take place at all only because the school "board has chosen to permit students to deliver a brief invocation and/or message." App. 104 (emphasis added). The elections thus "shall" be conducted "by the high school student council" and "[u]pon advice and direction of the high school principal." Id., at 104-105. The decision whether to deliver a message is first made by majority vote of the entire student body, followed by a choice of the speaker in a separate, similar majority election. Even though the particular words used by the speaker are not determined by those votes, the policy mandates that the "statement or invocation" be "consistent with the goals and purposes of this policy," which are "to solemnize the event, to promote good sportsmanship and student safety, and to establish the appropriate environment for the competition." Ibid.

In addition to involving the school in the selection of the speaker, the policy, by its terms, invites and encourages religious messages. The policy itself states that the purpose of the message is "to solemnize the event." A religious message is the most obvious method of solemnizing an event. Moreover, the requirements that the message "promote good citizenship" and "establish the appropriate environment for competition" further narrow the types of message deemed appropriate, suggesting that a solemn, yet nonreligious, message, such as commentary on United States foreign policy, would be prohibited. Indeed, the only type of message that is expressly endorsed in the text is an "invocation"--a term that primarily describes an appeal for divine assistance. In fact, as used in the past at Santa Fe High School, an "invocation" has always entailed a focused religious message. Thus, the expressed purposes of the policy encourage the selection of a religious message, and that is precisely how the students understand the policy. The results of the elections described in the parties' stipulation make it clear that the students understood that the central question before them was whether prayer should be a part of the pregame ceremony. We recognize the important role that public worship plays in many communities, as well as the sincere desire to include public prayer as a part of various occasions so as to mark those occasions' significance. But such religious activity in public schools, as elsewhere, must comport with the First Amendment.

The actual or perceived endorsement of the message, moreover, is established by factors beyond just the text of the policy. Once the student speaker is selected and the message composed, the invocation is then delivered to a large audience assembled as part of a regularly scheduled, school-sponsored function conducted on school property. The message is broadcast over the school's public address system, which remains subject to the control of school officials. It is fair to assume that the pregame ceremony is clothed in the traditional indicia of school sporting events, which generally include not just the team, but also cheerleaders and band members dressed in uniforms sporting the school name and mascot. The school's name is likely written in large print across the field and on banners and flags. The crowd will certainly include many who display the school colors and insignia on their school T-shirts, jackets, or hats and who may also be waving signs displaying the school name. It is in a setting such as this that "[t]he board has chosen to permit" the elected student to rise and give the "statement or invocation."

In this context the members of the listening audience must perceive the pregame message as a public expression of the views of the majority of the student body delivered with the approval of the school administration. In cases involving state participation in a religious activity, one of the relevant questions is "whether an objective observer, acquainted with the text, legislative history, and implementation of the statute, would perceive it as a state endorsement of prayer in public schools." Wallace, 472 U. S., at 73, 76 (O'Connor, J., concurring in judgment); see also Capital Square Review and Advisory Bd. v. Pinette, 515 U. S. 753, 777 (1995) (O'Connor, J., concurring in part and concurring in judgment). Regardless of the listener's support for, or objection to, the message, an objective Santa Fe High School student will unquestionably perceive the inevitable pregame prayer as stamped with her school's seal of approval.

The text and history of this policy, moreover, reinforce our objective student's perception that the prayer is, in actuality, encouraged by the school. When a governmental entity professes a secular purpose for an arguably religious policy, the government's characterization is, of course, entitled to some deference. But it is nonetheless the duty of the courts to "distinguis[h] a sham secular purpose from a sincere one." Wallace, 472 U. S., at 75 (O'Connor, J., concurring in judgment).

According to the District, the secular purposes of the policy are to "foste[r] free expression of private persons ... as well [as to] solemniz[e] sporting events, promot[e] good sportsmanship and student safety, and establis[h] an appropriate environment for competition." Brief for Petitioner 14. We note, however, that the District's approval of only one specific kind of message, an "invocation," is not necessary to further any of these purposes. Additionally, the fact that only one student is permitted to give a content-limited message suggests that this policy does little to "foste[r] free expression." Furthermore, regardless of whether one considers a sporting event an appropriate occasion for solemnity, the use of an invocation to foster such solemnity is impermissible when, in actuality, it constitutes prayer sponsored by the school. And it is unclear what type of message would be both appropriately "solemnizing" under the District's policy and yet non-religious.

Most striking to us is the evolution of the current policy from the long-sanctioned office of "Student Chaplain" to the candidly titled "Prayer at Football Games" regulation. This history indicates that the District intended to preserve the practice of prayer before football games. The conclusion that the District viewed the October policy simply as a continuation of the previous policies is dramatically illustrated by the fact that the school did not conduct a new election, pursuant to the current policy, to replace the results of the previous election, which occurred under the former policy. Given these observations, and in light of the school's history of regular delivery of a student-led prayer at athletic events, it is reasonable to infer that the specific purpose of the policy was to preserve a popular "state-sponsored religious practice." Lee, 505 U. S., at 596.

School sponsorship of a religious message is impermissible because it sends the ancillary message to members of the audience who are nonadherants "that they are outsiders, not full members of the political community, and an accompanying message to adherants that they are insiders, favored members of the political community." Lynch v. Donnelly, 465 U. S., at 688 (1984) (O'Connor, J., concurring). The delivery of such a message--over the school's public address system, by a speaker representing the student body, under the supervision of school faculty, and pursuant to a school policy that explicitly and implicitly encourages public prayer--is not properly characterized as "private" speech.

III

The District next argues that its football policy is distinguishable from the graduation prayer in Lee because it does not coerce students to participate in religious observances. Its argument has two parts: first, that there is no impermissible government coercion because the pregame messages are the product of student choices; and second, that there is really no coercion at all because attendance at an extracurricular event, unlike a graduation ceremony, is voluntary.

The reasons just discussed explaining why the alleged "circuit-breaker" mechanism of the dual elections and student speaker do not turn public speech into private speech also demonstrate why these mechanisms do not insulate the school from the coercive element of the final message. In fact, this aspect of the District's argument exposes anew the concerns that are created by the majoritarian election system. The parties' stipulation clearly states that the issue resolved in the first election was "whether a student would deliver prayer at varsity football games," App. 65, and the controversy in this case demonstrates that the views of the students are not unanimous on that issue.

One of the purposes served by the Establishment Clause is to remove debate over this kind of issue from governmental supervision or control. We explained in Lee that the "preservation and transmission of religious beliefs and worship is a responsibility and a choice committed to the private sphere." 505 U. S., at 589. The two student elections authorized by the policy, coupled with the debates that presumably must precede each, impermissibly invade that private sphere. The election mechanism, when considered in light of the history in which the policy in question evolved, reflects a device the District put in place that determines whether religious messages will be delivered at home football games. The mechanism encourages divisiveness along religious lines in a public school setting, a result at odds with the Establishment Clause. Although it is true that the ultimate choice of student speaker is "attributable to the students," Brief for Petitioner 40, the District's decision to hold the constitutionally problematic election is clearly "a choice attributable to the State," Lee, 505 U. S., at 587.

The District further argues that attendance at the commencement ceremonies at issue in Lee "differs dramatically" from attendance at high school football games, which it contends "are of no more than passing interest to many students" and are "decidedly extracurricular," thus dissipating any coercion. Brief for Petitioner 41. Attendance at a high school football game, unlike showing up for class, is certainly not required in order to receive a diploma. Moreover, we may assume that the District is correct in arguing that the informal pressure to attend an athletic event is not as strong as a senior's desire to attend her own graduation ceremony.

There are some students, however, such as cheerleaders, members of the band, and, of course, the team members themselves, for whom seasonal commitments mandate their attendance, sometimes for class credit. The District also minimizes the importance to many students of attending and participating in extracurricular activities as part of a complete educational experience. As we noted in Lee, "[l]aw reaches past formalism." 505 U. S., at 595. To assert that high school students do not feel immense social pressure, or have a truly genuine desire, to be involved in the extracurricular event that is American high school football is "formalistic in the extreme." Ibid. We stressed in Lee the obvious observation that "adolescents are often susceptible to pressure from their peers towards conformity, and that the influence is strongest in matters of social convention." Id., at 593. High school home football games are traditional gatherings of a school community; they bring together students and faculty as well as friends and family from years present and past to root for a common cause. Undoubtedly, the games are not important to some students, and they voluntarily choose not to attend. For many others, however, the choice between whether to attend these games or to risk facing a personally offensive religious ritual is in no practical sense an easy one. The Constitution, moreover, demands that the school may not force this difficult choice upon these students for "[i]t is a tenet of the First Amendment that the State cannot require one of its citizens to forfeit his or her rights and benefits as the price of resisting conformance to state-sponsored religious practice." Id., at 596.

Even if we regard every high school student's decision to attend a home football game as purely voluntary, we are nevertheless persuaded that the delivery of a pregame prayer has the improper effect of coercing those present to participate in an act of religious worship. For "the government may no more use social pressure to enforce orthodoxy than it may use more direct means." Id., at 594. As in Lee, "[w]hat to most believers may seem nothing more than a reasonable request that the nonbeliever respect their religious practices, in a school context may appear to the nonbeliever or dissenter to be an attempt to employ the machinery of the State to enforce a religious orthodoxy." Id., at 592. The constitutional command will not permit the District "to exact religious conformity from a student as the price" of joining her classmates at a varsity football game.

The Religion Clauses of the First Amendment prevent the government from making any law respecting the establishment of religion or prohibiting the free exercise thereof. By no means do these commands impose a prohibition on all religious activity in our public schools. See, e.g., Lamb's Chapel v. Center Moriches Union Free School Dist., 508 U. S. 384, 395 (1993); Board of Ed. of Westside Community Schools (Dist. 66) v. Mergens, 496 U. S. 226 (1990); Wallace v. Jaffree, 472 U. S. 38, 59 (1985). Indeed, the common purpose of the Religion Clauses "is to secure religious liberty." Engel v. Vitale, 370 U. S. 421, 430 (1962). Thus, nothing in the Constitution as interpreted by this Court prohibits any public school student from voluntarily praying at any time before, during, or after the schoolday. But the religious liberty protected by the Constitution is abridged when the State affirmatively sponsors the particular religious practice of prayer.

IV

Finally, the District argues repeatedly that the Does have made a premature facial challenge to the October policy that necessarily must fail. The District emphasizes, quite correctly, that until a student actually delivers a solemnizing message under the latest version of the policy, there can be no certainty that any of the statements or invocations will be religious. Thus, it concludes, the October policy necessarily survives a facial challenge.

This argument, however, assumes that we are concerned only with the serious constitutional injury that occurs when a student is forced to participate in an act of religious worship because she chooses to attend a school event. But the Constitution also requires that we keep in mind "the myriad, subtle ways in which Establishment Clause values can be eroded," Lynch, 465 U. S., at 694 (O'Connor, J., concurring), and that we guard against other different, yet equally important, constitutional injuries. One is the mere passage by the District of a policy that has the purpose and perception of government establishment of religion. Another is the implementation of a governmental electoral process that subjects the issue of prayer to a majoritarian vote.

The District argues that the facial challenge must fail because "Santa Fe's Football Policy cannot be invalidated on the basis of some `possibility or even likelihood' of an unconstitutional application." Brief for Petitioner 17 (quoting Bowen v. Kendrick, 487 U. S. 589, 613 (1988)). Our Establishment Clause cases involving facial challenges, however, have not focused solely on the possible applications of the statute, but rather have considered whether the statute has an unconstitutional purpose. Writing for the Court in Bowen, The Chief Justice concluded that "[a]s in previous cases involving facial challenges on Establishment Clause grounds, e.g., Edwards v. Aguillard, [482 U. S. 578 (1987)]; Mueller v. Allen, 463 U. S. 388 (1983), we assess the constitutionality of an enactment by reference to the three factors first articulated in Lemon v. Kurtzman, 403 U. S. 602, 612 (1971) ... . which guides `[t]he general nature of our inquiry in this area,' Mueller v. Allen, supra, at 394." 487 U. S., at 602. Under the Lemon standard, a court must invalidate a statute if it lacks "a secular legislative purpose." Lemon v. Kurtzman, 403 U. S. 602, 612 (1971). It is therefore proper, as part of this facial challenge, for us to examine the purpose of the October policy.

As discussed, supra, at 14-15, 17, the text of the October policy alone reveals that it has an unconstitutional purpose. The plain language of the policy clearly spells out the extent of school involvement in both the election of the speaker and the content of the message. Additionally, the text of the October policy specifies only one, clearly preferred message--that of Santa Fe's traditional religious "invocation." Finally, the extremely selective access of the policy and other content restrictions confirm that it is not a content-neutral regulation that creates a limited public forum for the expression of student speech. Our examination, however, need not stop at an analysis of the text of the policy.

This case comes to us as the latest step in developing litigation brought as a challenge to institutional practices that unquestionably violated the Establishment Clause. One of those practices was the District's long-established tradition of sanctioning student-led prayer at varsity football games. The narrow question before us is whether implementation of the October policy insulates the continuation of such prayers from constitutional scrutiny. It does not. Our inquiry into this question not only can, but must, include an examination of the circumstances surrounding its enactment. Whether a government activity violates the Establishment Clause is "in large part a legal question to be answered on the basis of judicial interpretation of social facts... . Every government practice must be judged in its unique circumstances ... ." Lynch, 465 U. S., at 693-694 (O'Connor, J., concurring). Our discussion in the previous sections, supra, at 15-18, demonstrates that in this case the District's direct involvement with school prayer exceeds constitutional limits.

The District, nevertheless, asks us to pretend that we do not recognize what every Santa Fe High School student understands clearly--that this policy is about prayer. The District further asks us to accept what is obviously untrue: that these messages are necessary to "solemnize" a football game and that this single-student, year-long position is essential to the protection of student speech. We refuse to turn a blind eye to the context in which this policy arose, and that context quells any doubt that this policy was implemented with the purpose of endorsing school prayer.

Therefore, the simple enactment of this policy, with the purpose and perception of school endorsement of student prayer, was a constitutional violation. We need not wait for the inevitable to confirm and magnify the constitutional injury. In Wallace, for example, we invalidated Alabama's as yet unimplemented and voluntary "moment of silence" statute based on our conclusion that it was enacted "for the sole purpose of expressing the State's endorsement of prayer activities for one minute at the beginning of each school day." 472 U. S., at 60; see also Church of Lukumi Babalu Aye, Inc. v. Hialeah, 508 U. S. 520, 532 (1993). Therefore, even if no Santa Fe High School student were ever to offer a religious message, the October policy fails a facial challenge because the attempt by the District to encourage prayer is also at issue. Government efforts to endorse religion cannot evade constitutional reproach based solely on the remote possibility that those attempts may fail.

This policy likewise does not survive a facial challenge because it impermissibly imposes upon the student body a majoritarian election on the issue of prayer. Through its election scheme, the District has established a governmental electoral mechanism that turns the school into a forum for religious debate. It further empowers the student body majority with the authority to subject students of minority views to constitutionally improper messages. The award of that power alone, regardless of the students' ultimate use of it, is not acceptable. Like the referendum in Board of Regents of Univ. of Wis. System v. Southworth, 529 U. S. ___ (2000), the election mechanism established by the District undermines the essential protection of minority viewpoints. Such a system encourages divisiveness along religious lines and threatens the imposition of coercion upon those students not desiring to participate in a religious exercise. Simply by establishing this school-related procedure, which entrusts the inherently nongovernmental subject of religion to a majoritarian vote, a constitutional violation has occurred. No further injury is required for the policy to fail a facial challenge.

To properly examine this policy on its face, we "must be deemed aware of the history and context of the community and forum," Pinette, 515 U. S., at 780 (O'Connor, J., concurring in part and concurring in judgment). Our examination of those circumstances above leads to the conclusion that this policy does not provide the District with the constitutional safe harbor it sought. The policy is invalid on its face because it establishes an improper majoritarian election on religion, and unquestionably has the purpose and creates the perception of encouraging the delivery of prayer at a series of important school events.

The judgment of the Court of Appeals is, accordingly, affirmed.

It is so ordered.

ZELMAN v. SIMMONS-HARRIS
U.S. Supreme Court, June 27, 2002

CHIEF JUSTICE REHNQUIST delivered the opinion of the Court.

The State of Ohio has established a pilot program designed to provide educational choices to families with children who reside in the Cleveland City School District. The question presented is whether this program offends the Establishment Clause of the United States Constitution. We hold that it does not.

There are more than 75,000 children enrolled in the Cleveland City School District. The majority of these children are from low-income and minority families. Few of these families enjoy the means to send their children to any school other than an inner-city public school. For more than a generation, however, Cleveland's public schools have been among the worst performing public schools in the Nation. In 1995, a Federal District Court declared a "crisis of magnitude" and placed the entire Cleveland school district under state control. See Reed v. Rhodes, No. 1:73 CV 1300 (ND Ohio, Mar. 3, 1995). Shortly thereafter, the state auditor found that Cleveland's public schools were in the midst of a "crisis that is perhaps unprecedented in the history of American education." Cleveland City School District Performance Audit 2-1 (Mar. 1996). The district had failed to meet any of the 18 state standards for minimal acceptable performance. Only 1 in 10 ninth graders could pass a basic proficiency examination, and students at all levels performed at a dismal rate compared with students in other Ohio public schools. More than two-thirds of high school students either dropped or failed out before graduation. Of those students who managed to reach their senior year, one of every four still failed to graduate. Of those students who did graduate, few could read, write, or compute at levels comparable to their counterparts in other cities.

It is against this backdrop that Ohio enacted, among other initiatives, its Pilot Project Scholarship Program, Ohio Rev. Code Ann. §§3313.974-3313.979 (Anderson 1999 and Supp. 2000) (program). The program provides financial assistance to families in any Ohio school district that is or has been "under federal court order requiring supervision and operational management of the district by the state superintendent." §3313.975(A). Cleveland is the only Ohio school district to fall within that category.

The program provides two basic kinds of assistance to parents of children in a covered district. First, the program provides tuition aid for students in kindergarten through third grade, expanding each year through eighth grade, to attend a participating public or private school of their parent's choosing. §§3313.975(B) and (C)(1). Second, the program provides tutorial aid for students who choose to remain enrolled in public school. §3313.975(A).

The tuition aid portion of the program is designed to provide educational choices to parents who reside in a covered district. Any private school, whether religious or nonreligious, may participate in the program and accept program students so long as the school is located within the boundaries of a covered district and meets statewide educational standards. §313.976(A)(3). Participating private schools must agree not to discriminate on the basis of race, religion, or ethnic background, or to "advocate or foster unlawful behavior or teach hatred of any person or group on the basis of race, ethnicity, national origin, or religion." §3313.976(A)(6). Any public school located in a school district adjacent to the covered district may also participate in the program. §3313.976(C). Adjacent public schools are eligible to receive a $2,250 tuition grant for each program student accepted in addition to the full amount of per-pupil state funding attributable to each additional student. §§3313.976(C), 3317.03(I)(1).1 All participating schools, whether public or private, are required to accept students in accordance with rules and procedures established by the state superintendent. §§3313.977(A)(1)(a)-(c).

Tuition aid is distributed to parents according to financial need. Families with incomes below 200% of the poverty line are given priority and are eligible to receive 90% of private school tuition up to $2,250. §§3313.978(A) and (C)(1). For these lowest-income families, participating private schools may not charge a parental co-payment greater than $250. §3313.976(A)(8).

For all other families, the program pays 75% of tuition costs, up to $1,875, with no co-payment cap. §§3313.976(A)(8), 3313.978(A). These families receive tuition aid only if the number of available scholarships exceeds the number of low-income children who choose to participate.2 Where tuition aid is spent depends solely upon where parents who receive tuition aid choose to enroll their child. If parents choose a private school, checks are made payable to the parents who then endorse the checks over to the chosen school. §3313.979.

The tutorial aid portion of the program provides tutorial assistance through grants to any student in a covered district who chooses to remain in public school. Parents arrange for registered tutors to provide assistance to their children and then submit bills for those services to the State for payment. §§3313.976(D), 3313.979(C). Students from low-income families receive 90% of the amount charged for such assistance up to $360. All other students receive 75% of that amount. §3313.978(B). The number of tutorial assistance grants offered to students in a covered district must equal the number of tuition aid scholarships provided to students enrolled at participating private or adjacent public schools. §3313.975(A).

The program has been in operation within the Cleveland City School District since the 1996-1997 school year. In the 1999-2000 school year, 56 private schools participated in the program, 46 (or 82%) of which had a religious affiliation. None of the public schools in districts adjacent to Cleveland have elected to participate. More than 3,700 students participated in the scholarship program, most of whom (96%) enrolled in religiously affiliated schools. Sixty percent of these students were from families at or below the poverty line. In the 1998-1999 school year, approximately 1,400 Cleveland public school students received tutorial aid. This number was expected to double during the 1999-2000 school year.

The program is part of a broader undertaking by the State to enhance the educational options of Cleveland's schoolchildren in response to the 1995 takeover. That undertaking includes programs governing community and magnet schools. Community schools are funded under state law but are run by their own school boards, not by local school districts. §§3314.01(B), 3314.04. These schools enjoy academic independence to hire their own teachers and to determine their own curriculum. They can have no religious affiliation and are required to accept students by lottery. During the 1999-2000 school year, there were 10 start-up community schools in the Cleveland City School District with more than 1,900 students enrolled. For each child enrolled in a community school, the school receives state funding of $4,518, twice the funding a participating program school may receive.

Magnet schools are public schools operated by a local school board that emphasize a particular subject area, teaching method, or service to students. For each student enrolled in a magnet school, the school district receives $7,746, including state funding of $4,167, the same amount received per student enrolled at a traditional public school. As of 1999, parents in Cleveland were able to choose from among 23 magnet schools, which together enrolled more than 13,000 students in kindergarten through eighth grade. These schools provide specialized teaching methods, such as Montessori, or a particularized curriculum focus, such as foreign language, computers, or the arts.

In 1996, respondents, a group of Ohio taxpayers, challenged the Ohio program in state court on state and federal grounds. The Ohio Supreme Court rejected respondents' federal claims, but held that the enactment of the program violated certain procedural requirements of the Ohio Constitution. Simmons-Harris v. Goff, 86 Ohio St. 3d 1, 8-9, 711 N. E. 2d 203, 211 (1999). The state legislature immediately cured this defect, leaving the basic provisions discussed above intact.

In July 1999, respondents filed this action in United States District Court, seeking to enjoin the reenacted program on the ground that it violated the Establishment Clause of the United States Constitution. In August 1999, the District Court issued a preliminary injunction barring further implementation of the program, 54 F. Supp. 2d 725 (ND Ohio), which we stayed pending review by the Court of Appeals, 528 U. S. 983 (1999). In December 1999, the District Court granted summary judgment for respondents. 72 F. Supp. 2d 834. In December 2000, a divided panel of the Court of Appeals affirmed the judgment of the District Court, finding that the program had the "primary effect" of advancing religion in violation of the Establishment Clause.

234 F. 3d 945 (CA6). The Court of Appeals stayed its mandate pending disposition in this Court. App. to Pet. for Cert. in No. 01-1779, p. 151. We granted certiorari, 533 U. S. 976 (2001), and now reverse the Court of Appeals.

The Establishment Clause of the First Amendment, applied to the States through the Fourteenth Amendment, prevents a State from enacting laws that have the "purpose" or "effect" of advancing or inhibiting religion. Agostini v. Felton, 521 U. S. 203, 222-223 (1997) ("[W]e continue to ask whether the government acted with the purpose of advancing or inhibiting religion [and] whether the aid has the `effect' of advancing or inhibiting religion" (citations omitted)). There is no dispute that the program challenged here was enacted for the valid secular purpose of providing educational assistance to poor children in a demonstrably failing public school system. Thus, the question presented is whether the Ohio program nonetheless has the forbidden "effect" of advancing or inhibiting religion.

To answer that question, our decisions have drawn a consistent distinction between government programs that provide aid directly to religious schools, Mitchell v. Helms, 530 U. S. 793, 810-814 (2000) (plurality opinion); id., at 841-844 (O'Connor, J., concurring in judgment); Agostini, supra, at 225-227; Rosenberger v. Rector and Visitors of Univ. of Va., 515 U. S. 819, 842 (1995) (collecting cases), and programs of true private choice, in which government aid reaches religious schools only as a result of the genuine and independent choices of private individuals, Mueller v. Allen, 463 U. S. 388 (1983); Witters v. Washington Dept. of Servs. for Blind, 474 U. S. 481 (1986); Zobrest v. Catalina Foothills School Dist., 509 U. S. 1 (1993). While our jurisprudence with respect to the constitutionality of direct aid programs has "changed significantly" over the past two decades, Agostini, supra, at 236, our jurisprudence with respect to true private choice programs has remained consistent and unbroken. Three times we have confronted Establishment Clause challenges to neutral government programs that provide aid directly to a broad class of individuals, who, in turn, direct the aid to religious schools or institutions of their own choosing. Three times we have rejected such challenges.

In Mueller, we rejected an Establishment Clause challenge to a Minnesota program authorizing tax deductions for various educational expenses, including private school tuition costs, even though the great majority of the program's beneficiaries (96%) were parents of children in religious schools. We began by focusing on the class of beneficiaries, finding that because the class included "all parents," including parents with "children [who] attend nonsectarian private schools or sectarian private schools," 463 U. S., at 397 (emphasis in original), the program was "not readily subject to challenge under the Establishment Clause," id., at 399 (citing Widmar v. Vincent, 454 U. S. 263, 274 (1981) ("The provision of benefits to so broad a spectrum of groups is an important index of secular effect")). Then, viewing the program as a whole, we emphasized the principle of private choice, noting that public funds were made available to religious schools "only as a result of numerous, private choices of individual parents of school-age children." 463 U. S., at 399-400. This, we said, ensured that " `no imprimatur of state approval' can be deemed to have been conferred on any particular religion, or on religion generally." Id., at 399 (quoting Widmar, supra, at 274)). We thus found it irrelevant to the constitutional inquiry that the vast majority of beneficiaries were parents of children in religious schools, saying:

"We would be loath to adopt a rule grounding the constitutionality of a facially neutral law on annual reports reciting the extent to which various classes of private citizens claimed benefits under the law." 463 U. S., at 401.

That the program was one of true private choice, with no evidence that the State deliberately skewed incentives toward religious schools, was sufficient for the program to survive scrutiny under the Establishment Clause.

In Witters, we used identical reasoning to reject an Establishment Clause challenge to a vocational scholarship program that provided tuition aid to a student studying at a religious institution to become a pastor. Looking at the program as a whole, we observed that "[a]ny aid ... that ultimately flows to religious institutions does so only as a result of the genuinely independent and private choices of aid recipients." 474 U. S., at 487. We further remarked that, as in Mueller, "[the] program is made available generally without regard to the sectarian-nonsectarian, or public-nonpublic nature of the institution benefited." 474 U. S., at 487. In light of these factors, we held that the program was not inconsistent with the Establishment Clause. Id., at 488-489.

Five Members of the Court, in separate opinions, emphasized the general rule from Mueller that the amount of government aid channeled to religious institutions by individual aid recipients was not relevant to the constitutional inquiry. 474 U. S., at 490-491 (Powell, J., joined by Burger, C. J., and Rehnquist, J., concurring) (citing Mueller, supra, at 398-399); 474 U. S., at 493 (O'Connor, J., concurring in part and concurring in judgment); id., at 490 (White, J., concurring). Our holding thus rested not on whether few or many recipients chose to expend government aid at a religious school but, rather, on whether recipients generally were empowered to direct the aid to schools or institutions of their own choosing.

Finally, in Zobrest, we applied Mueller and Witters to reject an Establishment Clause challenge to a federal program that permitted sign-language interpreters to assist deaf children enrolled in religious schools. Reviewing our earlier decisions, we stated that "government programs that neutrally provide benefits to a broad class of citizens defined without reference to religion are not readily subject to an Establishment Clause challenge." 509 U. S., at 8. Looking once again to the challenged program as a whole, we observed that the program "distributes benefits neutrally to any child qualifying as `disabled.' " Id., at 10. Its "primary beneficiaries," we said, were "disabled children, not sectarian schools." Id., at 12.

We further observed that "[b]y according parents freedom to select a school of their choice, the statute ensures that a government-paid interpreter will be present in a sectarian school only as a result of the private decision of individual parents." Id., at 10. Our focus again was on neutrality and the principle of private choice, not on the number of program beneficiaries attending religious schools. Id., at 10-11. See, e.g., Agostini, 521 U. S., at 229 ("Zobrest did not turn on the fact that James Zobrest had, at the time of litigation, been the only child using a publicly funded sign-language interpreter to attend a parochial school"). Because the program ensured that parents were the ones to select a religious school as the best learning environment for their handicapped child, the circuit between government and religion was broken, and the Establishment Clause was not implicated.

Mueller, Witters, and Zobrest thus make clear that where a government aid program is neutral with respect to religion, and provides assistance directly to a broad class of citizens who, in turn, direct government aid to religious schools wholly as a result of their own genuine and independent private choice, the program is not readily subject to challenge under the Establishment Clause. A program that shares these features permits government aid to reach religious institutions only by way of the deliberate choices of numerous individual recipients. The incidental advancement of a religious mission, or the perceived endorsement of a religious message, is reasonably attributable to the individual recipient, not to the government, whose role ends with the disbursement of benefits. As a plurality of this Court recently observed:

"[I]f numerous private choices, rather than the single choice of a government, determine the distribution of aid, pursuant to neutral eligibility criteria, then a government cannot, or at least cannot easily, grant special favors that might lead to a religious establishment." Mitchell, 530 U. S., at 810.

See also id., at 843 (O'Connor, J., concurring in judgment) ("[W]hen government aid supports a school's religious mission only because of independent decisions made by numerous individuals to guide their secular aid to that school, `no reasonable observer is likely to draw from the facts ... an inference that the State itself is endorsing a religious practice or belief' " (quoting Witters, supra, at 493 (O'Connor, J., concurring in part and concurring in judgment))). It is precisely for these reasons that we have never found a program of true private choice to offend the Establishment Clause.

We believe that the program challenged here is a program of true private choice, consistent with Mueller, Witters, and Zobrest, and thus constitutional. As was true in those cases, the Ohio program is neutral in all respects toward religion. It is part of a general and multifaceted undertaking by the State of Ohio to provide educational opportunities to the children of a failed school district. It confers educational assistance directly to a broad class of individuals defined without reference to religion, i.e., any parent of a school-age child who resides in the

Cleveland City School District. The program permits the participation of all schools within the district, religious or nonreligious. Adjacent public schools also may participate and have a financial incentive to do so. Program benefits are available to participating families on neutral terms, with no reference to religion. The only preference stated anywhere in the program is a preference for low-income families, who receive greater assistance and are given priority for admission at participating schools.

There are no "financial incentive[s]" that "ske[w]" the program toward religious schools. Witters, supra, at 487-488. Such incentives "[are] not present ... where the aid is allocated on the basis of neutral, secular criteria that neither favor nor disfavor religion, and is made available to both religious and secular beneficiaries on a nondiscriminatory basis." Agostini, supra, at 231. The program here in fact creates financial disincentives for religious schools, with private schools receiving only half the government assistance given to community schools and one-third the assistance given to magnet schools. Adjacent public schools, should any choose to accept program students, are also eligible to receive two to three times the state funding of a private religious school. Families too have a financial disincentive to choose a private religious school over other schools. Parents that choose to participate in the scholarship program and then to enroll their children in a private school (religious or nonreligious) must copay a portion of the school's tuition. Families that choose a community school, magnet school, or traditional public school pay nothing. Although such features of the program are not necessary to its constitutionality, they clearly dispel the claim that the program "creates ... financial incentive[s] for parents to choose a sectarian school." Zobrest, 509 U. S., at 10.3

Respondents suggest that even without a financial incentive for parents to choose a religious school, the program creates a "public perception that the State is endorsing religious practices and beliefs." Brief for Respondents Simmons-Harris et al. 37-38. But we have repeatedly recognized that no reasonable observer would think a neutral program of private choice, where state aid reaches religious schools solely as a result of the numerous independent decisions of private individuals, carries with it the imprimatur of government endorsement. Mueller, 463 U. S., at 399-399; Witters, 474 U. S., at 488-489; Zobrest, supra, at 10-11; e.g., Mitchell, supra, at 842-843 (O'Connor, J., concurring in judgment) ("In terms of public perception, a government program of direct aid to religious schools ... differs meaningfully from the government distributing aid directly to individual students who, in turn, decide to use the aid at the same religious schools"). The argument is particularly misplaced here since "the reasonable observer in the endorsement inquiry must be deemed aware" of the "history and context" underlying a challenged program. Good News Club v. Milford Central School, 533 U. S. 98, 119 (2001) (internal quotation marks omitted). See also Capitol Square Review and Advisory Bd. v. Pinette, 515 U. S. 753, 780 (1995) (O'Connor, J., concurring in part and concurring in judgment). Any objective observer familiar with the full history and context of the Ohio program would reasonably view it as one aspect of a broader undertaking to assist poor children in failed schools, not as an endorsement of religious schooling in general.

There also is no evidence that the program fails to provide genuine opportunities for Cleveland parents to select secular educational options for their school-age children. Cleveland schoolchildren enjoy a range of educational choices: They may remain in public school as before, remain in public school with publicly funded tutoring aid, obtain a scholarship and choose a religious school, obtain a scholarship and choose a nonreligious private school, enroll in a community school, or enroll in a magnet school. That 46 of the 56 private schools now participating in the program are religious schools does not condemn it as a violation of the Establishment Clause. The Establishment Clause question is whether Ohio is coercing parents into sending their children to religious schools, and that question must be answered by evaluating all options Ohio provides Cleveland schoolchildren, only one of which is to obtain a program scholarship and then choose a religious school.

Justice Souter speculates that because more private religious schools currently participate in the program, the program itself must somehow discourage the participation of private nonreligious schools. Post, at 19-22 (dissenting opinion).4 But Cleveland's preponderance of religiously affiliated private schools certainly did not arise as a result of the program; it is a phenomenon common to many American cities. See U. S. Dept. of Ed., National Center for Education Statistics, Private School Universe Survey: 1999-2000, pp. 2-4 (NCES 2001-330, 2001) (hereinafter Private School Universe Survey) (cited in Brief for United States as Amicus Curiae 24). Indeed, by all accounts the program has captured a remarkable cross-section of private schools, religious and nonreligious. It is true that 82% of Cleveland's participating private schools are religious schools, but it is also true that 81% of private schools in Ohio are religious schools. See Brief for State of Florida et al. as Amici Curiae 16 (citing Private School Universe Survey). To attribute constitutional significance to this figure, moreover, would lead to the absurd result that a neutral school-choice program might be permissible in some parts of Ohio, such as Columbus, where a lower percentage of private schools are religious schools, see Ohio Educational Directory (Lodging of Respondents Gatton et al., available in Clerk of Court's case file), and Reply Brief for Petitioners in No. 00-1751, p. 12, n. 1, but not in inner-city Cleveland, where Ohio has deemed such programs most sorely needed, but where the preponderance of religious schools happens to be greater. Cf. Brief for State of Florida et al. as Amici Curiae 17 ("[T]he percentages of sectarian to nonsectarian private schools within Florida's 67 school districts ... vary from zero to 100 percent"). Likewise, an identical private choice program might be constitutional in some States, such as Maine or Utah, where less than 45% of private schools are religious schools, but not in other States, such as Nebraska or Kansas, where over 90% of private schools are religious schools. Id., at 15-16 (citing Private School Universe Survey).

Respondents and Justice Souter claim that even if we do not focus on the number of participating schools that are religious schools, we should attach constitutional significance to the fact that 96% of scholarship recipients have enrolled in religious schools. They claim that this alone proves parents lack genuine choice, even if no parent has ever said so. We need not consider this argument in detail, since it was flatly rejected in Mueller, where we found it irrelevant that 96% of parents taking deductions for tuition expenses paid tuition at religious schools. Indeed, we have recently found it irrelevant even to the constitutionality of a direct aid program that a vast majority of program benefits went to religious schools. See Agostini, 521 U. S., at 229 ("Nor are we willing to conclude that the constitutionality of an aid program depends on the number of sectarian school students who happen to receive the otherwise neutral aid" (citing Mueller, 463 U. S., at 401)); see also Mitchell, 530 U. S., at 812, n. 6 (plurality opinion) ("[Agostini] held that the proportion of aid benefiting students at religious schools pursuant to a neutral program involving private choices was irrelevant to the constitutional inquiry"); id., at 848 (O'Connor, J., concurring in judgment) (same) (quoting Agostini, supra, at 229). The constitutionality of a neutral educational aid program simply does not turn on whether and why, in a particular area, at a particular time, most private schools are run by religious organizations, or most recipients choose to use the aid at a religious school. As we said in Mueller, "[s]uch an approach would scarcely provide the certainty that this field stands in need of, nor can we perceive principled standards by which such statistical evidence might be evaluated." 463 U. S., at 401.

This point is aptly illustrated here. The 96% figure upon which respondents and Justice Souter rely discounts entirely (1) the more than 1,900 Cleveland children enrolled in alternative community schools, (2) the more than 13,000 children enrolled in alternative magnet schools, and (3) the more than 1,400 children enrolled in traditional public schools with tutorial assistance. See supra, at 5-6. Including some or all of these children in the denominator of children enrolled in nontraditional schools during the 1999-2000 school year drops the percentage enrolled in religious schools from 96% to under 20%. See also J. Greene, The Racial, Economic, and Religious Context of Parental Choice in Cleveland 11, Table 4 (Oct. 8, 1999), App. 217a (reporting that only 16.5% of nontraditional schoolchildren in Cleveland choose religious schools). The 96% figure also represents but a snapshot of one particular school year. In the 1997-1998 school year, by contrast, only 78% of scholarship recipients attended religious schools. See App. to Pet. for Cert. in No. 01-1751, p. 5a. The difference was attributable to two private nonreligious schools that had accepted 15% of all scholarship students electing instead to register as community schools, in light of larger per-pupil funding for community schools and the uncertain future of the scholarship program generated by this litigation. See App. 59a-62a, 209a, 223a-227a.5 Many of the students enrolled in these schools as scholarship students remained enrolled as community school students, id., at 145a-146a, thus demonstrating the arbitrariness of counting one type of school but not the other to assess primary effect, e.g., Ohio Rev. Code Ann. §3314.11 (Anderson 1999) (establishing a single "office of school options" to "provide services that facilitate the management of the community schools program and the pilot project scholarship program"). In spite of repeated questioning from the Court at oral argument, respondents offered no convincing justification for their approach, which relies entirely on such arbitrary classifications. Tr. of Oral Arg. 52-60.6

Respondents finally claim that we should look to Committee for Public Ed. & Religious Liberty v. Nyquist, 413 U. S. 756 (1973), to decide these cases. We disagree for two reasons. First, the program in Nyquist was quite different from the program challenged here. Nyquist involved a New York program that gave a package of benefits exclusively to private schools and the parents of private school enrollees. Although the program was enacted for ostensibly secular purposes, id., at 773-774, we found that its "function" was "unmistakably to provide desired financial support for nonpublic, sectarian institutions," id., at 783 (emphasis added). Its genesis, we said, was that private religious schools faced "increasingly grave fiscal problems." Id., at 795. The program thus provided direct money grants to religious schools. Id., at 762-764. It provided tax benefits "unrelated to the amount of money actually expended by any parent on tuition," ensuring a windfall to parents of children in religious schools. Id., at 790. It similarly provided tuition reimbursements designed explicitly to "offe[r] ... an incentive to parents to send their children to sectarian schools." Id., at 786. Indeed, the program flatly prohibited the participation of any public school, or parent of any public school enrollee. Id., at 763-765. Ohio's program shares none of these features.

Second, were there any doubt that the program challenged in Nyquist is far removed from the program challenged here, we expressly reserved judgment with respect to "a case involving some form of public assistance (e.g., scholarships) made available generally without regard to the sectarian-nonsectarian, or public-nonpublic nature of the institution benefited." Id., at 783, n. 38. That, of course, is the very question now before us, and it has since been answered, first in Mueller, 463 U. S., at 398-399 ("[A] program ... that neutrally provides state assistance to a broad spectrum of citizens is not readily subject to challenge under the Establishment Clause" (citing Nyquist, supra, at 782, n. 38)), then in Witters, 474 U. S., at 487 ("Washington's program is `made available generally without regard to the sectarian-nonsectarian, or public-nonpublic nature of the institution benefited' " (quoting Nyquist, supra, at 782, n. 38)), and again in Zobrest, 509 U. S., at 12-13 ("[T]he function of the [program] is hardly `to provide desired financial support for nonpublic, sectarian institutions' " (quoting Nyquist, supra, at 782, n. 38)). To the extent the scope of Nyquist has remained an open question in light of these later decisions, we now hold that Nyquist does not govern neutral educational assistance programs that, like the program here, offer aid directly to a broad class of individual recipients defined without regard to religion.7

In sum, the Ohio program is entirely neutral with respect to religion. It provides benefits directly to a wide spectrum of individuals, defined only by financial need and residence in a particular school district. It permits such individuals to exercise genuine choice among options public and private, secular and religious. The program is therefore a program of true private choice. In keeping with an unbroken line of decisions rejecting challenges to similar programs, we hold that the program does not offend the Establishment Clause.

The judgment of the Court of Appeals is reversed.

It is so ordered.

NEW JERSEY v. T.L.O.
U.S. Supreme Court, 469 U.S. 325 (1985)

JUSTICE WHITE delivered the opinion of the Court.

We . . . here address . . . the questions of the proper standard for assessing the legality of searches conducted by public school officials and the application of that standard to the facts of this case.

I

On March 7, 1980, a teacher at Piscataway High School in Middlesex County, N. J., discovered two girls smoking in a lavatory. One of the two girls was the respondent T.L.O., who at that time was a 14-year-old high school freshman. Because smoking in the lavatory was a violation of a school rule, the teacher took the two girls to the Principal's office, where they met with Assistant Vice Principal Theodore Choplick. In response to questioning by Mr. Choplick, T.L.O.'s companion admitted that she had violated the rule. T.L.O., however, denied that she had been smoking in the lavatory and claimed that she did not smoke at all.

Mr. Choplick asked T.L.O. to come into his private office and demanded to see her purse. Opening the purse, he found a pack of cigarettes, which he removed from the purse and held before T.L.O. as he accused her of having lied to him. As he reached into the purse for the cigarettes, Mr. Choplick also noticed a package of cigarette rolling papers. In his experience, possession of rolling papers by high school students was closely associated with the use of marihuana. Suspecting that a closer examination of the purse might yield further evidence of drug use, Mr. Choplick proceeded to search the purse thoroughly. The search revealed a small amount of marihuana, a pipe, a number of empty plastic bags, a substantial quantity of money in one-dollar bills, an index card that appeared to be a list of students who owed T.L.O. money, and two letters that implicated T.L.O. in marihuana dealing.

Mr. Choplick notified T.L.O.'s mother and the police, and turned the evidence of drug dealing over to the police. At the request of the police, T.L.O.'s mother took her daughter to police headquarters, where T.L.O. confessed that she had been selling marihuana at the high school. On the basis of the confession and the evidence seized by Mr. Choplick, the State brought delinquency charges against T.L.O. in the Juvenile and Domestic Relations Court of Middlesex County. Contending that Mr. Choplick's search of her purse violated the Fourth Amendment, T.L.O. moved to suppress the evidence found in her purse as well as her confession, which, she argued, was tainted by the allegedly unlawful search. . . .

Having heard argument on the legality of the search of T.L.O.'s purse, we are satisfied that the search did not violate the Fourth Amendment.

II

In determining whether the search at issue in this case violated the Fourth Amendment, we are faced initially with the question whether that Amendment's prohibition on unreasonable searches and seizures applies to searches conducted by public school officials. We hold that it does.

It is now beyond dispute that "the Federal Constitution, by virtue of the Fourteenth Amendment, prohibits unreasonable searches and seizures by state officers." Elkins v. United States, 364 U.S. 206, 213 (1960); accord, Mapp v. Ohio, 367 U.S. 643 (1961); Wolf v. Colorado, 338 U.S. 25 (1949). Equally indisputable is the proposition that the Fourteenth Amendment protects the rights of students against encroachment by public school officials:

"The Fourteenth Amendment, as now applied to the States, protects the citizen against the State itself and all of its creatures - Boards of Education not excepted. These have, of course, important, delicate, and highly discretionary functions, but none that they may not perform within the limits of the Bill of Rights. That they are educating the young for citizenship is reason for scrupulous protection of Constitutional freedoms of the individual, if we are not to strangle the free mind at its source and teach youth to discount important principles of our government as mere platitudes." West Virginia State Bd. of Ed. v. Barnette, 319 U.S. 624, 637 (1943).

These two propositions - that the Fourth Amendment applies to the States through the Fourteenth Amendment, and that the actions of public school officials are subject to the limits placed on state action by the Fourteenth Amendment - might appear sufficient to answer the suggestion that the Fourth Amendment does not proscribe unreasonable searches by school officials. On reargument, however, the State of New Jersey has argued that the history of the Fourth Amendment indicates that the Amendment was intended to regulate only searches and seizures carried out by law enforcement officers; accordingly, although public school officials are concededly state agents for purposes of the Fourteenth Amendment, the Fourth Amendment creates no rights enforceable against them.

It may well be true that the evil toward which the Fourth Amendment was primarily directed was the resurrection of the pre-Revolutionary practice of using general warrants or "writs of assistance" to authorize searches for contraband by officers of the Crown. See United States v. Chadwick, 433 U.S. 1, 7-8 (1977); Boyd v. United States, 116 U.S. 616, 624-629 (1886).

But this Court has never limited the Amendment's prohibition on unreasonable searches and seizures to operations conducted by the police. Rather, the Court has long spoken of the Fourth Amendment's strictures as restraints imposed upon "governmental action" - that is, "upon the activities of sovereign authority." Burdeau v. McDowell, 256 U.S. 465, 475 (1921). Accordingly, we have held the Fourth Amendment applicable to the activities of civil as well as criminal authorities: building inspectors, see Camara v. Municipal Court, 387 U.S. 523, 528 (1967), Occupational Safety and Health Act inspectors, see Marshall v. Barlow's, Inc., 436 U.S. 307, 312-313 (1978), and even firemen entering privately owned premises to battle a fire, see Michigan v. Tyler, 436 U.S. 499, 506 (1978), are all subject to the restraints imposed by the Fourth Amendment. As we observed in Camara v. Municipal Court, supra, "[t]he basic purpose of this Amendment, as recognized in countless decisions of this Court, is to safeguard the privacy and security of individuals against arbitrary invasions by governmental officials." 387 U.S., at 528. Because the individual's interest in privacy and personal security "suffers whether the government's motivation is to investigate violations of criminal laws or breaches of other statutory or regulatory standards," Marshall v. Barlow's, Inc., supra, at 312-313, it would be "anomalous to say that the individual and his private property are fully protected by the Fourth Amendment only when the individual is suspected of criminal behavior." Camara v. Municipal Court, supra, at 530.

Notwithstanding the general applicability of the Fourth Amendment to the activities of civil authorities, a few courts have concluded that school officials are exempt from the dictates of the Fourth Amendment by virtue of the special nature of their authority over schoolchildren. See, e. g., R. C. M. v. State, 660 S. W. 2d 552 (Tex. App. 1983). Teachers and school administrators, it is said, act in loco parentis in their dealings with students: their authority is that of the parent, not the State, and is therefore not subject to the limits of the Fourth Amendment. Ibid.

Such reasoning is in tension with contemporary reality and the teachings of this Court. We have held school officials subject to the commands of the First Amendment, see Tinker v. Des Moines Independent Community School District, 393 U.S. 503 (1969), and the Due Process Clause of the Fourteenth Amendment, see Goss v. Lopez, 419 U.S. 565 (1975). If school authorities are state actors for purposes of the constitutional guarantees of freedom of expression and due process, it is difficult to understand why they should be deemed to be exercising parental rather than public authority when conducting searches of their students. More generally, the Court has recognized that "the concept of parental delegation" as a source of school authority is not entirely "consonant with compulsory education laws." Ingraham v. Wright, 430 U.S. 651, 662 (1977). Today's public school officials do not merely exercise authority voluntarily conferred on them by individual parents; rather, they act in furtherance of publicly mandated educational and disciplinary policies. See, e. g., the opinion in State ex rel. T.L.O., 94 N. J., at 343, 463 A. 2d, at 934, 940, describing the New Jersey statutes regulating school disciplinary policies and establishing the authority of school officials over their students. In carrying out searches and other disciplinary functions pursuant to such policies, school officials act as representatives of the State, not merely as surrogates for the parents, and they cannot claim the parents' immunity from the strictures of the Fourth Amendment.

III

To hold that the Fourth Amendment applies to searches conducted by school authorities is only to begin the inquiry into the standards governing such searches. Although the underlying command of the Fourth Amendment is always that searches and seizures be reasonable, what is reasonable depends on the context within which a search takes place. The determination of the standard of reasonableness governing any specific class of searches requires "balancing the need to search against the invasion which the search entails." Camara v. Municipal Court, supra, at 536-537. On one side of the balance are arrayed the individual's legitimate expectations of privacy and personal security; on the other, the government's need for effective methods to deal with breaches of public order.

We have recognized that even a limited search of the person is a substantial invasion of privacy. Terry v. Ohio, 392 U.S. 1, 24-25 (1967). We have also recognized that searches of closed items of personal luggage are intrusions on protected privacy interests, for "the Fourth Amendment provides protection to the owner of every container that conceals its contents from plain view." United States v. Ross, 456 U.S. 798, 822-823 (1982). A search of a child's person or of a closed purse or other bag carried on her person, no less than a similar search carried out on an adult, is undoubtedly a severe violation of subjective expectations of privacy.

Of course, the Fourth Amendment does not protect subjective expectations of privacy that are unreasonable or otherwise "illegitimate." See, e. g., Hudson v. Palmer, 468 U.S. 517 (1984); Rawlings v. Kentucky, 448 U.S. 98 (1980). To receive the protection of the Fourth Amendment, an expectation of privacy must be one that society is "prepared to recognize as legitimate." Hudson v. Palmer, supra, at 526. The State of New Jersey has argued that because of the pervasive supervision to which children in the schools are necessarily subject, a child has virtually no legitimate expectation of privacy in articles of personal property "unnecessarily" carried into a school. This argument has two factual premises: (1) the fundamental incompatibility of expectations of privacy with the maintenance of a sound educational environment; and (2) the minimal interest of the child in bringing any items of personal property into the school. Both premises are severely flawed.

Although this Court may take notice of the difficulty of maintaining discipline in the public schools today, the situation is not so dire that students in the schools may claim no legitimate expectations of privacy. We have recently recognized that the need to maintain order in a prison is such that prisoners retain no legitimate expectations of privacy in their cells, but it goes almost without saying that "[t]he prisoner and the schoolchild stand in wholly different circumstances, separated by the harsh facts of criminal conviction and incarceration." Ingraham v. Wright, supra, at 669. We are not yet ready to hold that the schools and the prisons need be equated for purposes of the Fourth Amendment.

Nor does the State's suggestion that children have no legitimate need to bring personal property into the schools seem well anchored in reality. Students at a minimum must bring to school not only the supplies needed for their studies, but also keys, money, and the necessaries of personal hygiene and grooming. In addition, students may carry on their persons or in purses or wallets such nondisruptive yet highly personal items as photographs, letters, and diaries. Finally, students may have perfectly legitimate reasons to carry with them articles of property needed in connection with extracurricular or recreational activities. In short, schoolchildren may find it necessary to carry with them a variety of legitimate, noncontraband items, and there is no reason to conclude that they have necessarily waived all rights to privacy in such items merely by bringing them onto school grounds.

Against the child's interest in privacy must be set the substantial interest of teachers and administrators in maintaining discipline in the classroom and on school grounds. Maintaining order in the classroom has never been easy, but in recent years, school disorder has often taken particularly ugly forms: drug use and violent crime in the schools have become major social problems. See generally 1 NIE, U.S. Dept. of Health, Education and Welfare, Violent Schools - Safe Schools: The Safe

School Study Report to the Congress (1978). Even in schools that have been spared the most severe disciplinary problems, the preservation of order and a proper educational environment requires close supervision of schoolchildren, as well as the enforcement of rules against conduct that would be perfectly permissible if undertaken by an adult. "Events calling for discipline are frequent occurrences and sometimes require immediate, effective action." Goss v. Lopez, 419 U.S., at 580. Accordingly, we have recognized that maintaining security and order in the schools requires a certain degree of flexibility in school disciplinary procedures, and we have respected the value of preserving the informality of the student-teacher relationship. See id., at 582-583; Ingraham v. Wright, 430 U.S., at 680-682.

How, then, should we strike the balance between the schoolchild's legitimate expectations of privacy and the school's equally legitimate need to maintain an environment in which learning can take place? It is evident that the school setting requires some easing of the restrictions to which searches by public authorities are ordinarily subject. The warrant requirement, in particular, is unsuited to the school environment: requiring a teacher to obtain a warrant before searching a child suspected of an infraction of school rules (or of the criminal law) would unduly interfere with the maintenance of the swift and informal disciplinary procedures needed in the schools. Just as we have in other cases dispensed with the warrant requirement when "the burden of obtaining a warrant is likely to frustrate the governmental purpose behind the search," Camara v. Municipal Court, 387 U.S., at 532-533, we hold today that school officials need not obtain a warrant before searching a student who is under their authority.

The school setting also requires some modification of the level of suspicion of illicit activity needed to justify a search. Ordinarily, a search - even one that may permissibly be carried out without a warrant - must be based upon "probable cause" to believe that a violation of the law has occurred. See, e. g., Almeida-Sanchez v. United States, 413 U.S. 266, 273 (1973); Sibron v. New York, 392 U.S. 40, 62-66 (1968). However, "probable cause" is not an irreducible requirement of a valid search. The fundamental command of the Fourth Amendment is that searches and seizures be reasonable, and although "both the concept of probable cause and the requirement of a warrant bear on the reasonableness of a search, . . . in certain limited circumstances neither is required." Almeida-Sanchez v. United States, supra, at 277 (POWELL, J., concurring). Thus, we have in a number of cases recognized the legality of searches and seizures based on suspicions that, although "reasonable," do not rise to the level of probable cause. See, e. g., Terry v. Ohio, 392 U.S. 1 (1968); United States v. Brignoni-Ponce, 422 U.S. 873, 881 (1975); Delaware v. Prouse, 440 U.S. 648, 654-655 (1979); United States v. Martinez-Fuerte, 428 U.S. 543 (1976); cf. Camara v. Municipal Court, supra, at 534-539. Where a careful balancing of governmental and private interests suggests that the public interest is best served by a Fourth Amendment standard of reasonableness that stops short of probable cause, we have not hesitated to adopt such a standard.

We join the majority of courts that have examined this issue in concluding that the accommodation of the privacy interests of schoolchildren with the substantial need of teachers and administrators for freedom to maintain order in the schools does not require strict adherence to the requirement that searches be based on probable cause to believe that the subject of the search has violated or is violating the law. Rather, the legality of a search of a student should depend simply on the reasonableness, under all the circumstances, of the search. Determining the reasonableness of any search involves a twofold inquiry: first, one must consider "whether the . . . action was justified at its inception," Terry v. Ohio, 392 U.S., at 20; second, one must determine whether the search as actually conducted "was reasonably related in scope to the circumstances which justified the interference in the first place," ibid. Under ordinary circumstances, a search of a student by a teacher or other school official will be "justified at its inception" when there are reasonable grounds for suspecting that the search will turn up evidence that the student has violated or is violating either the law or the rules of the school. Such a search will be permissible in its scope when the measures adopted are reasonably related to the objectives of the search and not excessively intrusive in light of the age and sex of the student and the nature of the infraction.

This standard will, we trust, neither unduly burden the efforts of school authorities to maintain order in their schools nor authorize unrestrained intrusions upon the privacy of schoolchildren. By focusing attention on the question of reasonableness, the standard will spare teachers and school administrators the necessity of schooling themselves in the niceties of probable cause and permit them to regulate their conduct according to the dictates of reason and common sense. At the same time, the reasonableness standard should ensure that the interests of students will be invaded no more than is necessary to achieve the legitimate end of preserving order in the schools.

IV

There remains the question of the legality of the search in this case. We recognize that the "reasonable grounds" standard applied by the New Jersey Supreme Court in its consideration of this question is not substantially different from the standard that we have adopted today. Nonetheless, we believe that the New Jersey court's application of that standard to strike down the search of T.L.O.'s purse reflects a somewhat crabbed notion of reasonableness. Our review of the facts surrounding the search leads us to conclude that the search was in no sense unreasonable for Fourth Amendment purposes.

The incident that gave rise to this case actually involved two separate searches, with the first - the search for cigarettes - providing the suspicion that gave rise to the second - the search for marihuana. Although it is the fruits of the second search that are at issue here, the validity of the search for marihuana must depend on the reasonableness of the initial search for cigarettes, as there would have been no reason to suspect that T.L.O. possessed marihuana had the first search not taken place. Accordingly, it is to the search for cigarettes that we first turn our attention.

The New Jersey Supreme Court pointed to two grounds for its holding that the search for cigarettes was unreasonable. First, the court observed that possession of cigarettes was not in itself illegal or a violation of school rules. Because the contents of T.L.O.'s purse would therefore have "no direct bearing on the infraction" of which she was accused (smoking in a lavatory where smoking was prohibited), there was no reason to search her purse.11 Second, even assuming that a search of T.L.O.'s purse might under some circumstances be reasonable in light of the accusation made against T.L.O., the New Jersey court concluded that Mr. Choplick in this particular case had no reasonable grounds to suspect that T.L.O. had cigarettes in her purse. At best, according to the court, Mr. Choplick had "a good hunch." 94 N. J., at 347, 463 A. 2d, at 942.

Both these conclusions are implausible. T.L.O. had been accused of smoking, and had denied the accusation in the strongest possible terms when she stated that she did not smoke at all. Surely it cannot be said that under these circumstances, T.L.O.'s possession of cigarettes would be irrelevant to the charges against her or to her response to those charges. T.L.O.'s possession of cigarettes, once it was discovered, would both corroborate the report that she had been smoking and undermine the credibility of her defense to the charge of smoking. To be sure, the discovery of the cigarettes would not prove that T.L.O. had been smoking in the lavatory; nor would it, strictly speaking, necessarily be inconsistent with her claim that she did not smoke at all. But it is universally recognized that evidence, to be relevant to an inquiry, need not conclusively prove the ultimate fact in issue, but only have "any tendency to make the existence of any fact that is of consequence to the determination of the action more probable or less probable than it would be without the evidence." Fed. Rule Evid. 401. The relevance of T.L.O.'s possession of cigarettes to the question whether she had been smoking and to the credibility of her denial that she smoked supplied the necessary "nexus" between the item searched for and the infraction under investigation. See Warden v. Hayden, 387 U.S. 294, 306-307 (1967). Thus, if Mr. Choplick in fact had a reasonable suspicion that T.L.O. had cigarettes in her purse, the search was justified despite the fact that the cigarettes, if found, would constitute "mere evidence" of a violation. Ibid.

Of course, the New Jersey Supreme Court also held that Mr. Choplick had no reasonable suspicion that the purse would contain cigarettes. This conclusion is puzzling. A teacher had reported that T.L.O. was smoking in the lavatory. Certainly this report gave Mr. Choplick reason to suspect that T.L.O. was carrying cigarettes with her; and if she did have cigarettes, her purse was the obvious place in which to find them. Mr. Choplick's suspicion that there were cigarettes in the purse was not an "inchoate and unparticularized suspicion or `hunch,'" Terry v. Ohio, 392 U.S., at 27; rather, it was the sort of "common-sense conclusio[n] about human behavior" upon which "practical people" - including government officials – are entitled to rely. United States v. Cortez, 449 U.S. 411, 418 (1981). Of course, even if the teacher's report were true, T.L.O. might not have had a pack of cigarettes with her; she might have borrowed a cigarette from someone else or have been sharing a cigarette with another student. But the requirement of reasonable suspicion is not a requirement of absolute certainty: "sufficient probability, not certainty, is the touchstone of reasonableness under the Fourth Amendment . . . ." Hill v. California, 401 U.S. 797, 804 (1971). Because the hypothesis that T.L.O. was carrying cigarettes in her purse was itself not unreasonable, it is irrelevant that other hypotheses were also consistent with the teacher's accusation. Accordingly, it cannot be said that Mr. Choplick acted unreasonably when he examined T.L.O.'s purse to see if it contained cigarettes.

Our conclusion that Mr. Choplick's decision to open T.L.O.'s purse was reasonable brings us to the question of the further search for marihuana once the pack of cigarettes was located. The suspicion upon which the search for marihuana was founded was provided when Mr. Choplick observed a package of rolling papers in the purse as he removed the pack of cigarettes.

Although T.L.O. does not dispute the reasonableness of Mr. Choplick's belief that the rolling papers indicated the presence of marihuana, she does contend that the scope of the search Mr. Choplick conducted exceeded permissible bounds when he seized and read certain letters that implicated T.L.O. in drug dealing. This argument, too, is unpersuasive. The discovery of the rolling papers concededly gave rise to a reasonable suspicion that T.L.O. was carrying marihuana as well as cigarettes in her purse. This suspicion justified further exploration of T.L.O.'s purse, which turned up more evidence of drug-related activities: a pipe, a number of plastic bags of the type commonly used to store marihuana, a small quantity of marihuana, and a fairly substantial amount of money. Under these circumstances, it was not unreasonable to extend the search to a separate zippered compartment of the purse; and when a search of that compartment revealed an index card containing a list of "people who owe me money" as well as two letters, the inference that T.L.O. was involved in marihuana trafficking was substantial enough to justify Mr. Choplick in examining the letters to determine whether they contained any further evidence. In short, we cannot conclude that the search for marihuana was unreasonable in any respect.

Because the search resulting in the discovery of the evidence of marihuana dealing by T.L.O. was reasonable, the New Jersey Supreme Court's decision to exclude that evidence from T.L.O.'s juvenile delinquency proceedings on Fourth Amendment grounds was erroneous. Accordingly, the judgment of the Supreme Court of New Jersey is

Reversed.

VERNONIA SCHOOL DIST. 47J v. ACTON
U.S. Supreme Court, 115 S. Ct. 2386 (1995)

JUSTICE SCALIA delivered the opinion of the Court.

The Student Athlete Drug Policy adopted by School District 47J in the town of Vernonia, Oregon, authorizes random urinalysis drug testing of students who participate in the District's school athletics programs. We granted certiorari to decide whether this violates the Fourth and Fourteenth Amendments to the United States Constitution.

I

A

Petitioner Vernonia School District 47J (District) operates one high school and three grade schools in the logging community of Vernonia, Oregon. As elsewhere in small-town America, school sports play a prominent role in the town's life, and student athletes are admired in their schools and in the community. . . .

In the mid-to-late 1980's, [Vernonia School District] teachers and administrators observed a sharp increase in drug use. . . .

[Eventually,] District officials began considering a drug-testing program. They held a parent "input night" to discuss the proposed Student Athlete Drug Policy (Policy), and the parents in attendance gave their unanimous approval. The school board approved the Policy for implementation in the fall of 1989. Its expressed purpose is to prevent student athletes from using drugs, to protect their health and safety, and to provide drug users with assistance programs.

B

The Policy applies to all students participating in interscholastic athletics. Students wishing to play sports must sign a form consenting to the testing and must obtain the written consent of their parents. Athletes are tested at the beginning of the season for their sport. In addition, once each week of the season the names of the athletes are placed in a "pool" from which a student, with the supervision of two adults, blindly draws the names of 10% of the athletes for random testing. Those selected are notified and tested that same day, if possible.

The student to be tested completes a specimen control form which bears an assigned number. Prescription medications that the student is taking must be identified by providing a copy of the prescription or a doctor's authorization. The student then enters an empty locker room accompanied by an adult monitor of the same sex. Each boy selected produces a sample at a urinal, remaining fully clothed with his back to the monitor, who stands approximately 12 to 15 feet behind the student. Monitors may (though do not always) watch the student while he produces the sample, and they listen for normal sounds of urination. Girls produce samples in an enclosed bathroom stall, so that they can be heard but not observed. After the sample is produced, it is given to the monitor, who checks it for temperature and tampering and then transfers it to a vial.

The samples are sent to an independent laboratory, which routinely tests them for amphetamines, cocaine, and marijuana. Other drugs, such as LSD, may be screened at the request of the District, but the identity of a particular student does not determine which drugs will be tested. The laboratory's procedures are 99.94% accurate. The District follows strict procedures regarding the chain of custody and access to test results. The laboratory does not know the identity of the students whose samples it tests. It is authorized to mail written test reports only to the superintendent and to provide test results to District personnel by telephone only after the requesting official recites a code confirming his authority. Only the superintendent, principals, vice-principals, and athletic directors have access to test results, and the results are not kept for more than one year.

If a sample tests positive, a second test is administered as soon as possible to confirm the result. If the second test is negative, no further action is taken. If the second test is positive, the athlete's parents are notified, and the school principal convenes a meeting with the student and his parents, at which the student is given the option of (1) participating for six weeks in an assistance program that includes weekly urinalysis, or (2) suffering suspension from athletics for the remainder of the current season and the next athletic season. The student is then retested prior to the start of the next athletic season for which he or she is eligible. The Policy states that a second offense results in automatic imposition of option (2); a third offense in suspension for the remainder of the current season and the next two athletic seasons.

C

In the fall of 1991, respondent James Acton, then a seventh-grader, signed up to play football at one of the District's grade schools. He was denied participation, however, because he and his parents refused to sign the testing consent forms. The Actons filed suit, seeking declaratory and injunctive relief from enforcement of the Policy on the grounds that it violated the Fourth and Fourteenth Amendments to the United States Constitution and Article I, 9, of the Oregon Constitution. After a bench trial, the District Court entered an order denying the claims on the merits and dismissing the action. 796 F. Supp., at 1355. The United States Court of Appeals for the Ninth Circuit reversed, holding that the Policy violated both the Fourth and Fourteenth Amendments and Article I, 9, of the Oregon Constitution. 23 F.3d 1514 (1994). We granted certiorari.

II

The Fourth Amendment to the United States Constitution provides that the Federal Government shall not violate "[t]he right of the people to be secure in their persons, houses, papers, and effects, against unreasonable searches and seizures, ..." We have held that the Fourteenth Amendment extends this constitutional guarantee to searches and seizures by state officers, Elkins v. United States, 364 U.S. 206, 213 (1960), including public school officials, New Jersey v. T. L. O., 469 U.S. 325, 336-337 (1985). In Skinner v. Railway Labor Executives' Assn., 489 U.S. 602, 617 (1989), we held that state-compelled collection and testing of urine, such as that required by the Student Athlete Drug Policy, constitutes a "search" subject to the demands of the Fourth Amendment. See also Treasury Employees v. Von Raab, 489 U.S. 656, 665 (1989).

As the text of the Fourth Amendment indicates, the ultimate measure of the constitutionality of a governmental search is "reasonableness." At least in a case such as this, where there was no clear practice, either approving or disapproving the type of search at issue, at the time the constitutional provision was enacted, whether a particular search meets the reasonableness standard "`is judged by balancing its intrusion on the individual's Fourth Amendment interests against its promotion of legitimate governmental interests.'" Skinner, supra, at 619 (quoting Delaware v. Prouse, 440 U.S. 648, 654 (1979)). Where a search is undertaken by law enforcement officials to discover evidence of criminal wrongdoing, this Court has said that reasonableness generally requires the obtaining of a judicial warrant, Skinner, supra, at 619. Warrants cannot be issued, of course, without the showing of probable cause required by the Warrant Clause. But a warrant is not required to establish the reasonableness of all government searches; and when a warrant is not required (and the Warrant Clause therefore not applicable), probable cause is not invariably required either. A search unsupported by probable cause can be constitutional, we have said, "when special needs, beyond the normal need for law enforcement, make the warrant and probable-cause requirement impracticable." Griffin v. Wisconsin, 483 U.S. 868, 873 (1987) (internal quotation marks omitted).

We have found such "special needs" to exist in the public-school context. There, the warrant requirement "would unduly interfere with the maintenance of the swift and informal disciplinary procedures [that are] needed," and "strict adherence to the requirement that searches be based upon probable cause" would undercut "the substantial need of teachers and administrators for freedom to maintain order in the schools." T. L. O., supra, at 340, 341. The school search we approved in T. L. O., while not based on probable cause, was based on individualized suspicion of wrongdoing. As we explicitly acknowledged, however, "`the Fourth Amendment imposes no irreducible requirement of such suspicion,'" id., at 342, n. 8 (quoting United States v. Martinez-Fuerte, 428 U.S. 543, 560-561 (1976)).

We have upheld suspicionless searches and seizures to conduct drug testing of railroad personnel involved in train accidents, see Skinner, supra; to conduct random drug testing of federal customs officers who carry arms or are involved in drug interdiction, see Von Raab, supra; and to maintain automobile checkpoints looking for illegal immigrants and contraband, Martinez-Fuerte, supra, and drunk drivers, Michigan Dept. of State Police v. Sitz, 496 U.S. 444 (1990).

III

The first factor to be considered is the nature of the privacy interest upon which the search here at issue intrudes. The Fourth Amendment does not protect all subjective expectations of privacy, but only those that society recognizes as "legitimate." T. L. O., 469 U.S., at 338. What expectations are legitimate varies, of course, with context, id., at 337, depending, for example, upon whether the individual asserting the privacy interest is at home, at work, in a car, or in a public park. In addition, the legitimacy of certain privacy expectations vis-a-vis the State may depend upon the individual's legal relationship with the State. For example, in Griffin, supra, we held that, although a "probationer's home, like anyone else's, is protected by the Fourth Amendmen[t]," the supervisory relationship between probationer and State justifies "a degree of impingement upon [a probationer's] privacy that would not be constitutional if applied to the public at large." 483 U.S., at 873, 875. Central, in our view, to the present case is the fact that the subjects of the Policy are (1) children, who (2) have been committed to the temporary custody of the State as schoolmaster.

Traditionally at common law, and still today, unemancipated minors lack some of the most fundamental rights of self-determination - including even the right of liberty in its narrow sense, i.e., the right to come and go at will. They are subject, even as to their physical freedom, to the control of their parents or guardians. See 59 Am. Jur. 2d 10 (1987). When parents place minor children in private schools for their education, the teachers and administrators of those schools stand in loco parentis over the children entrusted to them. In fact, the tutor or schoolmaster is the very prototype of that status. As Blackstone describes it, a parent "may . . . delegate part of his parental authority, during his life, to the tutor or schoolmaster of his child; who is then in loco parentis, and has such a portion of the power of the parent committed to his charge, viz. that of restraint and correction, as may be necessary to answer the purposes for which he is employed." 1 W. Blackstone, Commentaries on the Laws of England 441 (1769).

In T. L. O. we rejected the notion that public schools, like private schools, exercise only parental power over their students, which of course is not subject to constitutional constraints. T. L. O., 469 U.S., at 336. Such a view of things, we said, "is not entirely `consonant with compulsory education laws,'" ibid. (quoting Ingraham v. Wright, 430 U.S. 651, 662 (1977)), and is inconsistent with our prior decisions treating school officials as state actors for purposes of the Due Process and Free Speech Clauses, T. L. O., supra, at 336. But while denying that the State's power over schoolchildren is formally no more than the delegated power of their parents, T. L. O. did not deny, but indeed emphasized, that the nature of that power is custodial and tutelary, permitting a degree of supervision and control that could not be exercised over free adults. "[A] proper educational environment requires close supervision of schoolchildren, as well as the enforcement of rules against conduct that would be perfectly permissible if undertaken by an adult." 469 U.S., at 339. While we do not, of course, suggest that public schools as a general matter have such a degree of control over children as to give rise to a constitutional "duty to protect," see DeShaney v. Winnebago County Dept. of Social Servs., 489 U.S. 189, 200 (1989), we have acknowledged that for many purposes "school authorities ac[t] in loco parentis," Bethel School Dist. No. 403 v. Fraser, 478 U.S. 675, 684 (1986), with the power and indeed the duty to "inculcate the habits and manners of civility," id., at 681 (internal quotation marks omitted). Thus, while children assuredly do not "shed their constitutional rights . . . at the schoolhouse gate," Tinker v. Des Moines Independent Community School Dist., 393 U.S. 503, 506 (1969), the nature of those rights is what is appropriate for children in school. See, e.g., Goss v. Lopez, 419 U.S. 565, 581-582 (1975) (due process for a student challenging disciplinary suspension requires only that the teacher "informally discuss the alleged misconduct with the student minutes after it has occurred"); Fraser, supra, at 683 ("[I]t is a highly appropriate function of public school education to prohibit the use of vulgar and offensive terms in public discourse"); Hazlewood School Dist. v. Kuhlmeier, 484 U.S. 260, 273 (1988) (public school authorities may censor school-sponsored publications, so long as the censorship is "reasonably related to legitimate pedagogical concerns"); Ingraham, supra, at 682 ("[I]mposing additional administrative safeguards [upon corporal punishment] . . . would . . . entail a significant intrusion into an area of primary educational responsibility").

Fourth Amendment rights, no less than First and Fourteenth Amendment rights, are different in public schools than elsewhere; the "reasonableness" inquiry cannot disregard the schools' custodial and tutelary responsibility for children. For their own good and that of their classmates, public school children are routinely required to submit to various physical examinations, and to be vaccinated against various diseases. According to the American Academy of Pediatrics, most public schools "provide vision and hearing screening and dental and dermatological checks. . . . Others also mandate scoliosis screening at appropriate grade levels." Committee on School Health, American Academy of Pediatrics, School Health: A Guide for Health Professionals 2 (1987). In the 1991-1992 school year, all 50 States required public-school students to be vaccinated against diphtheria, measles, rubella, and polio. U.S. Dept. of Health & Human Services, Public Health Service, Centers for Disease Control, State Immunization Requirements 1991-1992, p. 1. Particularly with regard to medical examinations and procedures, therefore, "students within the school environment have a lesser expectation of privacy than members of the population generally." T.L.O., 469 U.S., at 348 (Powell, J., concurring).

Legitimate privacy expectations are even less with regard to student athletes. School sports are not for the bashful. They require "suiting up" before each practice or event, and showering and changing afterwards. Public school locker rooms, the usual sites for these activities, are not notable for the privacy they afford. The locker rooms in Vernonia are typical: no individual dressing rooms are provided; shower heads are lined up along a wall, unseparated by any sort of partition or curtain; not even all the toilet stalls have doors. As the United States Court of Appeals for the Seventh Circuit has noted, there is "an element of `communal undress' inherent in athletic participation," Schaill by Kross v. Tippecanoe County School Corp., 864 F.2d 1309, 1318 (1988).

There is an additional respect in which school athletes have a reduced expectation of privacy. By choosing to "go out for the team," they voluntarily subject themselves to a degree of regulation even higher than that imposed on students generally. In Vernonia's public schools, they must submit to a preseason physical exam (James testified that his included the giving of a urine sample, App. 17), they must acquire adequate insurance coverage or sign an insurance waiver, maintain a minimum grade point average, and comply with any "rules of conduct, dress, training hours and related matters as may be established for each sport by the head coach and athletic director with the principal's approval." Somewhat like adults who choose to participate in a "closely regulated industry," students who voluntarily participate in school athletics have reason to expect intrusions upon normal rights and privileges, including privacy. See Skinner, 489 U.S., at 627; United States v. Biswell, 406 U.S. 311, 316 (1972).

IV

Having considered the scope of the legitimate expectation of privacy at issue here, we turn next to the character of the intrusion that is complained of. We recognized in Skinner that collecting the samples for urinalysis intrudes upon "an excretory function traditionally shielded by great privacy." Skinner, 489 U.S., at 626. We noted, however, that the degree of intrusion depends upon the manner in which production of the urine sample is monitored. Ibid. Under the District's Policy, male students produce samples at a urinal along a wall. They remain fully clothed and are only observed from behind, if at all. Female students produce samples in an enclosed stall, with a female monitor standing outside listening only for sounds of tampering. These conditions are nearly identical to those typically encountered in public restrooms, which men, women, and especially school children use daily. Under such conditions, the privacy interests compromised by the process of obtaining the urine sample are in our view negligible. The other privacy-invasive aspect of urinalysis is, of course, the information it discloses concerning the state of the subject's body, and the materials he has ingested. In this regard it is significant that the tests at issue here look only for drugs, and not for whether the student is, for example, epileptic, pregnant, or diabetic. See Skinner, supra, at 617. Moreover, the drugs for which the samples are screened are standard, and do not vary according to the identity of the student. And finally, the results of the tests are disclosed only to a limited class of school personnel who have a need to know; and they are not turned over to law enforcement authorities or used for any internal disciplinary function. 796 F. Supp., at 1364; see also 23 F.3d, at 1521.

Respondents argue, however, that the District's Policy is in fact more intrusive than this suggests, because it requires the students, if they are to avoid sanctions for a falsely positive test, to identify in advance prescription medications they are taking. We agree that this raises some cause for concern. In Von Raab, we flagged as one of the salutary features of the Customs Service drug-testing program the fact that employees were not required to disclose medical information unless they tested positive, and, even then, the information was supplied to a licensed physician rather than to the Government employer. See Von Raab, 489 U.S., at 672-673, n. 2. On the other hand, we have never indicated that requiring advance disclosure of medications is per se unreasonable. Indeed, in Skinner we held that it was not "a significant invasion of privacy." Skinner, 489 U.S., at 626, n. 7. It can be argued that, in Skinner, the disclosure went only to the medical personnel taking the sample, and the Government personnel analyzing it, see id., at 609, but see id., at 610 (railroad personnel responsible for forwarding the sample, and presumably accompanying information, to the Government's testing lab); and that disclosure to teachers and coaches - to persons who personally know the student - is a greater invasion of privacy. Assuming for the sake of argument that both those propositions are true, we do not believe they establish a difference that respondents are entitled to rely on here.

The General Authorization Form that respondents refused to sign, which refusal was the basis for James's exclusion from the sports program, said only (in relevant part): "I . . . authorize the Vernonia School District to conduct a test on a urine specimen which I provide to test for drugs and/or alcohol use. I also authorize the release of information concerning the results of such a test to the Vernonia School District and to the parents and/or guardians of the student." App. 10-11. While the practice of the District seems to have been to have a school official take medication information from the student at the time of the test, see App. 29, 42, that practice is not set forth in, or required by, the Policy, which says simply: "Student athletes who . . . are or have been taking prescription medication must provide verification (either by a copy of the prescription or by doctor's authorization) prior to being tested." App. 8. It may well be that, if and when James was selected for random testing at a time that he was taking medication, the School District would have permitted him to provide the requested information in a confidential manner - for example, in a sealed envelope delivered to the testing lab. Nothing in the Policy contradicts that, and when respondents choose, in effect, to challenge the Policy on its face, we will not assume the worst. Accordingly, we reach the same conclusion as in Skinner: that the invasion of privacy was not significant.

V

Finally, we turn to consider the nature and immediacy of the governmental concern at issue here, and the efficacy of this means for meeting it. In both Skinner and Von Raab, we characterized the government interest motivating the search as "compelling." Skinner, supra, at 628 (interest in preventing railway accidents); Von Raab, supra, at 670 (interest in insuring fitness of customs officials to interdict drugs and handle firearms). Relying on these cases, the District Court held that because the District's program also called for drug testing in the absence of individualized suspicion, the District "must demonstrate a `compelling need' for the program." 796 F. Supp., at 1363. The Court of Appeals appears to have agreed with this view. See 23 F.3d, at 1526. It is a mistake, however, to think that the phrase "compelling state interest," in the Fourth Amendment context, describes a fixed, minimum quantum of governmental concern, so that one can dispose of a case by answering in isolation the question: Is there a compelling state interest here? Rather, the phrase describes an interest which appears important enough to justify the particular search at hand, in light of other factors which show the search to be relatively intrusive upon a genuine expectation of privacy. Whether that relatively high degree of government concern is necessary in this case or not, we think it is met.

That the nature of the concern is important - indeed, perhaps compelling can hardly be doubted. Deterring drug use by our Nation's schoolchildren is at least as important as enhancing efficient enforcement of the Nation's laws against the importation of drugs, which was the governmental concern in Von Raab, supra, at 668, or deterring drug use by engineers and trainmen, which was the governmental concern in Skinner, supra, at 628. School years are the time when the physical, psychological, and addictive effects of drugs are most severe. "Maturing nervous systems are more critically impaired by intoxicants than mature ones are; childhood losses in learning are lifelong and profound"; "children grow chemically dependent more quickly than adults, and their record of recovery is depressingly poor." Hawley, The Bumpy Road to Drug-Free Schools, 72 Phi Delta Kappan 310, 314 (1990). See also Estroff, Schwartz, & Hoffmann, Adolescent Cocaine Abuse: Addictive Potential, Behavioral and Psychiatric Effects, 28 Clinical Pediatrics 550 (Dec. 1989); Kandel, Davies, Karus, & Yamaguchi, The Consequences in Young Adulthood of Adolescent Drug Involvement, 43 Arch. Gen. Psychiatry 746 (Aug. 1986). And of course the effects of a drug-infested school are visited not just upon the users, but upon the entire student body and faculty, as the educational process is disrupted. In the present case, moreover, the necessity for the State to act is magnified by the fact that this evil is being visited not just upon individuals at large, but upon children for whom it has undertaken a special responsibility of care and direction. Finally, it must not be lost sight of that this program is directed more narrowly to drug use by school athletes, where the risk of immediate physical harm to the drug user or those with whom he is playing his sport is particularly high. Apart from psychological effects, which include impairment of judgment, slow reaction time, and a lessening of the perception of pain, the particular drugs screened by the District's Policy have been demonstrated to pose substantial physical risks to athletes. Amphetamines produce an "artificially induced heart rate increase, [p]eripheral vasoconstriction, [b]lood pressure increase, and [m]asking of the normal fatigue response," making them a "very dangerous drug when used during exercise of any type." Hawkins, Drugs and Other Ingesta: Effects on Athletic Performance, in H. Appenzeller, Managing Sports and Risk Management Strategies 90, 90-91 (1993). Marijuana causes "[i]rregular blood pressure responses during changes in body position," "[r]eduction in the oxygen-carrying capacity of the blood," and "[i]nhibition of the normal sweating responses resulting in increased body temperature." Id., at 94. Cocaine produces "[v]asoconstriction[,] [e]levated blood pressure," and "[p]ossible coronary artery spasms and myocardial infarction." Ibid.

As for the immediacy of the District's concerns: We are not inclined to question - indeed, we could not possibly find clearly erroneous - the District Court's conclusion that "a large segment of the student body, particularly those involved in interscholastic athletics, was in a state of rebellion," that "[d]isciplinary actions had reached `epidemic proportions,'" and that "the rebellion was being fueled by alcohol and drug abuse as well as by the student's misperceptions about the drug culture." 796 F. Supp., at 1357. That is an immediate crisis of greater proportions than existed in Skinner, where we upheld the Government's drug testing program based on findings of drug use by railroad employees nationwide, without proof that a problem existed on the particular railroads whose employees were subject to the test. See Skinner, 489 U.S., at 607. And of much greater proportions than existed in Von Raab, where there was no documented history of drug use by any customs officials. See Von Raab, 489 U.S., at 673; id., at 683 (SCALIA, J., dissenting).

As to the efficacy of this means for addressing the problem: It seems to us self-evident that a drug problem largely fueled by the "role model" effect of athletes' drug use, and of particular danger to athletes, is effectively addressed by making sure that athletes do not use drugs. Respondents argue that a "less intrusive means to the same end" was available, namely, "drug testing on suspicion of drug use." Brief for Respondents 45-46. We have repeatedly refused to declare that only the "least intrusive" search practicable can be reasonable under the Fourth Amendment. Skinner, supra, at 629, n. 9 (collecting cases). Respondents' alternative entails substantial difficulties - if it is indeed practicable at all. It may be impracticable, for one thing, simply because the parents who are willing to accept random drug testing for athletes are not willing to accept accusatory drug testing for all students, which transforms the process into a badge of shame. Respondents' proposal brings the risk that teachers will impose testing arbitrarily upon troublesome but not drug-likely students. It generates the expense of defending lawsuits that charge such arbitrary imposition, or that simply demand greater process before accusatory drug testing is imposed. And not least of all, it adds to the ever-expanding diversionary duties of schoolteachers the new function of spotting and bringing to account drug abuse, a task for which they are ill prepared, and which is not readily compatible with their vocation. Cf. Skinner, supra, at 628 (quoting 50 Fed. Reg. 31526 (1985)) (a drug impaired individual "will seldom display any outward `signs detectable by the lay person or, in many cases, even the physician.'"); Goss, 419 U.S., at 594 (Powell, J., dissenting) ("There is an ongoing relationship, one in which the teacher must occupy many roles - educator, adviser, friend, and, at times, parent-substitute. It is rarely adversary in nature . . .") (footnote omitted). In many respects, we think, testing based on "suspicion" of drug use would not be better, but worse.

VI

Taking into account all the factors we have considered above - the decreased expectation of privacy, the relative unobtrusiveness of the search, and the severity of the need met by the search - we conclude Vernonia's Policy is reasonable and hence constitutional.

We caution against the assumption that suspicionless drug testing will readily pass constitutional muster in other contexts. The most significant element in this case is the first we discussed: that the Policy was undertaken in furtherance of the government's responsibilities, under a public school system, as guardian and tutor of children entrusted to its care. Just as when the government conducts a search in its capacity as employer (a warrantless search of an absent employee's desk to obtain an urgently needed file, for example), the relevant question is whether that intrusion upon privacy is one that a reasonable employer might engage in, see O'Connor v. Ortega, 480 U.S. 709 (1987); so also when the government acts as guardian and tutor the relevant question is whether the search is one that a reasonable guardian and tutor might undertake. Given the findings of need made by the District Court, we conclude that in the present case it is.

We may note that the primary guardians of Vernonia's schoolchildren appear to agree. The record shows no objection to this districtwide program by any parents other than the couple before us here - even though, as we have described, a public meeting was held to obtain parents' views. We find insufficient basis to contradict the judgment of Vernonia's parents, its school board, and the District Court, as to what was reasonably in the interest of these children under the circumstances.

* * *

The Ninth Circuit held that Vernonia's Policy not only violated the Fourth Amendment, but also, by reason of that violation, contravened Article I, 9 of the Oregon Constitution. Our conclusion that the former holding was in error means that the latter holding rested on a flawed premise. We therefore vacate the judgment, and remand the case to the Court of Appeals for further proceedings consistent with this opinion.

It is so ordered.

BOARD OF EDUCATION v. EARLS
U.S. Supreme Court, June 27, 2002

JUSTICE THOMAS delivered the opinion of the Court.

The Student Activities Drug Testing Policy implemented by the Board of Education of Independent School District No. 92 of Pottawatomie County (School District) requires all students who participate in competitive extracurricular activities to submit to drug testing. Because this Policy reasonably serves the School District's important interest in detecting and preventing drug use among its students, we hold that it is constitutional.

I

The city of Tecumseh, Oklahoma, is a rural community located approximately 40 miles southeast of Oklahoma City. The School District administers all Tecumseh public schools. In the fall of 1998, the School District adopted the Student Activities Drug Testing Policy (Policy), which requires all middle and high school students to consent to drug testing in order to participate in any extracurricular activity. In practice, the Policy has been applied only to competitive extracurricular activities sanctioned by the Oklahoma Secondary Schools Activities Association, such as the Academic Team, Future Farmers of America, Future Homemakers of America, band, choir, pom pon, cheerleading, and athletics. Under the Policy, students are required to take a drug test before participating in an extracurricular activity, must submit to random drug testing while participating in that activity, and must agree to be tested at any time upon reasonable suspicion. The urinalysis tests are designed to detect only the use of illegal drugs, including amphetamines, marijuana, cocaine, opiates, and barbituates, not medical conditions or the presence of authorized prescription medications.

At the time of their suit, both respondents attended Tecumseh High School. Respondent Lindsay Earls was a member of the show choir, the marching band, the Academic Team, and the National Honor Society. Respondent Daniel James sought to participate in the Academic Team.1 Together with their parents, Earls and James brought a 42 U. S. C. §1983 action against the School District, challenging the Policy both on its face and as applied to their participation in extracurricular activities.2 They alleged that the Policy violates the Fourth Amendment as incorporated by the Fourteenth Amendment and requested injunctive and declarative relief. They also argued that the School District failed to identify a special need for testing students who participate in extracurricular activities, and that the "Drug Testing Policy neither addresses a proven problem nor promises to bring any benefit to students or the school." App. 9.

Applying the principles articulated in Vernonia School Dist. 47J v. Acton, 515 U. S. 646 (1995), in which we upheld the suspicionless drug testing of school athletes, the United States District Court for the Western District of Oklahoma rejected respondents' claim that the Policy was unconstitutional and granted summary judgment to the School District. The court noted that "special needs" exist in the public school context and that, although the School District did "not show a drug problem of epidemic proportions," there was a history of drug abuse starting in 1970 that presented "legitimate cause for concern." 115 F. Supp. 2d 1281, 1287 (2000). The District Court also held that the Policy was effective because "[i]t can scarcely be disputed that the drug problem among the student body is effectively addressed by making sure that the large number of students participating in competitive, extracurricular activities do not use drugs." Id., at 1295.

The United States Court of Appeals for the Tenth Circuit reversed, holding that the Policy violated the Fourth Amendment. The Court of Appeals agreed with the District Court that the Policy must be evaluated in the "unique environment of the school setting," but reached a different conclusion as to the Policy's constitutionality. 242 F. 3d 1264, 1270 (2001). Before imposing a suspicionless drug testing program, the Court of Appeals concluded that a school "must demonstrate that there is some identifiable drug abuse problem among a sufficient number of those subject to the testing, such that testing that group of students will actually redress its drug problem." Id., at 1278. The Court of Appeals then held that because the School District failed to demonstrate such a problem existed among Tecumseh students participating in competitive extracurricular activities, the Policy was unconstitutional. We granted certiorari, 534 U. S. 1015 (2001), and now reverse.

II

The Fourth Amendment to the United States Constitution protects "[t]he right of the people to be secure in their persons, houses, papers, and effects, against unreasonable searches and seizures." Searches by public school officials, such as the collection of urine samples, implicate Fourth Amendment interests. See Vernonia, supra, at 652; cf. New Jersey v. T. L. O., 469 U. S. 325, 334 (1985). We must therefore review the School District's Policy for "reasonableness," which is the touchstone of the constitutionality of a governmental search.

In the criminal context, reasonableness usually requires a showing of probable cause. See, e.g., Skinner v. Railway Labor Executives' Assn., 489 U. S. 602, 619 (1989). The probable-cause standard, however, "is peculiarly related to criminal investigations" and may be unsuited to determining the reasonableness of administrative searches where the "Government seeks to prevent the development of hazardous conditions." Treasury Employees v. Von Raab, 489 U. S. 656, 667-668 (1989) (internal quotation marks and citations omitted) (collecting cases). The Court has also held that a warrant and finding of probable cause are unnecessary in the public school context because such requirements " `would unduly interfere with the maintenance of the swift and informal disciplinary procedures [that are] needed.' " Vernonia, supra, at 653 (quoting T. L. O., supra, at 340-341).

Given that the School District's Policy is not in any way related to the conduct of criminal investigations, see Part II-B, infra, respondents do not contend that the School District requires probable cause before testing students for drug use. Respondents instead argue that drug testing must be based at least on some level of individualized suspicion. See Brief for Respondents 12-14. It is true that we generally determine the reasonableness of a search by balancing the nature of the intrusion on the individual's privacy against the promotion of legitimate governmental interests. See Delaware v. Prouse, 440 U. S. 648, 654 (1979). But we have long held that "the Fourth Amendment imposes no irreducible requirement of [individualized] suspicion." United States v. Martinez-Fuerte, 428 U. S. 543, 561 (1976). "[I]n certain limited circumstances, the Government's need to discover such latent or hidden conditions, or to prevent their development, is sufficiently compelling to justify the intrusion on privacy entailed by conducting such searches without any measure of individualized suspicion." Von Raab, supra, at 668; see also Skinner, supra, at 624. Therefore, in the context of safety and administrative regulations, a search unsupported by probable cause may be reasonable "when `special needs, beyond the normal need for law enforcement, make the warrant and probable-cause requirement impracticable.' " Griffin v. Wisconsin, 483 U. S. 868, 873 (1987) (quoting T. L. O., supra, at 351 (Blackmun, J., concurring in judgment)); see also Vernonia, supra, at 653; Skinner, supra, at 619.

Significantly, this Court has previously held that "special needs" inhere in the public school context. See Vernonia, supra, at 653; T. L. O., supra, at 339-340. While schoolchildren do not shed their constitutional rights when they enter the schoolhouse, see Tinker v. Des Moines Independent Community School Dist., 393 U. S. 503, 506 (1969), "Fourth Amendment rights ... are different in public schools than elsewhere; the `reasonableness' inquiry cannot disregard the schools' custodial and tutelary responsibility for children." Vernonia, supra, at 656. In particular, a finding of individualized suspicion may not be necessary when a school conducts drug testing.

In Vernonia, this Court held that the suspicionless drug testing of athletes was constitutional. The Court, however, did not simply authorize all school drug testing, but rather conducted a fact-specific balancing of the intrusion on the children's Fourth Amendment rights against the promotion of legitimate governmental interests. See 515 U. S., at 652-653. Applying the principles of Vernonia to the somewhat different facts of this case, we conclude that Tecumseh's Policy is also constitutional.

A

We first consider the nature of the privacy interest allegedly compromised by the drug testing. See id., at 654. As in

Vernonia, the context of the public school environment serves as the backdrop for the analysis of the privacy interest at stake and the reasonableness of the drug testing policy in general. See ibid. ("Central ... is the fact that the subjects of the Policy are (1) children, who (2) have been committed to the temporary custody of the State as schoolmaster"); see also id., at 665 ("The most significant element in this case is the first we discussed: that the Policy was undertaken in furtherance of the government's responsibilities, under a public school system, as guardian and tutor of children entrusted to its care"); ibid. ("[W]hen the government acts as guardian and tutor the relevant question is whether the search is one that a reasonable guardian and tutor might undertake").

A student's privacy interest is limited in a public school environment where the State is responsible for maintaining discipline, health, and safety. Schoolchildren are routinely required to submit to physical examinations and vaccinations against disease. See id., at 656. Securing order in the school environment sometimes requires that students be subjected to greater controls than those appropriate for adults. See T. L. O., supra, at 350 (Powell, J., concurring) ("Without first establishing discipline and maintaining order, teachers cannot begin to educate their students. And apart from education, the school has the obligation to protect pupils from mistreatment by other children, and also to protect teachers themselves from violence by the few students whose conduct in recent years has prompted national concern").

Respondents argue that because children participating in nonathletic extracurricular activities are not subject to regular physicals and communal undress, they have a stronger expectation of privacy than the athletes tested in Vernonia. See Brief for Respondents 18-20. This distinction, however, was not essential to our decision in Vernonia, which depended primarily upon the school's custodial responsibility and authority.3

In any event, students who participate in competitive extracurricular activities voluntarily subject themselves to many of the same intrusions on their privacy as do athletes.4 Some of these clubs and activities require occasional off-campus travel and communal undress. All of them have their own rules and requirements for participating students that do not apply to the student body as a whole. 115 F. Supp. 2d, at 1289-1290. For example, each of the competitive extracurricular activities governed by the Policy must abide by the rules of the Oklahoma Secondary Schools Activities Association, and a faculty sponsor monitors the students for compliance with the various rules dictated by the clubs and activities. See id., at 1290. This regulation of extracurricular activities further diminishes the expectation of privacy among schoolchildren. Cf. Vernonia, supra, at 657 ("Somewhat like adults who choose to participate in a closely regulated industry, students who voluntarily participate in school athletics have reason to expect intrusions upon normal rights and privileges, including privacy" (internal quotation marks omitted)). We therefore conclude that the students affected by this Policy have a limited expectation of privacy.

B

Next, we consider the character of the intrusion imposed by the Policy. See Vernonia, supra, at 658. Urination is "an excretory function traditionally shielded by great privacy." Skinner, 489 U. S., at 626. But the "degree of intrusion" on one's privacy caused by collecting a urine sample "depends upon the manner in which production of the urine sample is monitored." Vernonia, supra, at 658.

Under the Policy, a faculty monitor waits outside the closed restroom stall for the student to produce a sample and must "listen for the normal sounds of urination in order to guard against tampered specimens and to insure an accurate chain of custody." App. 199. The monitor then pours the sample into two bottles that are sealed and placed into a mailing pouch along with a consent form signed by the student. This procedure is virtually identical to that reviewed in Vernonia, except that it additionally protects privacy by allowing male students to produce their samples behind a closed stall. Given that we considered the method of collection in Vernonia a "negligible" intrusion, 515 U. S., at 658, the method here is even less problematic.

In addition, the Policy clearly requires that the test results be kept in confidential files separate from a student's other educational records and released to school personnel only on a "need to know" basis. Respondents nonetheless contend that the intrusion on students' privacy is significant because the Policy fails to protect effectively against the disclosure of confidential information and, specifically, that the school "has been careless in protecting that information: for example, the Choir teacher looked at students' prescription drug lists and left them where other students could see them." Brief for Respondents 24. But the choir teacher is someone with a "need to know," because during off-campus trips she needs to know what medications are taken by her students. Even before the Policy was enacted the choir teacher had access to this information. See App. 132. In any event, there is no allegation that any other student did see such information. This one example of alleged carelessness hardly increases the character of the intrusion.

Moreover, the test results are not turned over to any law enforcement authority. Nor do the test results here lead to the imposition of discipline or have any academic consequences. Cf. Vernonia, supra, at 658, and n. 2. Rather, the only consequence of a failed drug test is to limit the student's privilege of participating in extracurricular activities. Indeed, a student may test positive for drugs twice and still be allowed to participate in extracurricular activities. After the first positive test, the school contacts the student's parent or guardian for a meeting. The student may continue to participate in the activity if within five days of the meeting the student shows proof of receiving drug counseling and submits to a second drug test in two weeks. For the second positive test, the student is suspended from participation in all extracurricular activities for 14 days, must complete four hours of substance abuse counseling, and must submit to monthly drug tests. Only after a third positive test will the student be suspended from participating in any extracurricular activity for the remainder of the school year, or 88 school days, whichever is longer. See App. 201-202.

Given the minimally intrusive nature of the sample collection and the limited uses to which the test results are put, we conclude that the invasion of students' privacy is not significant.

C

Finally, this Court must consider the nature and immediacy of the government's concerns and the efficacy of the Policy in meeting them. See Vernonia, 515 U. S., at 660. This Court has already articulated in detail the importance of the governmental concern in preventing drug use by schoolchildren. See id., at 661-662. The drug abuse problem among our Nation's youth has hardly abated since Vernonia was decided in 1995. In fact, evidence suggests that it has only grown worse.5 As in Vernonia, "the necessity for the State to act is magnified by the fact that this evil is being visited not just upon individuals at large, but upon children for whom it has undertaken a special responsibility of care and direction." Id., at 662. The health and safety risks identified in Vernonia apply with equal force to Tecumseh's children. Indeed, the nationwide drug epidemic makes the war against drugs a pressing concern in every school.

Additionally, the School District in this case has presented specific evidence of drug use at Tecumseh schools. Teachers testified that they had seen students who appeared to be under the influence of drugs and that they had heard students speaking openly about using drugs. See, e.g., App. 72 (deposition of Dean Rogers); id., at 115 (deposition of Sheila Evans). A drug dog found marijuana cigarettes near the school parking lot. Police officers once found drugs or drug paraphernalia in a car driven by a Future Farmers of America member. And the school board president reported that people in the community were calling the board to discuss the "drug situation." See 115 F. Supp. 2d, at 1285-1286. We decline to second- guess the finding of the District Court that "[v]iewing the evidence as a whole, it cannot be reasonably disputed that the [School District] was faced with a `drug problem' when it adopted the Policy." Id., at 1287.

Respondents consider the proffered evidence insufficient and argue that there is no "real and immediate interest" to justify a policy of drug testing nonathletes. Brief for Respondents 32. We have recognized, however, that "[a] demonstrated problem of drug abuse ... [is] not in all cases necessary to the validity of a testing regime," but that some showing does "shore up an assertion of special need for a suspicionless general search program." Chandler v. Miller, 520 U. S. 305, 319 (1997). The School District has provided sufficient evidence to shore up the need for its drug testing program.

Furthermore, this Court has not required a particularized or pervasive drug problem before allowing the government to conduct suspicionless drug testing. For instance, in Von Raab the Court upheld the drug testing of customs officials on a purely preventive basis, without any documented history of drug use by such officials. See 489 U. S., at 673. In response to the lack of evidence relating to drug use, the Court noted generally that "drug abuse is one of the most serious problems confronting our society today," and that programs to prevent and detect drug use among customs officials could not be deemed unreasonable. Id., at 674; cf. Skinner, 489 U. S., at 607, and n. 1 (noting nationwide studies that identified on-the-job alcohol and drug use by railroad employees). Likewise, the need to prevent and deter the substantial harm of childhood drug use provides the necessary immediacy for a school testing policy. Indeed, it would make little sense to require a school district to wait for a substantial portion of its students to begin using drugs before it was allowed to institute a drug testing program designed to deter drug use.

Given the nationwide epidemic of drug use, and the evidence of increased drug use in Tecumseh schools, it was entirely reasonable for the School District to enact this particular drug testing policy. We reject the Court of Appeals' novel test that "any district seeking to impose a random suspicionless drug testing policy as a condition to participation in a school activity must demonstrate that there is some identifiable drug abuse problem among a sufficient number of those subject to the testing, such that testing that group of students will actually redress its drug problem." 242 F. 3d, at 1278. Among other problems, it would be difficult to administer such a test. As we cannot articulate a threshold level of drug use that would suffice to justify a drug testing program for schoolchildren, we refuse to fashion what would in effect be a constitutional quantum of drug use necessary to show a "drug problem."

Respondents also argue that the testing of nonathletes does not implicate any safety concerns, and that safety is a "crucial factor" in applying the special needs framework. Brief for Respondents 25-27. They contend that there must be "surpassing safety interests," Skinner, supra, at 634, or "extraordinary safety and national security hazards," Von Raab, supra, at 674, in order to override the usual protections of the Fourth Amendment. See Brief for Respondents 25-26. Respondents are correct that safety factors into the special needs analysis, but the safety interest furthered by drug testing is undoubtedly substantial for all children, athletes and nonathletes alike. We know all too well that drug use carries a variety of health risks for children, including death from overdose.

We also reject respondents' argument that drug testing must presumptively be based upon an individualized reasonable suspicion of wrongdoing because such a testing regime would be less intrusive. See id., at 12-16. In this context, the Fourth Amendment does not require a finding of individualized suspicion, see supra, at 5, and we decline to impose such a requirement on schools attempting to prevent and detect drug use by students. Moreover, we question whether testing based on individualized suspicion in fact would be less intrusive. Such a regime would place an additional burden on public school teachers who are already tasked with the difficult job of maintaining order and discipline. A program of individualized suspicion might unfairly target members of unpopular groups. The fear of lawsuits resulting from such targeted searches may chill enforcement of the program, rendering it ineffective in combating drug use. See Vernonia, 515 U. S., at 663-664 (offering similar reasons for why "testing based on `suspicion' of drug use would not be better, but worse"). In any case, this Court has repeatedly stated that reasonableness under the Fourth Amendment does not require employing the least intrusive means, because "[t]he logic of such elaborate less-restrictive-alternative arguments could raise insuperable barriers to the exercise of virtually all search-and-seizure powers." Martinez-Fuerte, 428 U. S., at 556-557, n. 12; see also Skinner, supra, at 624 ("[A] showing of individualized suspicion is not a constitutional floor, below which a search must be presumed unreasonable").

Finally, we find that testing students who participate in extracurricular activities is a reasonably effective means of addressing the School District's legitimate concerns in preventing, deterring, and detecting drug use. While in Vernonia there might have been a closer fit between the testing of athletes and the trial court's finding that the drug problem was "fueled by the `role model' effect of athletes' drug use," such a finding was not essential to the holding. 515 U. S., at 663; cf. id., at 684-685 (O'Connor, J., dissenting) (questioning the extent of the drug problem, especially as applied to athletes). Vernonia did not require the school to test the group of students most likely to use drugs, but rather considered the constitutionality of the program in the context of the public school's custodial responsibilities. Evaluating the Policy in this context, we conclude that the drug testing of Tecumseh students who participate in extracurricular activities effectively serves the School District's interest in protecting the safety and health of its students.

III

Within the limits of the Fourth Amendment, local school boards must assess the desirability of drug testing schoolchildren. In upholding the constitutionality of the Policy, we express no opinion as to its wisdom. Rather, we hold only that Tecumseh's Policy is a reasonable means of furthering the School District's important interest in preventing and deterring drug use among its schoolchildren. Accordingly, we reverse the judgment of the Court of Appeals.

It is so ordered.

Appendix B

A Note About Child Abuse

As a professional educator, you are a mandatory reporter of suspected child abuse. The law requires you to report suspected child abuse. States can revoke professional licenses for failure to report and/or investigate suspected child abuse (and they have indeed done so). If you think a child is being abused, you must report it to the state department that handles child abuse cases, or to the police.
Please remember three important points:

1. In most states, your legal duty as a mandatory reporter is continuous, 24 hours a day, 7 days a week, 12 months of the year. Wherever you see it, whether in school or not, you must report suspected child abuse.

2. Current estimates suggest that one in four children are abused in their homes or by some adult in their lives. Do not feel you are being overly cautious by watching all students carefully.

3. Abuse is not limited by economic status or education levels. It can happen to any child, anywhere.

The following is a list of some of the types of legally recognized child abuse along with suggestions regarding what to look for:

Physical Injury: Physical injury includes bruises, welts, burns, cuts, broken bones, sprains, bites, etc. which are intentionally inflicted. Injuries of this type often do not match the child's description of how they occurred (e.g., fracture from falling off sofa).

Neglect: Neglect is a failure to provide food, shelter, medicine, etc. to such a degree that a child's health and safety are endangered. Neglected children often do not want to leave school, are constantly tired, are left alone with no supervision, and/or have unmet physical, emotional, or medical needs.

Sexual Abuse and Sexual Exploitation: Any sexual contact in which a child is used to sexually stimulate another person is illegal. This may be anything from rape to fondling to involving a child in pornography. Victims often exhibit one or more of the following symptoms: difficulty walking or sitting; pain or itching in the genital area; torn, stained, or bloody underclothing; poor peer relationships; fantasy or infantile behavior; fear of being left with someone; inappropriate interest in or knowledge of sexual matters; sexual "acting out"; or any of the behavior problems listed below under Mental Injury.

Mental Injury: Mental Injury is a continuing pattern of rejecting, terrorizing, ignoring, isolating, or corrupting a child which results in serious damage to the child. Victims often have speech or sleep disorders, fail to grow normally, are very aggressive or withdrawn, and/or show an abnormal need for emotional support.

Child Selling: Child selling is buying, selling, or trading for legal or physical custody of a child. It does not apply to legitimate adoption or domestic relations planning.

Threat of Harm: This is any action, statement, written, or non-verbal message which is serious enough to make a child believe that he or she is in danger of being abused. Victims may exhibit any of the behaviors associated with any of the above forms of abuse.

Appendix C

Laws Affecting Education: Links and Summaries

I. Links

The US Constitution, state constitutions, and all federal and state laws and regulations are now available online via the following links:

Annotated US Constitution
www.findlaw.com/casecode/constitution/

Federal Civil Rights Laws and Regulations
fedlaw.gsa.gov/fedfra6.htm

Federal Education Laws and Regulations
fedlaw.gsa.gov/fedfra11.htm

General Federal Laws and Regulations (Indexed by Topic)
fedlaw.gsa.gov/intro2.htm

IDEA (This link also provides access to the administrative regulations.)
www4.law.cornell.edu/uscode/20/1400.html

State Laws and Court Cases (All 50 States)
www.findlaw.com/casecode/state.html

II. Summary of Federal Laws

The following are some of the major federal laws affecting education.

Section 1983 of the Civil Rights Act: Permits individuals to file civil lawsuits against school districts (as well as other government entities) for violations of constitutional or civil rights. Persons bringing such suits may seek to accomplish any or all of the following: recover damages, obtain injunctions, recover attorney fees. Section 1983 is often used in the courts to enforce civil rights conferred by the Constitution or other federal laws.

Title VI of the Civil Rights Act of 1964: Prohibits discrimination on the basis of race, color, or national origin, covers any school that receives any form of federal assistance.

Title IX of the Education Amendments of 1972: Prohibits discrimination on the basis of sex, covers any school receiving any form of federal financial assistance, covers discrimination against students and employees.

Title VII of the Civil Rights Act of 1964: Prohibits discrimination on the basis of race, color, national origin religion or sex against employees, covers employers with 15 or more employees.

Equal Pay Act: Prohibits discrimination against employees on the basis of sex, covers employee wages and fringe benefits.

Age Discrimination in Employment Act: Prohibits employers from discriminating against people of 40 years old, prohibits the following: failing or refusing to hire, discharging, or otherwise discriminating with respect to compensation, and terms, conditions, or privileges of employment.

Section 504 of the Rehabilitation Act of 1973 (Section 504): Prohibits discrimination against students or employees on the basis of disability. Schools must make courses, facilities, and programs available on an equal basis to all students. Schools must also make reasonable accommodations to insure that students with disabilities have an opportunity to participate fully in the school programs.

Americans with Disabilities Act (ADA): Prohibits discrimination against people with disabilities regarding employment, public services (including transportation), public accommodations, and services operated by private entities.

Individuals with Disabilities Education Act (IDEA): Entitles all students with disabilities to a free appropriate public education. Children with disabilities must receive education with their nondisabled peers to the extent possible. Students with disabilities must be provided with supportive services (such as the assistance of a teaching aid or use of a computer) if necessary for the student to participate in the regular school environment.

Equal Access Act of 1984: If a public secondary school allows one extracurricular club (during non-instructional time), it incurs the obligation to afford the same privileges (access to school facilities, announcements, etc.) to any other student club without discrimination based on the religious, political, philosophical or other orientation of the group. Note that religious groups must be formed by the students and not the school, and the school faculty must not participate in or promote the activities of religious groups.

III. Summary of State Laws

Most states have civil rights laws similar to the above-described federal laws. State laws and federal laws are not mutually exclusive, so citizens are usually protected simultaneously under all applicable provisions. The common types of state laws affecting education are as follows:

Employment Discrimination Laws: These laws prohibit discrimination in employment, usually on the following bases: race, religion, color, sex, national origin, disability, marital status, or age (usually if the employee is age 18 or older).

Work-Related Injury Laws: These laws prohibit discrimination against persons who are injured on the job and against employees who apply for workers' compensation benefits.

General Education-Related Anti-Discrimination Laws: These laws specifically prohibit discrimination by public schools.

Appendix D

Five Common Forms of Discrimination Found in Schools

1. Course and Program Offerings

Courses and programs should be available to all students. Educators should evaluate the reasons for the existence of any imbalance of students in particular courses or programs with regard to age, disability, national origin, race, marital status, religion, or sex. If educators discover that past discrimination, actions of discouragement by any particular educator, or some other such inappropriate cause exists for the imbalance, then remedial action must be taken.

2. Disproportionate Minority Referral to and Enrollment in Special Education

If the percentage of minority students referred to and found eligible for special education is disproportionate to the percentage of minority students in the school or district, a discrimination problem may exist. Consider whether teachers apply the same standards to all students, whether sufficient pre-referral/intervention strategies are used (and assure that these are documented), whether tests used for placement are appropriate and unbiased, and whether there is a clear and determinable legitimate reason for the imbalance.

3. Course or Program Access

Educators should investigate situations involving disproportions in student absences in certain classes or programs in order to assure that the reason us not due to a teacher's or a department's reputation or disregard for certain groups of students. Likewise, educators should assure that such situations are not due to differential grading, administration of improper testing, or a staff's advising students away from nontraditional classes for that group. If educators treat different protected categories of students differently in a class, such educators place the school in violation of the law. If a district fails to correct the situation, the district is also in violation of the law.

4. Segregation and Separation

Separating students on the basis of sex, race, etc., is unlawful. Separation is permitted by ability groupings, or by sex in contact sports. However, automatically separating all male and female students, for example, (such as for the entire physical education class) raises questions under the law. Likewise, violations of the law occur when educators segregate students who have a limited proficiency in English and place these students into certain reading groups when such placement is not necessary to address their educational needs. The same problem arises when educators segregate of children with disabilities simply because they are disabled. Students must be allowed to participate according to their individual needs and abilities.

5. Harassment

Harassment is an action or actions based on race, sex, or disability that are sufficiently severe or pervasive to limit a student's opportunity to benefit from the school program or activity. Schools must protect students from harassment, whether such harassment is committed by staff or by one student to another. School officials with knowledge or a report of alleged harassment have a duty to determine the nature of the problem and to take any necessary corrective action to prevent it.

Appendix E

Quick and Easy Help for Working with Students with IEPs

NOTE: Modification vs. Accommodation

It is important to distinguish between modification and accommodation. Modification is a change or reduction in curriculum, in the actual content. Accommodation, on the other hand, is merely a adaptation of how the information is taught.

For example, consider the four major components of the typical Earth Science curriculum: geology, meteorology, oceanography, and astronomy. If a student requires an actual reduction in all or part of one of these four components, then the curriculum has been modified. The student's grade should be based only on the reduced curriculum, but transcripts should clearly indicate that fact that the curriculum was modified.

On the other hand, consider the student who does indeed have the intellectual capacity to learn the entire Earth Science curriculum, but will not necessarily do so by reading chapters, completing written worksheets, spelling terms properly on tests, etc. In such a case, the materials and methods will be adapted. This is a case of accommodation. Since the student will be learning the regular material (albeit in a different manner or with different materials) the student should receive credit for the knowledge he or she demonstrates and such credit should not carry an indication of modification.

A. Students Who Require a Modified Curriculum:

If a student requires modification of curriculum, for example, if the student is not on a regular or standard diploma track, then the process is simple -- reduce the curriculum (after all, it is modified and the transcripts will say so). Is the student learning and trying (i.e., attending class, working on the modified curriculum, etc.)? If so, grade the student based on the modified curriculum, not based on the regular curriculum.

Remember, there is no rush; take as long as necessary to get through material, discuss, revise/edit, etc. (so long as student effort is evident).

Examples:

1. **Math & Language Arts:** Have the student learn at his/her own pace. In Language Arts, have the student work on one reading selection until it is finished and understood. Likewise, have the student work on one writing assignment until it is done (revised, edited, etc.). When finished, begin another. Another writing option is to grade work for specific writing conventions only, progressing to greater expectations as is appropriate given student progress.

2. **Other Areas:** Try limiting the curriculum by selecting a few units/chapters/projects etc. that you feel are the most important. Another option is to let the student select topics in which he/she is most interested.

3. **Materials:** Remember that the students may not be able to use the standard materials. They may need accommodations, like those discussed below.

B. Students Who Require Accommodations:

If a student requires accommodations, the important thing to remember is that the student's opportunity to learn and the student's grade cannot suffer merely because his or her disability requires changing how the student is taught.

Examples:

1. **Consult:** Ask special educators for help; their job is to help you.

2. **Focus:** Focus on what you really want – what are your actual curriculum goals (irrespective of materials and methods)? Remember, many of these students simply

cannot do too much at once. Can you read a book, write a letter, and conduct a conversation all at the same time? That is what doing "regular school work" is like for them. Try these suggestions:

a. **Forget About Spelling and Grammar:** If you want to see if a student knows something (other than spelling and grammar), then forget about spelling and grammar. They can always go back and make corrections later. These things simply don't matter in most contexts -- especially on tests.

b. **Forget About Taking Notes:** Many students with disabilities really, really, really cannot take notes and pay attention to what is going on in class at the same time. Do not make them do it. Even in college, they will not have to take notes (this is a standard accommodation at the college level). Let them pay attention. Give them your own notes or a copy of another student's notes. They will learn a lot more this way.

c. **Do Not Make Students with IEP's Read Aloud:** It is cruel to make students with reading disabilities read aloud. Spare them the embarrassment. If you really want a student with an IEP to read aloud (if this is really a course objective in which students must demonstrate mastery), then meet with the student privately a day ahead of time to show the student exactly what he/she will read the next day. Let the student practice it as homework so that when reading in class, he/she will do a good job.

d. **Cue for Oral Questions:** Some students need extra processing time before they even understand your oral questions. They often answer oral questions incorrectly. Speak with students privately to agree on a cue. (Example: Only ask them a question if you are standing in front of their seat.) The cue prompts them to filter-out everything else and focus on the next question. (The rest of the time they can focus on learning without anxiety.) Before long they may actually volunteer to answer questions.

3. **Reduce:** Reduce the impact of reading and writing by reducing reading and writing requirements. (Remember, students with disabilities in reading and writing have difficulty processing; overburdening them in this regard detracts from their focus on the subject matter. It is just like making a non-disabled student read a US History text written in German; the student would be so caught up in language difficulties that he/she would never have a chance to learn the history.) Here are some suggestions:

   a. **Assign only novels that you have on audio tape.**

   b. **Modify Assignments:** Examples: When you hand out a worksheet, cut down the number of questions; if there are 10 questions, circle the five you think are most important. Pick half of the week's assignments for the IEP student to complete. When you give a reading or writing assignment, be prepared to read it to the student, to reduce the assignment, to permit oral answers, etc. The point is that we must present curriculum to students and let students demonstrate knowledge without letting ourselves get stuck in peripheral reading and writing demands.

   c. **Use Alternatives:** Videos, oral reports, two or more students working together on assignments, individual or group projects, demonstrations, guest speakers, field trips, etc.

d. **Let Them Take it Home:** Do not assume that students with disabilities can work as fast as others; they may be just as smart, but doing much more processing. Let them take books and materials home.

4. **Modify Tests:** Allow extra time, do not count spelling or grammar, permit testing in alternative locations (e.g., the Special Education Center in the school, the Media Center, study halls or student group-work areas, etc.), permit open-book and open-note tests, read directions and questions orally, permit oral responses, send students to the special education staff (who can read to them, take dictation, or tape record oral answers).

5. **Let the Special Education Staff Help:** Your special education staff should have assistance available. They will help to students and the specialists should be available for consultation, collaboration, and co-planning.

C. Special Considerations for Students with ADD and ADHD

Parents, teachers, case managers, administrators, etc. often become frustrated to the point of infuriation when dealing with students with ADD and ADHD. But by remembering that the behavior of these students is a direct manifestation of their disability; you can remain calm and implement supportive practices that will help these students. To varying degrees, ADD and ADHD can cause students to have some of the following problems:

- **Forgetfulness** (to the point that some of us find incomprehensible). They will forget to do assignments, and, if they do them, they will forget to turn them in.

They will forget to relay messages, they will miss deadlines, etc. The list is endless.

- **Inability to begin working.** These students will often find it impossible to begin actually working on an assignment or task.

- **Inability to write.** Students often experience an inability to write. They may be able to explain answer orally, but cannot successfully engage in the process of reducing their thought to written form.

- **Unusually high or low activity level** (and correspondingly low attention span). Some of these students are up an about or extremely restless in their seats. Others seem like they're tranquilized. Either way, they have a great deal of difficulty following long discussions or engaging in any single activity for long periods of time. Note that the word "deficit" is misleading. One problem is that the some students attend to everything. They are unable to filter or to limit attention that produces the high activity level and the short attention span with regard to particular items. Other students do indeed experience a "deficit," requiring enormous stimulus in order to maintain attention.

- **General impulsiveness and distractibility.** Impulsivity can be seen in many ways, from blurting out statements in class, to pushing a button for no apparent reason (Why did you push the elevator button? -- I don't know; I just did.), to major life decisions. Distractibility is seen in virtually everything the student does; the student can be distracted by anything, from a mere thought, to a bird landing outside the classroom window, to a pencil scribbling in the back of the room.

So what can you do? First, remember that the student cannot help it; the student is not lazy, not irresponsible, not defiant, not stubborn, and certainly not dumb. The student has a disability. We need to help.

Second, try the following:

- **Do the student's remembering for him/her.** Until student acquires effective approaches (which may not be until late in high school, or even after high school), provide assignment sheets, remind the student to turn in his/her work, and provide assignment and other deadline information to parents and case managers. If you give the student an opportunity to forget, you are setting the student up for failure.

- **Specifically and individually prompt the student to begin working.** Then, from time to time, comment on what the student completed and provide reminders to continue working.

- **Give the student the opportunity to do oral work instead of written work.** Another excellent strategy is to let the student dictate ideas/answers onto an audio tape, and then have the student play the tape back (preferably with head phones on) and write down the answers. This method seems to overcome physiological processing problems and the use of head phones reduces distractions.

- **Let the student move around if they are not disruptive.** Contact parents and case managers to see what devices (such as a balloon filled with sand for the student to squeeze, etc.) have been approved or suggested for the student to use to control his or her over activity. Plan activities and assignments such that there is enough variety to overcome attention span problems. Prompt the student to refocus when attention wanes.

- **Provide the student with prompts to pull him or her back from distraction.** In special activities, such as drama and other oral presentations, remember that the student may need a "double prompt" (in other words, the student may not catch the "cue"; instead, the student may need to be prompted to attend to an upcoming cue). In order to assure that attention is refocused give some warning that the student is about to be called on or that there is only a few minutes left before they must do something.

The above is really a very basic overview. ADD and ADHD are complex. The difficulties these medical conditions present are as varied as the students who have them. Many of the more general suggestions above in sections A and B will also be helpful with students with ADD and ADHD. The three most important things to remember are to:

- be patient;

- keep trying; and

- make it a team effort with parents, case mangers, students, teachers, administrators, physicians, counselors, and anyone else who can help.

Appendix F

Internet Links Related to Education and Education Law

NOTE: Appendix C provides links to constitutions and statutes

1. Certification and Licensure
Fifty State Certification Requirements - www.uky.edu/Education/TEP/usacert.html

2. State Departments of Education
Fifty State DOE Links - www.ode.state.or.us/uslinks.htm

3. Disabilities
Disabilities and Special Education Info for all 50 States - www.nichcy.org/states.htm

General Disabilities Related Resources - www.hood.edu/seri/parents.htm

Information About Specific Disabilities - www.ode.state.or.us/sped/spedareas/specdis.htm

Special Education Law Web Site - www.SpecialEdLaw.net

Special Ed Site for Administrators - www.cosa.k12.or.us/special2.htm

4. Discrimination Categories
General Civil Rights (All Categories) - www.findlaw.com/01topics/36civil/index.html

Sexual Orientation Issues (Lambda Legal Defense Fund Site) - www.lambdalegal.org

5. Education Law (and Law in General)

Education Law Institute at Franklin Pierce Law Center – www.edlaw.fplc.edu

Federal Legal Information – www.findlaw.com/10fedgov/index.html

Fifty State Legal Info (by State) – www.findlaw.com/11stategov/index.html

FindLaw (virtually everything having to do with the law.) – www.findlaw.com

6. Employment/Job Search

Fifty State Education Job Opportunities – www.uky.edu/Education/TEP/usajobs.html

7. Employment Law Issues

Employment Law Links – www.lawmemo.com/emp

8. Professional Organizations and Unions

American Association of School Administrators – www.aasa.org

American Federation of Teachers – www.aft.org

National Education Association – www.nea.org

Appendix G

The Complaint in the Case *Henkle v. Gregory*

The following complaint was filed in January, 2000. Paragraph numbering begins at "5" and skips many numbers because the complaint has been edited to eliminate as much as possible of the purely procedural components required in such documents.

UNITED STATES DISTRICT COURT
DISTRICT OF NEVADA

COMPLAINT

DEREK R. HENKLE, Plaintiff,

vs.

ROSS GREGORY, in his official and individual capacity, and DENISE HAUSAUER, LORETTA RENDE, JOE ANASTASIO, ROBERT FLOYD, SERENA ROBB, ARNEL RAMILO, and GLEN SELBY, in their individual capacities, Defendants.

PRELIMINARY STATEMENT

5. This is a civil rights action against employees and officials of the Washoe County School District for depriving Plaintiff Derek R. Henkle of established constitutional, statutory and common law rights.

7. Specifically, this action challenges Defendants' denial of Plaintiff's rights secured under the First and Fourteenth Amendments to the United States Constitution, and 42 U.S.C. Section 1983, and Defendants' tortious negligence, negligent supervision and training, intentional infliction of emotional

distress, and negligent infliction of emotional distress under Nevada state law.

PARTIES

8. From August 1994 until February 1997, Plaintiff DEREK HENKLE was a student attending public schools in the Washoe County School District, County of Washoe, State of Nevada. Plaintiff currently is a citizen of the State of Georgia. Plaintiff is gay.

9. Defendants ROSS GREGORY, Principal, Galena High School; DENISE HAUSAUER, Assistant Vice Principal, Galena High School; LOUISE RENDE, Teacher, Galena High School; JOE ANASTASIO, Washoe County School District Director of Student Services; BOB FLOYD, Principal, Washoe High School; SERENA ROBB, Principal, Wooster High School, ARNEL RAMILO, Officer, Washoe County School Police; and GLEN SELBY, Officer, Washoe County School Police, are or were at all relevant times individuals working as employees and agents of the Washoe County School District, a public school district organized and operated under the laws of the State of Nevada. All Defendants currently are citizens of Nevada.

10. Plaintiff alleges that each of the Defendants performed, participated in, aided and/or abetted in some manner the acts averred herein, proximately caused the damages averred below, and is liable to Plaintiff for the damages and other relief sought herein.

11. Based upon information and belief, Plaintiff alleges that Defendant Gregory was responsible for the training and supervision of Defendants Hausauer and Rende.

12. Based upon information and belief, Plaintiff alleges that Defendant Hausauer was responsible for the training and supervision of Defendant Rende.

13. Based upon information and belief, Plaintiff alleges that Defendant Robb was responsible for the training and supervision of Defendants Ramilo and Selby.

STATEMENT OF FACTS

Galena High School

15. Plaintiff Derek R. Henkle attended Galena from August 1994 until January 1996. During that time, Ross Gregory ("Gregory") was the Principal at Galena, Denise Hausauer ("Hausauer") was the Assistant Vice Principal at Galena, and Louise Rende ("Rende") was a teacher at Galena.

16. Prior to attending Galena, Plaintiff was enrolled at Washoe County School District's Pine Middle School, in a gifted and talented program. Due to Plaintiff's intellectual abilities, Plaintiff skipped eighth grade and was enrolled at Galena in a special program for gifted and talented students.

17. In the early Fall of 1995, Plaintiff appeared on a local public access television program entitled "Set Free." On the show, he participated in a discussion on the subject of gay students and their experiences in high school.

18. From that point on until he was forced to leave Galena, Plaintiff experienced a constant barrage of anti-gay harassment, assaults, intimidation, and discrimination from Galena students.

19. The harassment, assaults, intimidation, and discrimination occurred during school hours and on school grounds.

20. Plaintiff made repeated reports directly to Defendants Hausauer and Rende about the incidents of harassment, assault, intimidation and discrimination.

21. Defendants Gregory, Hausauer and Rende were aware of the harassment, assaults, intimidation, and discrimination suffered by Plaintiff.

22. Defendants Gregory, Hausauer, and Rende had the authority to take corrective and preventative action to stop the harassment, assaults, intimidation, and discrimination suffered by Plaintiff.

23. Defendants Gregory, Hausauer, and Rende deliberately, purposefully and intentionally failed to take steps to end the harassment, assaults, intimidation, and discrimination suffered by Plaintiff.

24. Defendants Gregory, Hausauer and Rende failed to take the steps necessary to prevent future incidents of harm to Plaintiff that were foreseeable given the past incidents of harassment, assault, intimidation and discrimination.

25. Based upon information and belief, this failure to take action departed from school and district procedures for dealing with harassment, violence, abuse and/or discrimination.

26. The incidents at Galena included:

a. In the fall semester of 1995, Plaintiff was approached by several male Galena students on school property who called him "fag," "butt pirate," "fairy" and "homo." One of the students suggested that the group tie Plaintiff to the back of a truck and drag him down a nearby road. While on school property, the students pursued Plaintiff and succeeded in lassoing him around the neck with a rope three separate times. Plaintiff finally was able to escape to a classroom and immediately used an internal phone to contact Defendant Hausauer's office. Plaintiff waited almost two hours for anyone to come to the classroom where he hid in fear. When Defendant Hausauer finally arrived, she responded to Plaintiff's recounting of the incident with laughter. Defendant Gregory also was aware of the incident. Instead of conducting an immediate investigation and punishing the harassers, Defendants Gregory and Hausauer took no action against the students who assaulted Plaintiff for several months, despite knowing the identities of some of the students who were involved. Actions belatedly taken by Defendants Gregory and

Hausauer occurred only after Plaintiff had been driven from Galena.

b. During the fall semester of the 1995-1996 school year, Plaintiff was enrolled in a mandatory English class taught and supervised by Louise Rende. Throughout the semester, Plaintiff repeatedly was harassed, intimidated, and subjected to discrimination by other students based upon Plaintiff's sexual orientation, sex, and expression. Students in the class repeatedly wrote the word "fag" on the "white board" and sent notes to Plaintiff calling him a "fag." Students also drew pictures of men engaged in explicit sex acts on the "white board" and would call Plaintiff's attention to the pictures in front of other students. Defendant Rende was fully aware of the harassment, intimidation and discrimination as well as the identity of the harassers, but deliberately and purposefully took no steps to end the harassment or to discipline the harassers. Instead, Plaintiff was admonished by Defendant Rende that his sexuality was a private matter and he should not discuss it with other students. Defendant Hausauer also was aware of the incidents in Defendant Rende's English class and of Defendant Rende's acts and omissions, but made no effort to stop the harassment or to correct Defendant Rende's handling of the situation. Based on information and belief, Defendant Gregory also was aware of the incidents in Defendant Rende's English class and was aware of and endorsed Defendant Rende's acts and omissions, but made no effort to stop the harassment or to correct Defendant Rende's handling of the situation.

c. On or around December 1995, Plaintiff was in the Galena discipline office reporting another incident of harassment when several students ran by the office, shouted anti-gay epithets at him, and threw a metal object at him that missed Plaintiff and stuck in the wall. A school administrator witnessed the incident and filed a report. Defendant Hausauer was aware of the incident and deliberately and intentionally made no effort to investigate or discipline Plaintiff's attackers. This incident resulted in Plaintiff having an emotional breakdown in Defendant Hausauer's office. Based upon information and belief, Defendant Gregory also was aware of the incident and deliberately and intentionally made no effort to investigate or discipline Plaintiff's attackers.

27. During the fall semester of 1995, Plaintiff expressed himself about his gay sexual orientation. For example, he wore buttons on his backpack that stated "We Are Everywhere" and "Out." Plaintiff also spoke about his pro-gay viewpoints on various topics while at school.

28. Plaintiff's expression was fully protected by the First Amendment.

29. Defendants Gregory, Hausauer, and Rende were aware of the content and viewpoint of Plaintiff's expressive activity.

30. On more than one occasion, Defendants Hausauer and Rende told Plaintiff not to discuss his sexual orientation with other students.

31. Based upon information and belief, Defendant Gregory was aware of and endorsed Defendant Hausauer's acts and omissions in response to Plaintiff's repeated complaints of harassment, assault, intimidation, and discrimination, and to Plaintiff's expression.

32. Because of Defendants Gregory, Hausauer and Rende's failure to provide Plaintiff with an educational environment free from harassment and assaults and Plaintiff's resulting fear of further harassment and assaults, Plaintiff was unable to attend Galena any longer and Plaintiff asked to leave Galena at the end of the fall 1995 semester.

Washoe High School

33. Washoe High School is an alternative high school.

34. Washoe was not a suitable placement for Plaintiff.

35. Defendant Anastasio made the decision to transfer Plaintiff to Washoe High.

36. As a condition for a transfer out of Galena, Plaintiff was told by Defendant Anastasio that Plaintiff must treat his sexuality as a private matter and that he must not discuss it with anyone at his next school.

37. As a result of Defendants' purposeful efforts to silence Plaintiff's protected speech, Plaintiff was chilled and deterred from engaging in protected speech at Washoe on the subject of his sexual orientation, and, among other things, removed the buttons stating "We Are Everywhere" and "Out" from his backpack when he began attending Washoe.

38. Plaintiff attended Washoe High School from January 1996 through May of 1996. During that time, Defendant Bob Floyd was the principal at Washoe.

39. During his attendance at Washoe High, Defendant Floyd repeatedly told Plaintiff not to discuss his sexual orientation with others. In addition, during a meeting in Defendant Floyd's office, Defendant Floyd told Plaintiff to stop acting like a "fag."

40. While Plaintiff diminished his expression about his sexual orientation and of his pro-gay viewpoints, he did not totally succumb to Defendants' censorship efforts and still expressed his identity and viewpoints on certain occasions.

41. Plaintiff's expression was fully protected by the First Amendment.

42. Defendant Floyd was aware of the content and viewpoint of Plaintiff's expressive activity.

43. Frustrated by the lack of educational opportunity at Washoe, Plaintiff requested a transfer to a traditional high school that would provide him with an education suited to his intellectual abilities.

44. Plaintiff initially was told by Defendant Floyd that such a transfer was not possible because he was openly gay and that a traditional high school therefore would not be appropriate for him.

Wooster High School

45. Eventually, it was decided that Plaintiff would transfer to Wooster High School for the Fall 1996 school year.

46. Plaintiff was told by Defendant Floyd not to disclose his sexual orientation to others while at Wooster.

47. As a result of Defendant Floyd's purposeful effort to silence Plaintiff's speech, Plaintiff was chilled and deterred from engaging in protected expression related to his sexual orientation. He did not discuss his sexual orientation with or express pro-gay viewpoints to other students at Wooster during his first months there.

48. Plaintiff attended Wooster High School from August 1996 to February 1997. During that time, Defendant Serena Robb was principal of Wooster.

49. While at Wooster, Plaintiff experienced a constant barrage of anti-gay harassment, assaults, intimidation, and discrimination from his classmates, who learned of his sexual orientation from students who previously had attended Galena with Plaintiff.

50. The harassment, assaults, intimidation, and discrimination at Wooster occurred during school hours and on school grounds.

51. Plaintiff made repeated reports to school administrators about the incidents of harassment, assaults, intimidation and discrimination.

52. Defendant Robb was aware of the harassment, assaults, intimidation, and discrimination suffered by Plaintiff.

53. Defendant Robb had the authority to take corrective and preventative action to stop the harassment, assaults, intimidation, and discrimination suffered by Plaintiff.

54. Defendant Robb deliberately, purposefully, and intentionally failed to take steps necessary to end the harassment, assaults, intimidation, and discrimination suffered by Plaintiff.

55. Defendant Robb failed to take steps necessary to prevent future incidents of harm to Plaintiff that were foreseeable given the past incidents of harassment, assault, intimidation and discrimination.

56. Based upon information and belief, this failure to take action departed from district and school procedures for dealing with harassment, violence, abuse, and/or discrimination.

57. While at Wooster, Plaintiff was approached on school property by several students who began laughing at him and barraging him with anti-gay epithets. One of the students approached Plaintiff and began punching him in the face, calling him "bitch." The other students encouraged the student punching Plaintiff to continue his attack. As a result of the attack, Plaintiff began bleeding profusely from his lip, nose and head.

58. The attack on Plaintiff was witnessed by Defendants Ramilo and Selby, who were present at the scene but deliberately, purposefully and intentionally took no action to assist Plaintiff or discipline Plaintiff's harassers, despite having the authority and ability to do so.

59. Subsequently, Defendants Ramilo and Selby deliberately, purposefully and intentionally discouraged Plaintiff from filing a report and would not let him file a complaint without his mother's permission.

60. Defendants Ramilo and Selby also deliberately, purposefully, and intentionally discouraged Plaintiff from describing the incident as a hate crime and discouraged him from calling the

Reno Police Department to report the incident. They further refused to arrest his attacker despite knowing the identity of the attacker.

61. Based upon information and belief, Defendant Robb was aware of Defendants Ramilo and Selby's failure to take appropriate action in response to the attack on Plaintiff.

62. Plaintiff was forced to seek medical attention and to miss days of school as a result of the attack.

63. After his initial months of silence to other students, and in light of others' attacks on him, Plaintiff expressed himself about his sexual orientation to other students. Plaintiff also expressed pro-gay viewpoints to other students.

64. Plaintiff's expression was fully protected by the First Amendment.

65. Defendant Robb was aware of the content and viewpoint of Plaintiff's expressive activity.

66. Defendant Robb failed to provide Plaintiff with a safe educational environment free from constant harassment, discrimination and abuse.

67. Defendants Floyd and Anastasio agreed that Plaintiff should return to Washoe High School for the spring 1997 semester.

68. Defendant Floyd later reversed himself and would not accept Plaintiff at Washoe notwithstanding that there was space available at Washoe for Plaintiff at the time.

69. In February 1997, systematically deprived of the benefits of a high school education, 16 year-old Derek Henkle was placed in an adult education program at Truckee Meadows Community College at the direction of Defendants Anastasio and Floyd.

70. Because he was not enrolled in a public high school, Plaintiff was rendered ineligible for a high school diploma.

Federal Constitutional Claims

82. Upon information and belief, Defendants have policies and procedures to prevent and remedy harassment, discrimination, and/or violence suffered by all students, and take appropriate action to prevent and remedy such harms for non-gay students, yet did not do so for Plaintiff.

83. Upon information and belief, Defendants have policies and procedures to prevent and remedy harassment, discrimination, and/or violence suffered by all students, and take appropriate action to prevent and remedy such harms for female students, yet did not do so for Plaintiff.

84. The acts and omissions alleged above by Defendants were committed with deliberate indifference towards the well-being and rights of Plaintiff.

85. All of the acts or omissions alleged above by Defendants were committed intentionally and purposefully because of Plaintiff's sexual orientation.

86. The acts and omissions alleged above by Defendants were committed intentionally and purposefully because of Plaintiff's sex.

87. The acts and omissions alleged above by Defendants were committed intentionally and purposefully because of the content and viewpoint of Plaintiff's expression about his sexual orientation.

FIRST CLAIM FOR RELIEF

U.S. Constit. Amend. XIV, Equal Protection on the Basis of Sexual Orientation 42 U.S.C. Section 1983
(Against Defendant Gregory in his official capacity and Defendants Anastasio, Gregory, Hausauer, Rende, Floyd, Robb, Ramilo and Selby in their individual capacities)

92. The above-described conduct by Defendants violated the right of Plaintiff not to be deprived of equal protection of the laws on the basis of sexual orientation under the Fourteenth Amendment to the United States Constitution.

SECOND CLAIM FOR RELIEF

U.S. Constit. Amend. XIV, Equal Protection on the Basis of Sex
42 U.S.C. Section 1983
(Against Defendant Gregory in his official capacity and Defendants Anastasio, Gregory, Hausauer, Rende, Floyd, Robb, Ramilo and Selby in their individual capacities)

95. The above-described conduct by Defendants violated the right of Plaintiff not to be deprived of equal protection of the laws on the basis of sex under the Fourteenth Amendment to the United States Constitution.

THIRD CLAIM FOR RELIEF

U.S. Constit. Amend. I, Freedom of Speech 42 U.S.C. Section 1983
(Against Defendant Gregory in his official capacity and Defendants Anastasio, Gregory, Hausauer, Rende, Floyd, Ramilo and Selby in their individual capacities)

98. The above-described conduct by Defendants violated Plaintiff's right to freedom of speech under the First Amendment of the United States Constitution by censoring and chilling Plaintiff's speech and deterring him from exercising his First Amendment rights.

FOURTH CLAIM FOR RELIEF

U.S. Constit. Amend. I, Freedom of Speech 42 U.S.C. Section 1983

(Against Defendant Gregory in his official capacity and Defendants Anastasio, Gregory, Hausauer, Rende, Floyd, Robb, Ramilo and Selby in their individual capacities)

101. The above-described conduct by Defendants violated the right of Plaintiff to be free from retaliatory treatment based upon the exercise of his freedom of speech under the First Amendment to the United States Constitution.

REQUEST FOR RELIEF

WHEREFORE, Plaintiff respectfully requests that the Court:

(a) Issue an injunction ordering Defendant Gregory in his official capacity to ensure that Plaintiff is awarded a Washoe County School District diploma.

(b) Award compensatory damages in an amount to be determined according to proof by Plaintiff against all Defendants in their individual capacities;

(c) Award punitive damages in such other amount as the jury may determine is sufficient to punish them for and deter others from committing the constitutional violations alleged herein.

(d) Award Plaintiff his costs, expenses, and reasonable attorneys' fees pursuant to, inter alia, 42 U.S.C. Section 1988 and other federal and state laws.

(e) Grant such other and further relief as the Court may deem just and proper.

Dated: January ____, 2000

Respectfully submitted

References

Alexander, K., & Alexander, M.D. (1984). The law of schools, students, and teachers. St. Paul, MN: West.

Americans with Disabilities Act, 42 U.S.C secs. 12,101 et seq.

Axelrod, L. H., & Zvi, J. C. (1997, February). The ability of college students to effectively communicate the specific nature of their own learning disability. Paper presented at Poster Session #1 of the Learning Disabilities Association of America International Conference, Chicago, IL. (ERIC Document Reproduction Service No. ED 407 756)

Battle, D. A., & Murphy, S. C. (1996, October). Communication: Teaching middle grades exception students to become self-advocates. Paper presented at the 88th Annual Convention of the National Rural Education Association, San Antonio, TX. (ERIC Document Reproduction Service No. ED 410 730)

Bell v. Board of Education of New York, 687 N.E.2d 1325 (N.Y. 1997).

Belman, D., Gunderson, M. & Hyatt, D. (Eds.). (1996). Public sector employment in a time of transition. Madison, WI: Industrial Relations Research Association, University of Wisonsin.

Black, H.C. (1990). Black's law dictionary (6th Ed.). St. Paul, MN: West.

Board of Education v. Pico, 457 U.S. 853 (1982).

Board of Education v. Earls, U.S. Supreme Court (2002).

Bob Jones University v. United States, 461 U.S. 574 (1983).

Boyd, P. (1997, Fall). Self-advocacy: Practical advice to the adult with LD. Linkages - linking Literacy and learning disabilities, 4(2), 5-7.

Boyle, J.R., Weishaar, M (2001). Special education law with cases. Needham Heights, MA: Allyn & Bacon.

Brown v. Board of Education, 347 U.S. 483 (1954).

Burnette, J. (1996). Including students with disabilities in general education classrooms: From policy to practice. ERIC Review: Inclusion 4(3).

Carey v. Piphus, 435 U.S. 247 (1978).

Civil Rights Act of 1964, 42 U.S.C. secs. 2000e et seq.

Constitution of the United States

Cooper v. Eugene School District, 301 Or. 358 (1986) appeal dismissed 480 U.S. 942 (1987).

Cotton, K. (2000). Research you can use to improve results. Association for Supervision and Curriculum Development; Northwest Regional Educational Laboratory.

Crocket, Special Education: The Least Restrictive Environment and The 1997 IDEA Amendments and Federal Regulations, 28 J. L. & Educ. 543, (1999).

Dean v. Town of Waterford, 523 A.2d 1059 (Md. App. 1987).

Durlak, C. M., Rose, E., & Bursuck, W. D. (1994, January). Preparing high school students with learning disabilities for the transition to postsecondary education: Teaching the skills of self-determination. Journal of learning disabilities, 27(1), 51-59.

Earls v. Board of Education of Tecumseh Public School District, 242 F.3d 1264 (10th Cir. 2001).

Eisel v. Board of Education of Montgomery County, 597 A.2d 447 (Md. 1991).

Essex, N.L. (1999). School law and the public schools: A practical guide for educational leaders. Needham Heights, MA: Allyn and Bacon.

Everson v. Board of Education of the Township of Ewing, 330 U.S. 1 (1947).

Family Educational Rights and Privacy Act, 20 U.S.C. secs. 1232 et seq.

Fischer, L., Schimmel, D. & Kelly, C. (1995). Teachers and the law (4th Ed.). White Plains, NY: Longman Publishers.

Friend, M., & Bursuck, W. D. (1996). Including students with special needs - a practical Guide for classroom teachers. Boston: Allyn and Bacon.

Fuentes v. Shevin, 407 U.S. 67 (1972).

Garcia, E.E., (2001). Hispanic education in the United States. Lanham, MD: Rowmant and Littlefield.

Goldberg v. Kelly, 397 U.S. 254 (1970).

Gonzaga University v. Doe, U.S. Supreme Court (2002).

Gonzalez v. Mackler, 241 N.Y.S.2d 254 (App. Div. 1963).

Goss v. Lopez, 419 U.S. 565 (1975).

Greene v. McElroy, 360 U.S. 474 (1959).

Grisso, T., & Vierling, L. (1978). Minors' consent to treatment: A developmental perspective. Professional psychology, 9, 412-427.

Gutman, A. (1987). Democratic education. Princeton, NJ: Princeton University Press.

Halloran, W. D., & Simon, M. Y. (1995). The transition services requirement: A federal perspective on issues, implication, and challenges. The journal for vocational special needs education, 17, 94-97. National Association of Vocational Special Needs Education.

Haralambie, A.M. (1993). The child's attorney: A guide to representing children in custody, adoption, and protection cases. Chicago, IL: American Bar Association.

Hazelwood School District v. Kuhlmeier, 484 U.S. 260 (1988).

Imber, M., van Geel, T. (2000). Education law (2d Ed.). Mahwah, NJ: Lawrence Erlbaum Associates, Inc.

Individuals with Disabilities Education Act, 20 U.S.C. secs. 1400 et seq.

Jorgensen, C.M. (1997). Curriculum and its impact on inclusion and the achievement of students with disabilities. Consortium on inclusive schooling practices issue brief 2(2).

Kaplin, W.A., Lee, B. A. (1997). A legal guide for student affairs professionals. San Francisco, CA: Jossey-Bass.

Knoff, H. M., Batsche, G. M. (1994). Project ACHIEVE: A collaborative, school-based school reform process improving the academic and social progress of at-risk and underachieving students. (ERIC Document Reproduction Service No. ED 383 963)

Knoff, H. M., Curtis, M. J. (1996). Organizational change and school reform: School psychology at a professional crossroad: Introduction to the mini-series. School Psychology Review, 25 n4 406-08.

Knoff, H. M. (1999). Project ACHIEVE and the need to create effective building-based social skills, discipline/behavior management, and school safety systems. (ERIC Document Reproduction Service No. ED 445 464)

Lau v. Nichols, 414 U.S. 563 (1974).

Lee, Searching for Patterns and Anomalies in the ADA Employment Constellation: Who is a Qualified Individual with a Disability and What Accommodations are Courts Really Demanding?, 13 The Labor Lawyer 149 (1997).

Lee v. Weisman, 505 U.S. 577 (1992).

Lemon v. Kurtzman, 42 U.S. 602 (1971).

Loewy, School Prayer, Neutrality, and the Open Forum: Why We Don't Need a Constitutional Amendment, 61 N. Car. L. Rev. 141 (1982).

Mann, H. (1846, 1848). The education of free men. Taking sides: Clashing views on controversial educational issues (10th Ed.) (1999), 68-71. Guilford, CT: McGraw-Hill.

Mathews v. Eldridge, 424 U.S. 319 (1976).

Mazurek, N., & Shoemaker, A. (1997). Career self-efficacy in college students with disabilities: Implications for secondary and post-secondary service providers. Unpublished manuscript, St. Ambrose University. (ERIC Document Reproduction Service No. ED 412 708)

Milliken v. Bradley, 418 U.S. 717 (1974).

Mullane v. Central Hanover Trust Co., 339 U.S. 306 (1950).

New Jersey v. T.L.O., 469 U.S. 325 (1985).

Newdow v. U.S. Congress, 9th Circuit Court of Appeals (2002).

NLRB v. Weingarten, Inc., 420 U.S. 251 (1975).

Note, The Judicial Role in Attacking Racial Discrimination in Tax-Exempt Private Schools, 93 Harv. L. Rev. 378 (1979).

Osborne, A.G. (1996). Legal issues in special education. Needham Heights, MA: Allyn& Bacon.

Peloza v. Capistrano Unified School District, 37 F3d 517 (9th Cir 1994), cert den, 115 S. Ct. 2640 (1995).

Pfeffer, L. (1967). Church, state and freedom. Boston, MA: Beacon Press.

Pierce v. Society of Sisters, 268 U.S. 510 (1925).

Plessy v. Ferguson, 163 U.S. 537 (1896).

Price v. Young, 580 F. Supp. 1 (E.D. Ark. 1983).

Romer v. Evans, U.S. Supreme Court, 1996.

Rothstein, L.F. (2000). Special education law. New York, NY: Addison Wesley Longman.

San Antonio School District v. Rodriguez, 411 U.S. 1 (1973).

Santa Fe Independent School District v. Doe, US Supreme Court (2000).

"Section 1983" of the Civil Rights Act of 1871, 42 U.S.C. sec. 1983.

Senate Committee on Labor and Human Resources, Report to accompany the Individuals with Disabilities Education Act Amendments of 1997. Section V. Explanation of bill and committee overviews.

Spring, J. (1989). American education: An introduction to social and political aspects. White Plains, NY: Longman.

Tilton v. Richardson, 403 U.S. 672 (1971).

Tinker v. Des Moines School District, 393 U.S. 503 (1969).

Titus v. Lindberg, 49 N.J. 66, 228 A.2d 65 (1967).

Twenty-Second Annual Report to Congress on the Implementation of the Individuals with Disabilities Education Act (2000), U.S. Department of Education.

Twenty-Third Annual Report to Congress on the Implementation of the Individuals with Disabilities Education Act (2001), U.S. Department of Education.

Vernonia School District 47J v. Acton, 115 S. Ct. 2386 (1995)

Wehmeyer, M. L. (1998). The spirit of the IDEA mandate: Student involvement in transition planning. Beyond high school: Transition from school to work, 206-233. Wadsworth Publishing Co.

West Virginia Board of Education v. Barnette, 319 U.S. 624 (1943).

Wood, J. (1998). Adapting instruction to accommodate students in inclusive settings. Upper Saddle River, NJ: Prentice Hall.

Yudof, M.G., Kirp, D.L., Levin, B. (1992). Educational policy and the law (3d Ed.). St. Paul, MN: West.

Zelman v. Simmons-Harris, U.S. Supreme Court (2002).